positions asia critique

**the good life in late-socialist asia:
aspirations, politics, and possibilities**

volume 32   number 1   february 2024

Contents

Guest Editors' Introduction

Minh T. N. Nguyen, Phill Wilcox, and Jake Lin

The emergent quest for the good life in late-socialist Asia is deeply implicated in the contradictions and double-sidedness of its political economic transformations over the last several decades. While continuing to be governed by the Communist Party, throughout the 1980s and 1990s Laos, China, and Vietnam replaced their centrally planned economy with a market economy via economic reforms. The ensuing economic growth and global integration have opened up new vistas of aspiration and desire. Wealth, consumption, higher education, global travel, and private housing, once beyond reach for most, have become common pursuits for many. With deepening privatization, market logics increasingly prevail. People are drawn into competitive striving and the accumulation of private wealth to keep up with market demands, even as the socialist ethos of harmony, equality, and mutuality continue to be highlighted in official and popular discourse. Meanwhile,

positions 32:1 DOI 10.1215/10679847-10889921

growing social inequality and ecological decline have started to expose the darker sides of the countries' development, which has relied on natural resource extraction and the devaluation of labor, especially migrant labor. The breathtaking pace of change has generated an imminent perception of moral decline, distrust and anxiety, especially in much-richer China (Ci 2014; Zhang 2020).

These emerging social and political economic issues, however, have dampened neither national leaders' talk of the "dream" of their countries nor ordinary people's aspirations to a good life. For many, life under late socialism is less concerned with surviving or making ends meet than it was during the pre-reform time of economic stagnation and isolation. Whether they subscribe to their leaders' dream or not, there is a broad expectation of a better future, despite greater uncertainty and anxiety (Wilcox, Rigg, and Nguyen 2021). This dynamic might be reminiscent of Berlant's (2011) influential notion of *cruel optimism*, which refers to a situation in which "what people desire is that which prevents them from flourishing." Berlant portrays the postindustrial social condition in which people persist futilely in a precarious world, as they continue to be attached to the waning liberal-capitalist social order's fantasies of upward social mobility and meritocratic achievements, leading to pain, trauma, and suffering. In late-socialist Asia, in contrast, while the present might be as precarious, it holds out new spaces, desires, and opportunities that would have been unthinkable in the time of central planning and draconian state control, engendering a pervasive sense of abundant possibilities for future making (High 2014; Rofel 2007; Wilcox, Rigg, and Nguyen 2021).

As we shall see in our authors' contributions, the double-sidedness of late-socialist transformations turns people's quest for the good life into a "field of struggles" (Jackson 2011) that is riddled with trade-offs and conflicting values. Our contributors critically engage with the notion of the good life and its ramifications in late-socialist social life from the perspectives of people and communities living amid the changes and juggling different value frameworks. Underlying socialism is a vision of the good life in which people are freed from alienated labor to fulfill their needs by engaging in socially meaningful work. Although its dream of reconciling human self-interest with collective goals has proven as elusive as the capitalist dream of self-determination and individual freedom (Freud and Strachey (1962) 2010; Marcuse 1964), socialism is an attempt to find the good life. In response to capitalist consumer society's alienation and domination of the individual (Marcuse 1964), socialist citizens are supposed to flourish as part of a collective unified in the work of building a common future. While this vision of the good life may have receded in the market economy, giving way to one guided by individualized goals of private accumulation and self-interest, it continues to influence the ways in which people evaluate their actions. Concurrently, the socialist vision increasingly contradicts the harsh realities of life in precarity for the millions of working men and women whose labor is essential to the foundations of any good life. This contradiction places limits on the pursuit of the good life as a common project of living well *together* (Arendt 1998), as people's varying abilities to traverse between seemingly incommensurable "social orders" (Gershon 2019) make up a central axis of inequality production.

By addressing the aspiring subject in its social contexts (Appadurai 2013; Robbins 2013), we underscore a politics of aspiration emerging from the realities of people negotiating between multiple value frameworks to create meanings in their lives. This politics of aspiration is rather distinct from the politics of disillusion underlying Berlant's notion of cruel optimism, although the latter is also emerging along with increasing ecological and social constraints on people's lives. Further, the politics of aspiration in late socialism is intimately connected to subtle changes in governance. According to Zhang and Ong (2008), the postreform governing mode of "socialism from afar" is characterized by the realignment of the state and the market to promote consumption and self-entrepreneurism as paths for actualizing the power of the self. Its product is a self-choosing subject governable by the state (see also High 2014; Schwenkel and Leshkowich 2012). Our analyses, however, suggest the emergence of an ethical citizen as the subject of governance (Derks and Nguyen 2020), which reactivates collectivist ideas of social life through the idiom of care. As both a moral discourse and a social value (Nguyen, Zavoretti, and Tronto 2017), care seems well suited to the work of linking personally with collectively oriented actions, both of which are foregrounded by late-socialist citizens.

The term *late socialism* here is shorthand for the period that started with the three countries' respective reforms at around the time when the Soviet Union disintegrated. Their populations, economic strength, and global positioning undoubtedly differ. At one end of the spectrum China has a vast, powerful economy, while at the other the Lao economy remains relatively modest, depending largely on investment from China and Vietnam, with Vietnam lying somewhere between the two. What they share is the trajectory of marketization under the continued single-party rule following a long period of central planning and collectivization that we refer to as *state socialism*. Their shared trajectory has generated comparable and interrelated dynamics of change (see also Hansen, Bekkevold, and Nordhaug 2020). While the term *postsocialism* is more widely used by international scholarship as an analytical frame, scholars and policymakers within these countries tend to reject the term as an incorrect portrayal that dismisses the endurance of major socialist institutions, preferring to refer to *market socialism* instead. Taking their insistence on the socialist character of the current governing regimes seriously, we also use the term *late socialism*, as it suggests less of the rupture experienced by the postsocialist societies of Eastern Europe.

Conceptualizing the Good Life

Sociologists and anthropologists tend to be reticent about making hope, well-being, and the good life topics of inquiry (Bauman in Jacobsen 2014; Ortner 2016; Robbins 2013). Oriented toward uncovering hidden dynamics of alienation, dispossession, and inequality, we commonly produce analyses that take human suffering as a point of departure. This overemphasis on the suffering subject sometimes causes us to lose sight of what Appadurai (2013: 179) terms a *capacity to aspire*, namely the ways in which humans engage with their own future. The recent turn to "the good," "well-being," and "the good life" in anthropology (Fisher 2014; Jackson 2011; Robbins 2013), however, is not only a recognition of ordinary people's future making. It is also a critical response to the omnipresence of performative happiness in advertising and social media, positive psychology's celebration of positive emotions, and the economistic logics of happiness rankings and indexes (Ahmed 2009; Davies 2015; Zhang 2020). Unsettling the idea of the good life as defined by individual choices and preferences, these works reground it in larger value frameworks founded on beliefs about life and death, human dignity and morality, interpersonal relationships, and relationships between humans and nature (Appadurai 2013).

Aspiration, as we recognize, is itself a morally laden concept that cannot be taken as a universal expression of the human experience. The neoliberal aspirational discourse often attributes poverty and suffering to low or lack of aspirations; the expectation that people be aspirational is a familiar logic of restructuring. For example, a common dictum in Vietnam today is that one can never "escape from poverty" without the "consciousness to rise" above one's circumstances (Nguyen 2018a), which in turn aligns with "the will to improve" (Li 2007) of governments and brokers of development as a national modernization project. Growing authoritarianism in late socialism also politicizes aspirations: anyone questioning the nation's dream can easily be cast as unpatriotic, especially in China. They would become what Ahmed (2009) refers to as "affect aliens" in her analysis of immigrants who refuse to assimilate with their new surroundings, feminists who question the family as a happiness-bearing institution, and queer subjects who refuse to be unhappy. Ahmed underscores the exclusionary effect of normalized notions of happiness while questioning it as the ultimate goal of human existence. That said, we shall make the case for reflecting on how people actively infuse dominant visions of the good life with their own meanings by weaving together the very contradictory value frameworks of late socialism. The "dream" propagated by national leaders is thus met by a great diversity of what Li Zhang (afterword, this issue) calls "bottom-up dreams," simultaneously crafted out of people's historical experiences of war, state intervention in private life, decades of being deemed to be swimming in the backwaters of global modernity, and the sense of national rejuvenation afforded by sustained economic growth.

This special issue considers the aspiring subject as shaping and shaped by the political economy of late socialism. In contrast to the positivist science of measuring happiness as a given condition, ours is an inquiry into how the aspiring subject grapples with the contradictions of their time and place with a view to living well, and the possible outcomes of that struggle. The central question we ask is, *What possibilities do people have to shape a life that they consider worth living?* Such a question presupposes the active role of the aspiring subject as the agent of both change and continuity. This subject, living out the contradictions and limits of late socialism, also manages to circulate between seemingly incommensurable social orders, rendering the boundaries between them porous and productive (Gershon 2019). Often the capacity to aspire is unevenly distributed; the elite tend to be better positioned institutionally and culturally to navigate the horizons of possibilities and connect concrete wants to larger schemes of distinction (Appadurai 2013). The idea of the good life, according to Jackson (2011), constitutes a field of struggle in which diverse social groups partake with their own strategies and repertoires of meaning from their social positions. The possibilities for living well together thus emerge from the frictions between differing visions of the good life and how people "move objects, forms and ideas across boundaries using consciously calibrated strategies" (Gershon 2019: 405), and in so doing generate new social forms.

We define the good life as *conceptions of a life that is considered worth striving for within the horizons of possibilities in a particular time and place.* Aspiration to the good life, we argue, is a force of social change as much as it is effected by it. We show that the good life is a site of emergent struggles and politics between citizens and the state, between social classes and genders, which contribute to the paradoxical dynamics of late socialism. It is these social struggles around evolving realities, social orders, and contradictory value frameworks coming alive in people's everyday actions that we seek to capture.

What Really Matters?

Our authors address a broad range of topics. Kirsten W. Endres begins with an account of how electrical home appliances, once curiosities, have become daily necessities for the Vietnamese. Arve Hansen takes us to the foodscape of Hanoi, where diverse dining avenues have emerged alongside the arrival of global food chains and the upgrading of street food for middle-class consumption. Roberta Zavoretti tells of urban Chinese women contesting the imperative of heteronormative marriage through their strategies for ensuring personal autonomy and cultivating social relationships. Sandra Kurfürst shows how Vietnamese female rappers defy gender norms in carving out an autonomous space to make their careers in hip-hop music in a male-dominated industry. Jiazhi Fengjiang's analysis of grassroots philanthropy (*caogen gongyi*) in China shows how charitable and volunteering activities offer opportunities for working people to gain the sense of public engagement that is central to their definition of a good life. Charlotte Bruckermann addresses ambivalent aspirations to a green life in the encounter between urban volunteers and rural people involved in afforestation projects sponsored by the Chinese state and large corporations. Elizabeth M. Elliott portrays how the Laos concept of well-being, *sabai*, which locates a person in their social and spiritual worlds, shapes rural people's health care–seeking practices. Fan Zhang introduces us to the lifeworld of Tibetan opera performers, whose performances underscore a vision of the good life that incorporates the logics of the state and the market into local ideas about cosmological balance. Michael Kleinod-Freudenberg and Sypha Chanthavong's figure of the *bangbot*, a forest spirit endowed with morality, embodies a criticism of how commercially motivated deforestation is foreclosing ecology-based visions of the good life, while at the same time inducing nostalgia for it.

What do these seemingly disparate topics have to do with the good life? Following Arendt (1998), who views the good life through the prism of actions aimed at living well together, we underscore how people articulate their ideas of the good life through everyday actions which, we argue, are shaped by the social expectations deriving from existing value frameworks. The broad range of our authors' analyses can be defined as four intertwining domains of action: comfort and pleasure, caring and being cared for, cosmology and nature, and autonomy and freedom. These domains of action constitute the material and social spaces where social groups articulate their aspirations, act out what they consider worth striving for, and evaluate their lives. How people act in these domains and what drives their actions not only indicate circulation and movement among multiple social orders (Ghershon 2019). They also defy the commonly assumed boundaries between individual and collective, self-interest and reciprocity, and public and private, indicating the ambivalence and multivocality of the aspiring subject.

Comfort and Pleasure

It is hard for people born since the end of central planning to imagine a life without electricity, the internet, or motorized transport, or one in which food is rationed and a black-and-white television may be a well-off family's most valuable asset. In Endres's account of "living electrically," the arrival of the electric fan in colonial Vietnam was nothing short of a miracle—nowadays even air-conditioning is commonplace. Hansen's analysis describes, in contrast to the severe food shortage a couple of decades ago, a bustling foodscape in which the Hanoian middle classes avail themselves of endless dining choices. They can command both the authenticity of street food and the exclusiveness of upmarket restaurants, or summon their favorite food with a few touches on their smartphones. Most people in China, and to a lesser degree in Laos, would relate well to similar accounts of major material changes in their daily life.

State socialism frowned upon comfort and pleasure as bourgeois weaknesses; pleasure-seeking was marked out as morally problematic and antirevolutionary. In the centrally planned economies that downplayed consumption due to imminent shortages, compounded by the aftermath of war and serious natural disasters in Vietnam and Laos, comfort and pleasure were also out of the reach of ordinary people. The market economy has not only made comfort and pleasure conceivable but has also turned them into respectable pursuits, backed by party-states keen to keep the middle class growing and yet politically inactive. Exclusive spaces of consumption such as gated housing and international travel are made increasingly available to the middle class, who, according to some authors, "born of high GDP and nurtured by a culture of consumption," trade purchasing power and consumption choices for political self-awareness (Ci 2014; Dai and Rofel 2018: 44; Nguyen-Vo 2008). Whatever political energy there is in the middle classes, it seems to be channeled into protecting their own interests against the bureaucratic failure of state and market actors to ensure the security of their private interests and properties (Dai and Rofel 2018; Zhang 2010). Endres's informants adamantly complain about not being able to use their appliances due to a power cut, prompting her to ask how people had coped without them previously. The same can be asked about the internet, air-conditioning, smartphones, flat-screen televisions, refrigerators, electric stoves, and personal computers, the use of which requires proper living spaces and a constant supply of electricity, which used to be rationed for lighting only. Such morphing of wants into needs can be similarly observed in food consumption. As with travel, dining out has become a field of practices in which the ability to authenticate one's experiences and to embrace global trends is a means of social distinction (Hansen, this issue). Desire for comfort and pleasure has been normalized under marketization, and consumption has turned into a citizen's quasi-duty (Nguyen-Vo 2008; Osburg 2013). It is equally pursued by working people, whose higher income allows them to acquire certain aspects of middle-class life, and whose expectations are raised by the middle-class projection of such consumption (Nguyen 2015, 2018b; Otis 2012).

One might see in these the rise of Herbert Marcuse's (1964) one-dimensional man, the tamed subject of techno-capitalism who finds its soul and identity in consumer objects and lifestyle, bereft of any capacity for critical reflection and transformative action. Yet late-socialist subjects' desire for comfort and pleasure, we argue, is connected to broader aspirations to modernity, progress, and development in contexts where people had long felt that they were lagging behind in the global world (Derks and Nguyen 2020; Harms 2016). Endres suggests that electrical appliances carry major implications for gendered notions of the good life that are inseparable from the meaning of electricity as liberating society from labor, darkness, and backwardness. Take the electric stove, for instance; apart from being a labor- and timesaving device, it helps to remove the dirt common to older methods of cooking on coal and wood. The removal of dirt is essential to a shiny and presentable middle-class kitchen aligned with the notion of the modern middle-class woman, who is able to manage her home scientifically with the right technology and knowledge (Nguyen 2015). Similarly, the ability to traverse global and local dining spaces, to own vehicles and technological devices, to travel internationally for leisure or work (Kürfurst, this issue) signify conscious engagement with the global world and assertion of one's place, and by extension one's country's place, within it (see also Rofel 2007). As much as it concerns individual wants, therefore, the desire for comfort and pleasure is also a yearning to belong to a larger whole, and can be a space for transformative action. With it, the aspiring subject seeks to overcome past experiences of isolation, dependency, and poverty, and to achieve recognition as one who is in tandem with the vanguards of global modernity. The much-derided rise of conspicuous consumption by the few in such rapidly transforming locations does not need to equate with the broader-based quest for improved living standards by the many who are still without access to the comfort of goods and services easily available to those—not least academics—critiquing it (Miller 2001).

Caring and Being Cared For

Broadly defined, *care* constitutes "processes of creating, sustaining and reproducing bodies, selves and social relationships" (Nguyen, Zavoretti, and Tronto 2017: 202). Care encompasses what we do to sustain our world in order to live well (Tronto 1993). More than just the needs of the sick and the infirm, it also refers to the complex relationships between social groups, citizens and states, humans and their environment. Late-socialist Asia experiences a common shift in the care relation between citizens and states: government programs such as health insurance and old-age pension are reexpanding, seeming to contradict the privatization and restructuring mentioned. Contributory health insurance is now almost universal in China, and covers a large majority of the population in Laos and Vietnam. It appears that the socialist state is once again picking up on its promises of universal care after years of leaving it to the market. However, the expansion of these new welfare programs makes it even more imperative for individuals and families to rely on their own resources and networks for access to care and social protection (Nguyen and Chen 2017; Lin and Nguyen 2021). The reemphasis on familialism is coupled with pervasive messages from state and market institutions about people's responsibility to care for the disadvantaged and the environment. Socialist ethos of mutuality and solidarity are actively deployed to mobilize individual contributions to social and environmental care (Nguyen 2018b; Palmer and Winiger 2019). These shifts have major implications for the realities and practices of caring and being cared for.

Elliott's analysis shows how rural people in Laos negotiate between the care provided by traditional healers, who are more attentive to patients' personal needs, and public hospitals, which appear inattentive and cold. The difference is linked to state incentive structures that neither recognize traditional healers nor incentivize attentive care among public medical professionals, leaving it to people to address their own needs. Zavoretti's account of unmarried women in urban China, often referred to as "leftover women" (*shengnu*), highlights the predominance of heteronormative marriage through which property ownership, reproductive labor, and care are regulated in official conceptions of the good life. This helps to enhance familialism for the sake of late-socialist welfare restructuring. Concurrently, as Fengjiang and Bruckermann show, even people struggling with their own livelihoods are drawn into the work of improving the lives of the more disadvantaged Other or protecting the environment sponsored by state and market institutions such as the online commerce giant Alibaba. Care, it seems, functions as a moral discourse that smooths out the increased burdens, social conflicts, and inequalities induced by economic and welfare restructuring (Nguyen, Zavoretti, and Tronto 2017).

Meanwhile, caring and being cared for are also central to how people seek meaning, mutual support, and social validation in their lives. Even as they delay marriage and having children for the sake of personal autonomy, Kürfurst's Vietnamese female hip-hop artists emphasize caring for their parents and husbands as an important aspect of their lives. In the same vein, the unmarried urban Chinese women discussed by Zavorretti challenge the imperative of marriage by invoking the importance of care for their own families and for themselves. Amid the turn to private responsibility, their moral commitment to care can be a matter of survival for their parents in old age, as it is for the mother of one of Zavoretti's (2017) informants, who survives only due to her daughter's support. The stronger familial basis of social protection in more competitive social environments also translates into increased personal and financial investment in children's all-around development and their academic suitability for higher education, especially in China (Kipnis 2011; Kuan 2013).

These dynamics of caring and being cared for reverberate beyond family and kinship. Elliott's village healers in Laos not only provide physical treatment but also care for their patients' souls by seeking to recreate the harmony between the body and external forces. Such care demands time and effort and is poorly remunerated, yet they derive strong motivation from the social prestige thus gained. Actively caring for disadvantaged others as part of the broader schema of "doing good" is also a source of meanings for Fengjiang's informants, working men struggling with their livelihoods in Wenzhou. Being a "greenwood hero" (*lulin haohan*)—a righteous outlaw acting on behalf of the weak—yet also seeking state recognition has implications for what it means to be a working man in China today, where prestige and desirability are reserved for men with wealth and power. Likewise, caring for the environment, whether by planting a virtual tree from their office desk or flying to rural frontiers to plant trees physically, helps Bruckermann's urban middle-class volunteers to encounter the alienation of urban life and work, even though some might only do it in response to workplace pressure. In the face of rampant natural resource extraction in Laos, Kleinod-Freudenberg and Chanthavong note a similar form of environmentalism with which the urban middle class and intellectual elite express disenchantment at the ecological decline and call for the return of past moral behavior. When taking part in the work of sustaining bodies and relationships and protecting the environment, therefore, people tend to ground their actions in the ambivalent and multilayered logics of care. As argued below, these logics are closely intertwined with ecological traditions and practices in the region.

Cosmology and Nature

Late-socialist societies are confronted by ecological decline that has led to both growing environmental conflicts and increased yearning to reconnect with nature. As people become more anxious about ecological problems, late-socialist governments have stepped up their "environmental rule" (McElwee 2016). The Chinese government, for example, has been championing a state-led form of environmentalism called *ecological civilization* (Bruckermann, this issue), with which the state seeks to monopolize knowledge production and interventions in environmental issues. The emphasis on improving people's environmental consciousness across these contexts often diverts attention from the disproportionate environmental burdens and costs incurred by certain populations (Bruckermann, this issue). However, grass-roots environmentalism does not always align with the state's environmental rule. Sometimes environmentally motivated popular protests spill out into regime critique; for example, protests following the fish kill due to a chemical spillage from a Formosa factory off the central coast of Vietnam in 2016 developed into demand for government transparency. More importantly, people across the region experience deep-rooted concerns about cosmology and nature; cosmological traditions premised on human situatedness in the natural and supernatural worlds have long existed. Despite centuries of encounters with modernist assumptions of human supremacy over nature, not least through state socialism's destructive industrialization schemes, they continue to shape local ideas about being and living in the world.

According to Elliott, sabai, the Laotian sense of well-being, is only possible when people act as part of a cycle of care with other humans and the spirit world. Thus health can only be sustained by maintaining both the boundedness of the body and its harmony with the surrounding environment, including the spirit world. Kleinod-Freudenberg and Chanthavong tell us more about this form of transcendental reciprocity through the imaginary of the bangbot—a forest spirit representing a "moral superhuman" that provides a potential role model for human behavior. Linking morality with the undisturbed forest, the bangbot carries a critique of the moral degradation resulting from the ecological decline caused by capitalist extraction. Similarly, Fan Zhang's Tibetan opera performers act out a notion of the good life defined by the work of accumulating virtuous merits and respecting the land and nature for the sake of their karma. Similar to sabai and bangbot, Zhang shows, karma beliefs and practices do not rule out local people's occupation with material possessions, state care, and pleasure and comfort. Yet local people incorporate these worldly elements into their enduring logics of cosmological balance rather than giving up on the latter for the allure of the modern material world.

Our authors also show that these ecologically based notions of the good life provide people with the resources to articulate critiques of the commercialization of nature and the impacts of national development on local ecologies (Kleinod-Freudenberg and Chanthavong, this issue). The insistence on the mutual constitution of the human body and its ecological sphere implied in the embrace of sabai (Elliott, this issue) brings into question forms of well-being that deny the reciprocity between human and nature (see also Fan Zhang, this issue). Even as Bruckermann's urban eco-volunteers may be the subjects of state environmentalism when planting a virtual tree or participating in a workplace-organized volunteering excursion, their encounters with rural people allow for reflection on the work that the latter do for the common good. The nostalgic evocation of ecological imaginaries such as bangbot (Kleinod-Freudenberg and Chanthavong, this issue) thus might be underscored by genuine yearning for a "green life" (Bruckermann, this issue) and reconnection with nature prompted by the alienation of urban life. The renewed turn to religion-inspired ideas can be fraught with power manipulation and complexity (Esler 2020), and the recentering of concepts and imageries such as karma, sabai, or bangbot may be just a reaction to the fast pace of change. Yet unlike in the postindustrial West, where they are selectively adopted as optimizing techniques for the sake of capitalist productivity (Marcuse 1964), these concepts are internal to local worldviews. They have proven resilient in the face of successive attempts by those in power to deride them throughout various historical eras. Instead of simply being "digested by the status quo as part of a healthy diet" (Marcuse 1964: 16), they do hold potentials for driving people to action and providing them with counterarguments against pro-growth development, competitive striving, and even state power.

Freedom and Autonomy

The breathtaking pace of change and the emergence of contradictory value frameworks have resulted in a widespread perception of moral crisis in late-socialist Asia, as highlighted by Jiwei Ci's (2014) analysis of China, echoed by similar perceptions in Vietnam and Laos. If a crisis of the good is common in most societies, as he posits, postreform China has been undergoing a crisis of justice and order with daily violations of "elementary norms of co-existence" becoming normalized (Ci 2014). It is the result of a vicious circle in which certain people gain unfair advantages from the violations without being corrected, leading even those with no objections to the norms to emulate their transgressions. Ci traces this situation to a double-layered breakdown in the political authority and exemplarity of the party-state through widespread corruption and rent seeking. In a society where moral education through exemplarity is central to social life, credible moral exemplars for a notion of the good based on collective goals seem in short supply as people forgo them for private wealth and pleasure. Consequently inequality and anxiety rise, at times prompting nostalgia for the relative equality and apparent absence of corruption under state socialism. However, as nobody wishes to relive the privations of life under Mao, the nostalgia merely reflects the alienation and vacuity of what Ci (2014: 36) terms "wealth-chasing and pleasure-seeking subjects." The only way out for him is to cultivate "agency through freedom," namely people's capacity to embrace meaningful and responsible action without coercion (5). Ci, however, is hardly upbeat about this in a society where "a leader-centered morality has lost its foundation and yet an alternative, superego-centered morality is not there to take its place" (214).

Yet as argued earlier, the pursuit of pleasure and wealth does not necessarily rule out moral agency and yearning for transformative action. In fact, people are continually on the lookout for spaces in which to articulate critiques of power. Kurfürst's female Vietnamese hip-hop dancers and Zavoretti's unmarried urban women defy the male dominance of the music industry and the state-sponsored, market-promoted hegemony of heterosexual marriage by carving out autonomous spaces for their private and professional lives. What appear as personal efforts irrelevant to public life are indeed actions that gradually undermine the hegemony of heterosexual marriage, and thus its state-sponsored patriarchal foundations. Despite their struggles with the pressures of the modern workplace and the difficult realities of making a living, Fengjiang's and Bruckermann's volunteers find their space for transformation in the work of relieving suffering and caring for the environment. Central to people's yearning for a pure past, as expressed by the bangbot (Kleinod-Freudenberg and Chanthavong, this issue), a reconnection to nature, seen in the eco-volunteering movement in China (Bruckermann, this issue), the Laos concept of sabai (Elliott, this issue), or the emphasis on accumulating merit in the Tibetan concept of karma (Fan Zhang, this issue) are indeed moral critiques from reflexive, meaning-seeking actors. As we discuss below, the coexistence of authoritarian government, neoliberal governmentality, and the modality of private accumulation simply renders their actions more complex and ambivalent than the portrayal of a morally vacuous citizen.

The Politics of Aspiration in Late-Socialist Asia

Ceaselessly projected by market institutions, the idea of the good life as a private state of satisfaction to be achieved by pursuing self-interest, making the right market choices, and applying appropriate methods of self-improvement has taken hold. It is an idea in which the postreform state is complicit for good reason: it helps to sustain state rule by marking out the limits of individual aspirations (High 2014; Nguyen-Vo 2008; Zhang and Ong 2008). However, people's ideas about how to live well have never been defined solely by the state. Even during the height of state socialism, they continued to draw from enduring institutions and communities of meaning such as family, kinship, and the home place. The socialist vision of the good life, meanwhile, continues to provide social and political resources for critiques of market-induced social problems; its emphasis on collective values has become part of what count as traditional repertoires of meaning. Adding to this picture is the tension between cosmopolitan desires arising out of transnational encounters, and the nationalist sentiment of citizens living in a globalized world in which people are more connected and yet immersed in shifting hierarchies of power (Boute and Pholsena 2017; Dai and Rofel 2018; Hoang 2015; Rofel 2007). All these movements and crosscurrents between different social orders give rise to contradictory values that people draw from in crafting their aspirations, engendering politics that are particular to late socialism.

The Ethical Citizen of Late Socialism

While Ci's (2014) analysis offers a good overview of the late-socialist moral landscape, it does not capture the moral life of the person unfolding at the interstices between multiple value frameworks and transcending the dualism between the good and the right. Instead of the "reflective freedom" (Laidlaw 2013) that Ci seems to be talking about, we underscore the Arendtian notion of freedom based on action. According to Arendt (1998), it is in embarking on actions that defy conventional and political givens that people come together to form new beginnings that gradually undermine existing structures. It is a form of freedom that people have to wrestle from the confines of their social position in everyday actions. We argue that it is in the very work of incrementally building this space for freedom through action that many, particularly weaker groups, find meaning in their lives (Fengjiang, this issue; Kürfurst, this issue; Zavorreti, this issue; see also Hsu and Madsen 2019). In doing so, they turn to moral ideas that are often marginalized in national and global projects of modernity. Concepts such as karma and sabai or the bangbot imaginaries thereby emerge from the margins to enter into dialogue with the logics of growth and accumulation, at times providing the very moral resources that society needs.

However, this on-the-ground struggle for spaces of action is complicated by the production of a moral subject akin to Muehlebach's (2012) ethical citizen, the self-responsible and compassionate subjecthood that is necessary for restructuring and privatization. Devoted to nurturing families and bodies (Elliott, this issue; Kürfurst, this issue; Zavoretti, this issue), the ethical citizen of late socialism is also supposed to possess an ecological consciousness (Bruckermann, this issue), the benevolent heart of a greenwood hero (Fengjiang, this issue) or the generous soul of a village healer shouldering the health care needs of their community (Elliott, this issue). Above all, this ethical citizen is shaped by the moral discourse of caring coconstituted by state, market, and other social institutions. Caring for the disadvantaged or the environment through donations, charity, and volunteering provides the moral distinction needed by anyone wishing for validation of their success. As people come to grapple with the alienating and ecologically eroding forces of development, the "choosing subject," governable by the state (Zhang and Ong 2008) seems to have receded, allowing this ethical citizen to come to the fore. Zhang and Ong's (2008) "socialism from afar" has morphed into a mode of governmentality through caring that features an intimate relationship among market rationalities, the socialist ethos, and enduring ideas of moral life. It explains the simultaneous reactivation of socialist exemplarity and values and the rolling out of privatization and restructuring in the last decade (Nguyen 2018b; Palmer and Winiger 2019; Schwenkel and Leshkowich 2012). This very conjuncture between contradicting value frameworks unleashes complex politics and struggles, not just between social groups and regions but also in the very actions of the same individual, group, or community.

Politics and Possibilities

The contradictions of late-socialist political economy become apparent in the moral quandaries behind people's actions. The motivated social engagement of Fengjiang's greenwood heroes is damped by its competition for time and energy. Unlike wealthy philanthropists, they experience a visible tension between providing for their family and caring for disadvantaged others in society. Aspiring to a cosmological balance whose material progress is enabled by the very natural resource extraction that disturbs it, people's concern with cosmology and nature (Bruckermann, this issue; Kleinod-Freudenberg and Chanthavong, this issue; Fan Zhang, this issue) is also contradicted by their own consumption, be it of travel, food, or leading "electrical lives" (Endres, this issue; Hansen, this issue). The energy-intensive life promoted by the state and the market depletes resources and further damages the environment (Endres, this issue). Even as Zavoretti's unmarried urban women or Kürfurst's female rappers in Hanoi articulate their actions in terms of self-determination or critiques of commodification, their logics tend to gravitate toward market rationalities of flexibility, self-responsibility, and self-enterprise. Concurrently, their actions are underscored by a longing for state recognition, a desire also observed by Elliott among the village healers who wish for political support even as their work falls outside the bounds of state governance. A certain cultural intimacy (Herzfeld 2005; Wilcox 2021) is observable between late-socialist states and their citizens, which at once nurtures the aspiring subject and sets its boundaries.

The limits of the aspiring subject are also drawn by the consolidation of class and gender politics of late socialism. Many people are bound by the need to labor to earn a living, which constrains their capacity and time for performing public-oriented actions. Conversely, the good life, in whatever form, depends on the labor and sacrifices of these very people. The energy-intensive life that Endres describes relies on the steady supply of electricity made possible by countless rural people being uprooted or losing their livelihoods to the installation of hydropower dams across the region (Dao 2011). A green life, as imagined by Bruckermann's urban white-collar eco-volunteers, would not be possible without the labor of the rural people who plant the trees and keep them growing. Their participation in reforestation clearly differs: for the former it is an opportunity for self-improvement, for the latter a matter of survival. Similarly, the life blessed with abundant food possibilities (Hansen, this issue) would be unthinkable without the toil of the farmers and the multitude of rural migrants who provide cheap labor for the urban food industry (Nguyen and Wei 2023). In countries where domestic servitude was condemned until recently, numerous rural women have been leaving their villages to care for urban middle-class homes in China and Vietnam (Nguyen 2015; Sun 2009), providing the urban middle class with the comfort and pleasure of a smoothly run domestic life. In short, the good life is only possible because certain people are there to shoulder its costs or the dirty, messy, and strenuous activities required to sustain it. In late-socialist Asia, these people are consistently rural people and migrant laborers. Meanwhile, both at home and in the labor market, women continue to be the main providers of care and domestic labor for the sake of reproducing healthy bodies and livable homes (Nguyen 2015; Sun 2009). While urban women may challenge the imperative of marriage and domesticity (Kürfurst, this issue; Zavoretti, this issue), they are the ones picking up the arising care needs of their own families.

The development model that devalues migrant labor for the sake of industrialization and urbanization has given rise to a laboring class whose social and political standing is fundamentally different from that of the socialist working class (Lin 2019; Nguyen and Locke 2014). However, this very laboring class is equally under the spell of the aspiring subject. For example, Bruckermann's tree-planting peasants dream about the consumption enjoyed by the urban volunteers they encounter, and Fengjiang's cabdrivers strive to serve the greater good in order to achieve a publicly recognized career such as those available to people with ample resources. With the expanding service economy, people of the laboring class find themselves in intimate encounters with the wealth projection and class distinction practices of the people they serve, with implications for their own aspirations (Hoang 2015; Nguyen 2015; Otis 2012; Sun 2009). Working people tend to view the precarity and exploitation they experience as trade-offs and sacrifices necessary for a better future, if not for themselves, then for their children (Wilcox, Rigg, and Nguyen 2021). Yet this belief in future making only holds to the extent that state-promoted dreams correspond with the possibility of realizing their own dreams, however long this may take. After all, people are only ready to make sacrifices for state-led national development goals as long as they see themselves living in countries that deliver the good life and enable them to be part of the modern world (Dai and Rofel 2018; Harms 2016).

Conclusion

The aspiring late-socialist subject's imagination is captured by an encounter between the "utopian dreams of socialism and the fictional expectations of capitalism" (Wilcox, Rigg, and Nguyen 2021: 12; see also Beckert 2016) whose goals are inherently contradictory. While each of these goals has brought about specific forms of disenchantment and unfreedom (Berlant 2011; Ahmed 2009; Marcuse 1964), their coming together under late socialism has generated a plurality of ideas and practices that emerge from people's very struggles with contradictory value frameworks. These struggles give rise to particular politics of aspiration between gendered social groups, people and the state, and the local and the global.

The most notable of these is the disconnection between the socialist ideal of the good life premised on liberating the working class, and the latter's reality of laboring in precarity and exploitation for the sake of others' pursuit of the good life. This disconnection is disguised through the production of the ethical citizen via the combination of socialist ethos, market rationalities, and past exemplars. Even as citizens pursue private accumulation and satisfaction, they are called on to care for themselves, others, communities, and the environment, and at times to make sacrifices in support of national goals. People, especially working people, do respond to these imperatives because they resonate with the emphasis on mutuality and solidarity that remains a staple of social memory, despite the foregrounding of private responsibility.

The shaping of the late-socialist ethical citizen via state and market institutions does not foreclose the possibility of freedom through action in the Arendtian sense. People's actions, however, must be understood in their everyday circulation between different social orders and strategic underscoring of certain value frameworks "at different moments and for different purposes" (Gershon 2019: 413). Our authors' analyses show that people tend to see caring for the self and others as their space for transformative action in ways that defy the separation between care as a moral discourse and care as a social value (Nguyen, Zavoretti, and Tronto 2017; see also Hsu and Madsen 2019). As Zhang (2020) suggests in *Anxious China*, even as many Chinese seek out the individualized interventions of psychotherapy to improve their private well-being, they do so to be able to care better for their families and social relations. The recentering of hitherto marginal concepts and imaginaries such as karma, sabai, or bangbot in everyday actions indicates a political reckoning with the dark sides of development and material progress. It has the potential to reactivate ecologically based conceptions of the good life. Under late socialism, where party-state and market powers are intimately connected, spaces of freedom are by no means readily given, however; they have to be constantly fought for and at times sacrificed for, and it is often in these very struggles and sacrifices that people see possibilities for generating meanings that are central to their definition of the good life.

Notes

This special issue is the outcome of a conference under the same title at the Bielefeld University's Center for Interdisciplinary Research (ZIF) in September 2019. Funding for the conference was made available through a research project funded by the European Research Council's starting grant (WelfareStruggles, no. 803614) and a conference grant from the Center for Interdisciplinary Research . We would like to thank the conference participants and discussants for their stimulating inputs, particularly by Susanne Brandstädter, Ian Baird, Kirsten W. Endres, Hy Van Luong, Andrew Kipnis, and Jonathan Rigg. We also thank Arve Hansen, Michael Kleinod-Freudenberg, Sandra Kürfurst, and Roberta Zavoretti for their comments on the introduction, and Zhenwei Wang for her research assistance.

References

Ahmed, Sara. 2009. *The Promise of Happiness*. Durham, NC: Duke University Press.

Appadurai, Arun. 2013. *The Future as Cultural Fact: Essays on the Global Condition*. New York: Verso.

Arendt, Hannah. 1998. *The Human Condition*. Chicago: University of Chicago Press.

Beckert, Jens. 2016. *Imagined Futures: Fictional Expectations and Capitalist Dynamics*. Cambridge, MA: Harvard University Press.

Berlant, Lauren. 2011. *Cruel Optimism*. Durham, NC: Duke University Press.

Boute, Vanina, and Vatthana Pholsena. 2017. *Changing Lives in Laos: Society, Politics, and Culture in a Post-socialist State*. Singapore: NUS Press.

Ci, Jiwei. 2014. *Moral China in the Age of Reform*. New York: Cambridge University Press.

Dai, Jinhua, and Lisa Rofel. 2018. *After the Post–Cold War: The Future of Chinese History*. Durham, NC: Duke University Press.

Dao, Nga. 2011. "Damming Rivers in Vietnam: A Lesson Learned in the Tây Bắc Region." *Journal of Vietnamese Studies* 6, no. 2: 106–40.

Davies, William. 2015. *The Happiness Industry: How Governments and Businesses Sold Us Well-Being*. London: Verso.

Derks, Annuska, and Minh T. N. Nguyen, eds. 2020. "Beyond the State? The Moral Turn of Development in South East Asia." Special issue, *South East Asian Research* 28, no. 1.

Esler, Joshua. 2020. *Tibetan Buddhism among Han Chinese: Mediation and Superscription of the Tibetan Tradition in Contemporary Chinese Society*. Lanham, MD: Lexington.

Fisher, Edward. 2014. *The Good Life: Aspiration, Dignity, and the Anthropology of Well-Being*. Stanford, CA: Stanford University Press.

Freud, Sigmund, and James Strachey. (1962) 2010. *Civilization and Its Discontents*. New York: W. W. Norton and Company.

Gershon, Ilana. 2019. "Porous Social Orders." *American Ethnologist* 46, no. 4: 404–16.

Hansen, Arve, Jo Inge Bekkevold, and Kristen Nordhaug, eds. 2020. *The Socialist Market Economy in Asia: Development in China, Vietnam, and Laos*. Singapore: Palgrave.

Harms, Erik. 2016. *Luxury and Rubble: Civility and Dispossession in the New Saigon*. Berkeley: University of California Press.

Herzfeld, Michael. 2005. *Cultural Intimacy: Social Poetics in the Nation-State*. New York: Routledge.

High, Holly. 2014. *Fields of Desire: Poverty and Policy in Laos*. Singapore: National University of Singapore Press.

Hoang, Kimberly Kay. 2015. *Dealing in Desire: Asian Ascendancy, Western Decline, and the Hidden Currencies of Global Sex Work*. Berkeley: University of California Press.

Hsu, Becky Yang, and Richard Madsen, eds. 2019. *The Chinese Pursuit of Happiness: Anxieties, Hopes, and Moral Tensions in Everyday Life*. Berkeley: University of California Press.

Jackson, Michael. 2011. *Life within Limits: Well-Being in a World of Want*. Durham, NC: Duke University Press.

Jacobsen, Michael H. 2014. "Sociology and Happiness: An Interview with Zygmunt Bauman." *Journal of Happiness and Well-Being* 2, no. 1: 85–94.

Kipnis, Andrew B. 2011. *Governing Educational Desire: Culture, Politics, and Schooling in China*. Chicago: University of Chicago Press.

Kuan, Teresa. 2013. *Love's Uncertainty: The Politics and Ethics of Child Rearing in Contemporary China*. Berkeley: University of California Press.

Laidlaw, James. 2013. *The Subject of Virtue: An Anthropology of Ethics and Freedom*. Cambridge: Cambridge University Press.

Li, Tania M. 2007. *The Will to Improve: Governmentality, Development, and the Practice of Politics*. Durham, NC: Duke University Press.

Lin, Jake. 2019. *Chinese Politics and Labor Movements*. Cham, Switzerland: Springer International.

Lin, Jake, and Minh T. N. Nguyen. 2021. "The Cycle of Commodification: Migrant Labour, Welfare, and the Market in Global China and Vietnam." *Global Public Policy and Governance* 1: 321–39.

Marcuse, Herbert. 1964. *One-Dimensional Man*. London: Routledge.

McElwee, Pamela D. 2016. *Forests Are Gold: Trees, People, and Environmental Rule in Vietnam*. Seattle: University of Washington Press.

Miller, Daniel. 2001. "The Poverty of Morality." *Journal of Consumer Culture* 1, no. 2: 225–43.

Muehlebach, Andrea. 2012. *The Moral Neoliberal: Welfare and Citizenship in Italy*. Chicago: University of Chicago Press.

Nguyen, Minh T. N. 2015. *Vietnam's Socialist Servants: Domesticity, Gender, Class, and Identity*. London: Routledge.

Nguyen, Minh T. N. 2018a. "Vietnam's 'Socialization' Policy and the Moral Subject in a Privatizing Economy." *Economy and Society* 47, no. 4: 627–47.

Nguyen, Minh T. N. 2018b. *Waste and Wealth: An Ethnography of Labor, Value, and Morality in a Vietnamese Recycling Economy*. Oxford: Oxford University Press.

Nguyen, Minh T. N., and Meixuan Chen. 2017. "The Caring State? On Welfare Governance in Rural Vietnam and China." *Ethics and Social Welfare* 11, no. 3: 230–47.

Nguyen, Minh T. N., and Catherine Locke. 2014. "Rural-Urban Migration in China and Vietnam: Gendered Householding, Space Production, and the State." *Journal of Peasant Studies* 41, no. 5: 855–76.

Nguyen, Minh T. N., and Lan Wei. 2023. "Peasant Traders, Migrant Workers and 'Supermarkets': Low-Cost Provisions and the Reproduction of Migrant Labor in China." *Economic Anthropology*. https://doi.org/10.1002/sea2.12292.

Nguyen, Minh T. N., Roberta Zavoretti, and Joan Tronto. 2017. "Beyond the Global Care Chain: Boundaries, Institutions, and Ethics of Care." Special issue introduction, *Ethics and Social Welfare* 11, no. 3: 199–212.

Nguyen-Vo, Thu-Huong. 2008. *The Ironies of Freedom: Sex, Culture, and Neoliberal Governance in Vietnam*. Seattle: University of Washington Press.

Ortner, Sherry B. 2016. "Dark Anthropology and Its Others: Theory since the Eighties." *HAU: Journal of Ethnographic Theory* 6, no. 1: 47–73.

Osburg, John. 2013. *Anxious Wealth: Money and Morality among China's New Rich*. Stanford, CA: Stanford University Press.

Otis, Eileen M. 2012. *Markets and Bodies: Women, Service Work, and the Making of Inequality in China*. Stanford, CA: Stanford University Press.

Palmer, David A., and Fabian Winiger. 2019. "Neo-socialist Governmentality: Managing Freedom in the People's Republic of China." *Economy and Society* 48, no. 4: 554–78.

Robbins, Joel. 2013. "Beyond the Suffering Subject: Toward an Anthropology of the Good." *Journal of the Royal Anthropological Institute* 19, no. 3: 447–62.

Rofel, Lisa. 2007. *Desiring China: Experiments in Neoliberalism, Sexuality, and Public Culture*. Durham, NC: Duke University Press.

Schwenkel, Christina, and Ann Marie Leshkowich. 2012. "How Is Neoliberalism Good to Think Vietnam? How Is Vietnam Good to Think Neoliberalism?" *positions: east asia critique* 20, no. 2: 379–401.

Sun, Wanning. 2009. *Maid in China: Media, Mobility, and the Cultural Politics of Boundaries*. London: Routledge.

Tronto, Joan. 1993. *Moral Boundaries: A Political Argument for an Ethic of Care*. New York: Routledge.

Wilcox, Phill. 2021. *Heritage and the Making of Political Legitimacy in Laos: The Past and the Present of the Lao Nation*. Amsterdam: Amsterdam University Press.

Wilcox, Phill, Jonathan Rigg, and Minh T. N. Nguyen, eds. 2021. "Rural Life in Late Socialist Asia: Politics of Development and Imaginaries of the Future." Special issue, *European Journal of East Asian Studies* 20, no. 1.

Zavoretti, Roberta. 2017. *Rural Origins, City Lives: Place and Class in Contemporary China*. Seattle: University of Washington Press.

Zhang, Li. 2010. *In Search of Paradise: Middle-Class Living in a Chinese Metropolis*. Ithaca, NY: Cornell University Press.

Zhang, Li. 2020. *Anxious China: Inner Revolution and Politics of Psychotherapy*. Oakland: University of California Press.

Zhang, Li, and Aihwa Ong. 2008. *Privatizing China: Socialism from Afar*. Ithaca, NY: Cornell University Press.

Plugged into the Good Life:

Living Electrically through the Ages in Urban Vietnam

Kirsten W. Endres

The quest for the good life is a universal expression of human endeavor and aspiration. It has been closely linked to questions of virtue and morality since the times of Confucius and Aristotle (Back 2018; Fischer 2014; Morris 2012; Gregory 2018; see also Nguyen, Wilcox, and Lin, this issue). In economic theory and development thinking, ideas of the good life have been correlated with material well-being and growth in consumption, both of which are unthinkable without electricity. Electrification has played a key role in the global spread of modern lifestyles since the late nineteenth century, although the results have been uneven across regions. Electricity's association with light and lightness, speed and connectivity, and freedom from drudgery has also been implicated in nation-building and modernization projects. Whereas colonial states emphasized its positive features as emblems of Western civilizational and technological superiority (Lar-

positions 32:1   DOI 10.1215/10679847-10889934
Copyright 2024 by Duke University Press

kin 2008: 7), socialist states turned them into icons of national belonging and liberation from feudal and colonial oppression. Today, electricity and electrification have come to signify state sovereignty, efficiency, and global integration, and universal access to an electric power supply is perceived as an essential prerequisite for civilized life and human progress (Abram, Winthereik, and Yarrow 2019: 11; see also Winther 2008). In many parts of the world, including Vietnam, growing middle-class populations and incomes foster an ever-increasing demand for domestic appliances and, consequently, household electricity (Hansen, Nielson, and Wilhite 2016; Wilhite 2008: 4). As a result, life without the comforts and conveniences of electricity and electric appliances has almost become unimaginable.

This article explores the history of domestic electrification and attitudes toward home appliances in urban Vietnam from the colonial period until the present. Inspired by recent advances in the anthropology of electricity (e.g., Cross et al. 2017), I reflect on the availability, significance, and role of electric appliances through the ages and ask if, how, and why some of them have come to define what it means to live a good life. According to Daniel Miller (2001: 1), "It is the material culture within our home that appears as both our appropriation of the larger world and often as the representation of that world within our private domain."

In Vietnam, the advancement and proper use of things electric was underpinned by discourses of civilizational achievement until the late 1980s. With the onset of Đổi Mới, Vietnam's economic reforms, Vietnamese urbanites grew evermore accustomed to living their lives electrically. Today modern Vietnamese households are equipped with an increasing number of electric appliances that cook and store food efficiently, provide physical comfort and relief from climatic conditions, allow for flexible work schedules, and connect people in unprecedented ways.[1] Some of these gadgets, as well as some specific brands, have even become symbols of conspicuous consumption and markers of social distinction and achievement among the privileged urban classes (Veblen [1899] 2009; see also Bourdieu 1984).

Throughout time and history, technological advancement and innovation in domestic appliances have thus contributed to imaginaries of and aspirations for a good life, which promises ever more material comfort, convenience, efficiency, and pleasure. Today some of the most common electric appliances seem almost to be natural extensions of their users' bodies and minds. But the unlimited pursuit of these aspirations comes at a price that future generations will have to pay. The specter of the Anthropocene already looms large across the globe, and Vietnam is among the countries most vulnerable to climate-change impacts and other environmental risks (Feeny, Trinh, and Zhu 2021: 3), the effects of which are unevenly felt across different social groups in the country. These existing inequalities are likely to be further exacerbated in the future, imposing certain limits on the pursuit of the good life as a collective project of contemporary socialist modernity (Nguyen, Wilcox, and Lin, this issue). In the current era, living electrically in urban Vietnam therefore also reflects a global sense of what Berlant (2011) calls *cruel optimism*, in which middle-class urbanites become ever more attached to certain understandings of what constitutes a good life that are unsustainable in the long run and detrimental to both their individual and their collective well-being.

The Colonial Making of Electrified Lives

Histories of national and domestic electrification have an important place in the study of technological systems (e.g., Chappels and Shin 2018; Hughes 1983; Nye 1990). The evolution of electric power systems in Western societies and their introduction into the domestic sphere roughly coincided with the heyday of European colonial expansion and rule, and it was during this time that electricity, along with other "tentacles of modernity" (Headrick 1988), penetrated colonized territories. Despite its transformative effects on colonial societies, however, there has been relatively little research on colonial electrification and broader issues of infrastructure development in the non-Western world (Hasenoehrl 2018: 5). Researchers in the humanities and social sciences have only recently begun to address this gap and to look at the emergence of colonial and postcolonial energy systems and electricity grids.

Vietnam's electrification during the French colonial era began as early as 1892 with the installation of electric lighting in the streets of Haiphong, with Hanoi following suit three years later (Drouin 1938; Tertrais 2002). For a long time, however, the transmission of electric power remained a purely local affair limited to major urban centers. The first power plant installed on the banks of Hanoi's Hoan Kiem Lake in 1895 generated only enough electricity to provide lighting in the main streets and administrative buildings, with private access to electricity remaining a privilege enjoyed mostly by the French, a small group of Vietnamese elites, and Chinese merchant-entrepreneurs.[2] In 1939, the French geographer Charles Robequain noted that "electricity provides the white population with infinitely valuable opportunities for comfort and resistance to tropical climate through its multiple domestic applications (ventilation, easy ice making, food preservation, etc.); it is highly valued in cities by indigenous traders, and even more so by the Chinese" (quoted in Tertrais 2002: 591; my translation).

Apart from electric lamps, one of the first home appliances that appeared in Vietnam in the early twentieth century was the electric fan. The following ruminations of a Frenchman during the early days of electrification indicate how quickly consumers grew accustomed to the comforts of electric lighting and ventilation in the colonial city: "When one is used to electric lighting and fans, one suffers when one is deprived of them in the bush" (*L'éveil économique de l'Indochine* 1918). In 1938, however, the number of fans powered by the rudimentary electrical grid that the Société Indochinoise d'Electricité had by then established in the Red River Delta was reported to total not more than 26,500, of which 16,800 were ceiling fans (Drouin 1938: 485).[3] Given that the urban population of Hanoi and Haiphong was around 219,000 at the time (Banens, Bassino, and Egretaud 1998), and that electric fans were mainly moving the air in administrative and public buildings, this was a very low number, and certainly electricity was something for rural folks to marvel at. In a cartoon published in 1933 in the Hanoi weekly *Phong Hóa*, Lý Toét, a rustic visitor to the rapidly transforming city who "struggled (usually unsuccessfully) to comprehend the modern" (Dutton 2007: 81), reasons about the usefulness of the fan as an indicator of his level of intoxication. Holding a glass of liquor in his hand, he sits in front of a table fan and wonders, "If it turns out that it is not spinning, then I'm drunk.... If it is truly spinning, then I'm not drunk" (my translation). Familiarity with electric appliances and their functions thus also came to indicate a high level of cultural sophistication that was closely associated with modern colonial urbanity. For those who could afford to purchase them, the new technologies provided ample opportunity to put their aspirations to a modern way of life on display. When radio broadcasting started in the late 1920s, those who were able to purchase a radio set usually placed it in a prominent spot in the home to make sure "that both neighbors and strangers could hear—and sometimes see—[it] in order to demonstrate their own social and cultural arrival" (DeWald 2012: 149).

Meanwhile, domestic electrification and household technification were well underway in other parts of Asia. Japan was in the global vanguard: 89 percent of its households had access to electric lighting in 1935, compared to only 68 percent in the United States (Morris-Suzuki 1994: 130). Moreover, the Japanese Sekaitsu Kaizen (life reform) movement of the late 1910s and 1920s was already propagating the use of electric appliances as a way of raising the standard of living (Yoshimi 1999: 154). Household electrification was further propelled by an oversupply of electricity in those years and the subsequent efforts of electricity-generation companies "to develop and proliferate the use of electricity for purposes other than lighting" (153). Japanese domestic production reached a peak in the 1930s, and included electric cooking stoves, cookie machines, water pumps, sewing machines, washing machines, vacuum cleaners, and refrigerators. In the mid-1950s, Japanese electric companies targeted women in particular with advertisements promising that "electric appliances in the home will fill [your life] with joy" (158). After the First Indochina War in 1954, their products eventually also reached South Vietnam. The Democratic Republic of Vietnam (DRV, or North Vietnam) turned to other suppliers to fill people's homes with this kind of "joy."

Technifying the Urban Home during Socialism

Whereas Vietnam's colonial electrification had mainly served the purpose of signifying Western civilizational superiority and consolidating the power and wealth of ruling elites, the aim of the government of the DRV was to make electricity accessible to all citizens in both urban and rural areas (Schwenkel 2019: 110). This also lent authority and support to the Communist Party and government. As Schwenkel notes, "Under the banner 'Đảng là ánh sáng' (The Party is the light), electrification projects brought new legitimacy and meaning to the postcolonial government's moral promise to rescue the population from the darkness of colonization" (111). During the Vietnam War, however, the newly evolving electricity supply networks became key targets for destruction. Between 1965 and 1972 American warplanes conducted 1,652 air-raids on power-supply facilities, destroying or severely damaging many. US military estimates hold that these raids reduced North Vietnam's national energy capacity by more than 70 percent (102; Griffith 1994). The devastating effect of the war on Hanoi's electric power system left domestic consumers without sufficient supply to meet demand: "The limited amount of power available [through the national system and portable generators] was probably supplied only to priority users, such as the more important industrial installations, foreign embassies, and selected government buildings in Hanoi" (Griffith 1994: 40).

After the war ended in 1975, energy production gradually increased, the majority derived from thermal power plants and hydroelectric dams (Gough 1990: 134). Postwar reconstruction included the implementation of grid expansion projects and the connection of rural industries to electric power supplies. It also included the intensification of official and unofficial commercial ties with socialist Eastern Bloc countries, where the gospel of household technification had already been received and adapted to suit socialist objectives. In the Soviet Union under Khrushchev (1953–64), the electrification of housework was supposed to bring the scientific-technological revolution into people's homes, "inculcating the scientific consciousness requisite for the transition to communism" (Reid 2005: 313). Yet it wasn't until the Brezhnev period (1964–82) that the production of domestic appliances was stepped up and "urban ownership of classic household appliances such as washing machines, vacuum cleaners, refrigerators, and television sets climbed to meaningful levels" (Chernyshova 2011: 192).[4]

Vietnamese who came to the USSR or to Eastern Europe as students or on temporary labor contracts would usually ship home some locally produced consumer goods that were highly coveted in Vietnam, such as sewing machines, pressing irons, electric kettles, radios, and refrigerators.[5] The arrival of these gadgets in Vietnamese households attracted the attention of neighbors, who would gather in large numbers to marvel at these latest technological advancements (Schlecker 2011). Seen as prestige items, they also enhanced their owners' status. As Beresford and Dang (2000: 74) note, "These small assets brought back from overseas were sufficient to guarantee that the returnee became one of the social elite" (see also Schwenkel 2022). Even familiar items such as the table fan were still exotic enough to inspire awe and admiration. Fifty-two-year-old Hàng remembers how the people in her hometown, Nam Định, lauded the arrival of Russian "elephant ear" fans during the high socialist period. "They enjoyed the breeze so much that they moved to and fro along with the oscillating fan head!" Hàng giggles, hastening to add "But my family was more civilized, we didn't do that!" In 1986 her family received their first refrigerator, shipped to Nam Định all the way from Kiev, where Hàng's sister was studying. "When it arrived at our home, we marveled at it as something incredible!" Hàng recounts. At that time, however, the family neither had money for meat or other things that could be stored in the refrigerator, nor could they afford the electricity to run it. "We put a flower vase on top and used it as decoration until we sold it two months later," she says. Some urbanites found better uses for their refrigerators, using them as a source of additional income by producing small quantities of ice to sell to tea shops and drink stands.[6] At the height of socialism, however, electricity was rationed, and people mainly used it for lighting and listening to the radio. Only those who had a priority grid or illegal connection to the electricity supply of a privileged household or production facility were able to use it for other purposes as well.[7]

Plugged into the Good Life in the Contemporary Era

Vietnam's shift to a market-oriented socialist economy in the mid-1980s marked a turning point in every respect. The extensive growth of the country's economy was accompanied by rapid increases in both energy production and consumption. In the twenty years from 1995 to 2014, the proportion of households without electricity decreased from 50 to only 2 percent (Asian Development Bank 2016: 6–7). Producing almost 40 percent of the total national electricity production, today hydropower is one of the most important sources of Vietnam's power supply. In the past two decades hundreds of hydropower dams have been constructed, predominately in the north and the central highlands. Their benefits to the national economy notwithstanding, these projects have also incurred huge human and environmental costs and contributed to the production of new inequalities (see Dao 2011). Meanwhile, Vietnam's hunger for electricity continued to soar: by the year 2000, the residential sector had seen the greatest increase in electricity consumption compared to the industrial and agricultural sectors (Scott and Greenhill 2014). From 2010 to 2015, annual per-capita electricity use grew by more than 50 percent from 998 to 1546 kwh (Neefjes and Dang 2017). In 2016, residential electricity accounted for 35 percent of Vietnam's total power consumption (Le and Pitts 2019). Rising middle-class living standards, changing notions of good and desirable lifestyles, and, more recently, rising temperatures brought on by climate change have led to a gradual "retreat from the street" (Harms 2009) in urban centers. This turn inward to the home has played a significant role in boosting consumer demand for domestic appliances such as refrigerators, air conditioners, and home entertainment devices. New images of the modern urban lifestyle circulated through the media and advertisements, serving as instruction manuals for "dealing with an ever more complex world in which there is greatly expanded choice" (Drummond 2004: 174). Concomitantly, they also contributed to standardizing people's aspirations to the good life (Elsaesser 2006: 28). Along with other consumer goods such as houses, motorbikes, and cars, electric appliances have become an important index of middle-class civility and family happiness (Leshkowich 2012: 100; fig. 1).

Today, urban middle-class Vietnamese homes are generally well equipped with a wide range of domestic electric and electronic devices. Data from the General Statistics Office of Vietnam show a continued increase in the ownership of electric appliances between 2002 and 2016.[8] Over this period, ownership of refrigerators increased by 157 percent, of washing machines by 340 percent, and of air conditioners by more than 1,000 percent. Electric fans are now ubiquitous throughout the country, and 25 percent of Vietnamese urban households were equipped with an air conditioner in 2016. Urban households generally own more than two telephones (including mobile phones), and many are equipped with more than one television set. My own twenty-one structured interviews conducted with a random sample in urban and peri-urban Hanoi in March 2019 confirm a clear trend toward a continuous increase in urban domestic appliance ownership.[9] While mass

Figure 1 Electricity meters on the outer wall of a multistory building in Hanoi, 2019.

production and cheap imports from China have democratized the general consumption of appliances, class distinctions are now defined by appliance brands and origins (Endres 2019: 59–60; Vann 2003).

Besides refrigerators, washing machines, air conditioners, and television sets, small appliances such as rice cookers, microwaves, water kettles, and pressing irons have become the norm rather than the exception.[10] In addition, all the homes in my small survey were equipped with Wi-Fi routers to connect their inhabitants' smartphones, laptops, and tablets to the internet. More than half of the survey participants also reported owning other small appliances such as ovens, portable induction cooktops, blenders, and vacuum cleaners, but fewer than 50 percent possessed equipment such as desktop computers (47 percent, often in addition to laptops), DVD/CD players (28 percent), radios (24 percent), or dishwashers (14 percent). Electric ceramic/induction stoves were used by the majority of households in the city center, while roughly two-thirds of households, primarily in peri-urban Hanoi, cooked on propane gas. Below I discuss some of the appliances that the survey participants considered most indispensable for a good life, grouping them into three categories for convenience: communicating/connecting, cooking/storing, and cooling.

Communicating/Connecting

As elsewhere in the world, smartphones have become essential in Vietnamese society, and life without one seems next to impossible.[11] Smartphones of highly valued and prestigious brands that are difficult to obtain through official channels are often smuggled into the country as *hàng xách tay* (hand-carried goods) and circulate via networks of family, friends, and peers (Nguyen 2016). Street peddlers use them to coordinate their business, app-based taxi drivers depend on them to provide their services, and academics use them to check their emails and find information online. Facebook, Zalo, and YouTube are popular platforms not only for online socializing and networking but also increasingly for all sorts of entrepreneurial and trading activities. This trend of smartphone penetration into Vietnamese society was reflected in the choices of my interviewees, for more than half of whom the smartphone occupied a central role in their everyday routine. The majority, in particular those working in the service and trade sectors, explained that they depended on their smartphones for work matters. Tùng, for example, works as a delivery man for an organic vegetable company and uses his smartphone for both professional and private purposes. In his free time he enjoys watching videos on YouTube and playing online games. Other private uses include communicating with family and friends, connecting with social networks, reading the news, and playing games.

Another important item in this category is the laptop. In present-day Vietnam the laptop signifies autonomy and entrepreneurship, especially among educated and globally connected enterprising young professionals. A third of the interviewees in my survey, of which four were academics, two worked for telecommunication companies, and one was an entrepreneur, regarded the laptop as indispensable for a good life. They all used them for work matters, which of course raises the question of the significance of work in the good life as such. But another important factor at play may be the flexibility a laptop provides by allowing people to work from their place of choice at any time of day. Vietnamese academics, for example, spend little time in their institutes or departments, and even there they prefer to use their laptops rather than the desktop computers installed in their office. They also tend to enjoy greater comfort and tranquility in the privacy of their homes than in their shared offices, where they are prone to frequent distractions and the disruption of their workflow.

Cooking/Storing

Imaginaries and practices of the good life under market socialism also require a shiny, presentable, and well-provisioned domestic sphere. In the words of Nguyen (2015: 112), "The home now must be both a sanctuary of relaxation and nurturance, and a window to its occupants' standards of living and their social status." As the heart of the home, the kitchen plays a key role in facilitating the good life. Food and eating are more than just basic human needs; they are central to social life and "partake in processes of cultural production, reproduction, and negotiation" (Avieli 2012: 15). Preparing and cooking food are also essential parts of caring for and nurturing the self and others, both of which are central elements of meaning making in people's lives (Nguyen, Wilcox, and Lin, this issue). It is therefore not surprising that appliances for cooking and storing food are high on the list of most important household objects. Even though restaurants and street food outlets are omnipresent in urban Vietnam, with many Hanoians eating at least one meal a day outside the home (see Hansen, this issue), cooking appliances are still seen as essential devices in the kitchen. More than 70 percent of respondents nominated an electric cooking appliance as one of the three most important items for a good life, eight choosing the cooking stove and seven the rice cooker, which can also be used to prepare other types of food (fig. 2).

With changing food provisioning infrastructure and new habits of consumption, the refrigerator-freezer has become another indispensable element of the modern Vietnamese kitchen (Le and Pitts 2019; Rinkinen, Shove, and Smits 2019). A recent article published on the Vietnamese news

Figure 2 Rice cookers on display at an electronics supermarket in Hanoi, 2019.

website *Báo Mới* highlights some of the benefits conferred by the appearance of the refrigerator in Vietnam, in particular with regard to easing the burden of housework for women: "They no longer have to go to the market every day, neither do they need to worry about cooking the right amount of food, because left-overs can be kept in the fridge" (Giang Quốc Hoàng 2019; my translation). Women remain primarily responsible for household duties, and notions of the good life in the domestic sphere are highly charged with gendered assumptions. Moreover, the increased use of modern kitchen gadgets does not necessarily mean that women spend less time on housework, as Ruth Schwartz Cowan (1983) cogently shows in *More Work for Mother*. As standards of cleanliness and sanitation rise, new expectations and needs can increase the amount of domestic work required, adding to women's burden.

Some items can lose their distinctive meaning as status markers when they become commonly available to and affordable for the majority (Beng-

Huat 2000; Earl 2014). While an ordinary refrigerator-freezer costing roughly 6,000,000 VND (250 USD) may no longer be seen as a symbol of wealth and social status, a high-tech German refrigerator with an integrated wine cabinet still has considerable potential to convey a sense of achievement and social distinction. As Catherine Earl (2014: 174) points out, it is not the consumer product itself that creates status but its appropriate use and its symbolic meaning as a marker of cultural sophistication and cosmopolitan middle-class civility. Yet with the rapid development of new technologies, devices quickly lose their novelty and become outdated. On the individual level, this may lead to what Thomas Hylland Eriksen (2016) describes as "treadmill competition" in an overheated world: an endless spiral of consumption in pursuit of the latest gadgets that enhance the consumer's personal comfort and social status but sooner or later end up as electronic waste, posing a risk to human health and the environment.

Cooling

As elsewhere in Southeast Asia, Vietnam's urban expansion and the associated change in land use have had a profound impact on the urban climate, and city dwellers are increasingly relying on air conditioning for their physical comfort (Hansen, Nielsen, and Wilhite 2016: 12; Sahakian 2014; Winter 2013). This has led to "a hardening of the physical and social boundaries between home and surroundings" (Wilhite 2009: 86), with people preferring the comfort of their air-conditioned homes to spending recreational time outdoors. The desire to stay cool during the summer months also creates a negative feedback loop: the waste heat emitted from air-conditioners not only affects the urban air temperature and contributes to more pronounced urban heat islands where the air is up to 10 degrees warmer than in surrounding city districts (see Hansen, Nielsen, and Wilhite 2016), but it also results in city dwellers facing ever higher electricity bills. As a result of the rapid increase in residential electricity consumption, Vietnamese households also experienced a ninefold increase in electricity prices between 2009 and 2018, and another steep hike of 8.36 percent in 2019 (Feeny, Trinh, and Zhu 2021; Hoai Thu 2019). Electricity consumption thus imposes a significant financial burden on households, and some lower-income families have to think twice before running domestic appliances (Lê Bảo 2020; see also Ha-Duong 2021).[12]

Urbanites who can afford an energy-intensive lifestyle increasingly do so at the expense of those who earn their livelihoods in the streets, be they street vendors, construction workers, or motorcycle-taxi drivers. Although anxieties about a sustainable environmental future are growing across the region (Sands 2019; see also Bruckermann, this issue; Kleinod-Freudenberg and Chanthavong, this issue), including critical perspectives on energy consumption and its effects on the environment, the desire for individual comfort and social status expressed through lifestyle choices still "outweighs a desire to achieve globally-valued sustainability" (Earl 2013: 21).[13] Here we might see Lauren Berlant's (2011: 51) *cruel optimism* most clearly at work: "Optimism is cruel when it takes shape as an affectively stunning double bind: a binding to fantasies that block the satisfactions they offer, and a binding to the promise of optimism as such that the fantasies have come to represent." The continuous increase in air temperature in Hanoi over the past two decades clearly indicates that our fantasy of the good life as an electrically powered life may ultimately become an obstacle to the flourishing of humanity. To some people it certainly already has.[14]

Conclusion

Questions addressed in the 2017 issue of *Cultural Anthropology*'s Theorizing the Contemporary series entitled "Our Lives with Electrical Things" included "Can we still imagine the possibility of lives without electric things? Can electric things help us to address the possibilities and limits of life with electricity? Can our lives with electricity ever be disentangled from electric things?" (Cross et al. 2017). Domestic appliances have been shaping human notions of comfort and well-being ever since their invention. In Vietnam, as elsewhere, electricity has facilitated the emergence of what Reyes (2012: 195) calls the technological infrastructure of the good life—a life that is increasingly difficult to imagine without the modern comforts that electricity provides. I still remember the frequent blackouts in the village where I conducted fieldwork in the mid-1990s. It was a hot and humid summer, and whenever the electric ventilator stopped in the middle of an interview, people frantically reached for their traditional hand-held fans and waved them vigorously in front of their faces. How, I wondered, had they survived before being connected to the grid? The villagers had quickly come to take the comfort of electrically powered heat relief for granted.

Today in late-socialist Vietnam, electric household appliances have become essential material components of the good life. This is most apparent in urban and peri-urban areas, where the country's growing middle class is concentrated. However, it is hard to pin down the cultural, social, and economic particularities of electric lives under the conditions of late socialism. The electrically powered lifestyles that have emerged in Vietnam's metropoles have much in common with cosmopolitan middle-class lifestyles in other Asian cities. In the future, these lifestyles are likely to become more difficult to achieve or maintain. But adopting a less energy-intensive lifestyle, whether by force or voluntarily, might ultimately be crucial to mitigating the negative effects of environmental pollution on people's lives and well-being. As Lauren Berlant (2011: 69) asks, "What is the good life when the world that was to have been delivered by upward mobility and collective uplift that national/capitalism promised goes awry in front of one?" With climate change looming large, an answer to this question is urgently needed, not just in Asia but across the globe.

Notes

This research was funded by the Max Planck Institute for Social Anthropology, Halle/ Saale. I would like to thank the editors of this special issue and the anonymous reviewers for their many insightful comments and suggestions. Huge thanks also to Nguyễn Thị Thanh Bình and Trần Hoài for their help with the survey.

1   Rural households tend to possess fewer appliances than their urban counterparts, not only because they cannot afford to pay high electricity bills but also because the supply voltage in the countryside is often too low or unstable to operate high-energy devices.

2   Hanoi's electric tramway lines, first inaugurated in 1901, were powered by a separate power station.

3   The number of refrigerators, in contrast, was estimated at 829.

4   This was not only true for the Soviet Union but also for postwar Western Europe, where few households had been equipped with, for instance, refrigerators and washing machines during the 1950s (Chernyshova 2011: 193).

5 Television sets and other entertainment devices only became common after the collapse of the Soviet Union (Schlecker 2011: 125; for an account of the arrival of television at an individual household, see Nguyen-Thu 2019: viii–ix).

6 Thanks to Minh T. N. Nguyen for this information.

7 Thanks to Minh T. N. Nguyen and Thi Phuong Thao Vu for this information.

8 Until recently, these data were available on the website of the General Statistics Office. The new website has only archived some of them: https://www.gso.gov.vn/en/population-and-houses-census/publication/.

9 This sample is of course not representative of the full spectrum of urban dwellers in Hanoi. Fifteen of the interviewees were female and six were male. Two-thirds lived in houses of varying degrees of affluence, and about one-third owned or rented apartments in modern high-rise buildings. Professions ranged from university professors and researchers to business owners, company employees, two retirees, an event manager, a cleaner, a domestic helper, and a Grab taxi driver. Household incomes varied from 11–15 million VND (about 470–650 USD) to over 40 million VND (about 1,700 USD) per month, with two-thirds of interviewees in the 31 million VND (about 1,300 USD) and above range.

10 While the fact that grid connections and electric appliances are available to everyone should not blind us to the fact that not everyone has the means to pay the electricity bills incurred when using these items, this is beyond the scope of this article and is therefore not discussed in depth.

11 According to the Nielsen Việt Nam Smartphone Insights Report 2017, 95 percent of urban dwellers in key cities own a mobile phone, of which 84 percent are smartphones. In rural areas, mobile phones have also become the norm rather than the exception.

12 Poor households are eligible for a so-called "lifeline tariff" if they consume no more than 50 kWh per month; see http://www.meconproject.com/wp-content/uploads/report/[Task%206 -Electricity%20pricing%20in%20the%20residential%20sector]%20Vietnam%20country%20 report.pdf.

13 The growing use of air conditioners has not completely replaced the use of electric fans in their various forms. Although all twenty-one survey participants were equipped with air-conditioning, five chose the fan as one of three items they considered most indispensable for a good life, while only four chose the air conditioner.

14 Between 1990 and 2010, the monthly mean surface air temperature in Hanoi's city center increased by 0.35° C and is predicted to rise further by 0.7° C in the coming decade (see Doan, Kusaka, and Nguyen 2019).

References

Abram, Simone, Brit Ross Winthereik, and Thomas Yarrow. 2019. "Current Thinking— An Introduction." In *Electrifying Anthropology. Exploring Electrical Practices and Infrastruc-*

tures, edited by Simone Abram, Brit Ross Winthereik, and Thomas Yarrow, 3–24. New York: Bloomsbury Academic.

Asian Development Bank. 2016. *Viet Nam. Energy Sector Assessment, Strategy, and Road Map.* Manila: Asian Development Bank. https://www.adb.org/documents/viet-nam-energy-sector-assessment-strategy-and-road-map.

Avieli, Nir. 2012. *Rice Talks: Food and Community in a Vietnamese Town.* Bloomington: Indiana University Press.

Back, Youngsun. 2018. "Virtue and the Good Life in the Early Confucian Tradition." *Journal of Religious Ethics* 46, no. 1: 37–62.

Banens, Maks, Jean-Pascal Bassino, and Eric Egretaud. 1998. "Estimating Population and Labour Force in Vietnam under French Rule (1900–1954)." Discussion paper no. D98-7, Institute of Economic Research, Hitotsubashi University. http://hermes-ir.lib.hit-u.ac.jp/rs/handle/10086/14693.

Beng-Huat, Chua. 2000. "Consuming Asians: Ideas and Issues." In *Consumption in Asia. Lifestyles and Identities*, edited by Chua Beng-Huat, 1–34. New York: Routledge.

Beresford, Melanie, and Dang Phong. 2000. *Economic Transition in Vietnam: Trade and Aid in the Demise of a Centrally Planned Economy.* Cheltenham, UK: Elgar.

Berlant, Laurent. 2011. *Cruel Optimism.* Durham, NC: Duke University Press.

Bourdieu, Pierre. 1984. *Distinction: A Social Critique of the Judgement of Taste.* Translated by Richard Nice. Cambridge, MA: Harvard University Press.

Chappels, Heather, and Hiroki Shin. 2018. "Making Material and Cultural Connections: The Fluid Meaning of 'Living Electrically' in Japan and Canada 1920–1960." *Science Museum Group Journal* 9. http://journal.sciencemuseum.org.uk/browse/issue-09/making-material-and-cultural-connections/.

Chernyshova, Natalya. 2011. "Consuming Technology in a Closed Society: Household Appliances in Soviet Urban Homes of the Brezhnev Era." *Ab Imperio* 2: 188–220.

Cross, Jamie, Simone Abram, Mike Anusas, and Lea Schick. 2017. "Introduction: Our Lives with Electric Things." Theorizing the Contemporary, *Fieldsights*, December 19. https://culanth.org/fieldsights/introduction-our-lives-with-electric-things.

Dao, Nga. 2011. "Damming Rivers in Vietnam: A Lesson Learned in the Tây Bắc Region." *Journal of Vietnamese Studies* 6, no. 2: 106–40.

DeWald, Erich. 2012. "Taking to the Waves: Vietnamese Society Around the Radio in the 1930s." *Modern Asian Studies* 46, no. 1: 143–65.

Doan, Q. Van, Hiroyuki Kusaka, and Tuong M. Nguyen. 2019. "Roles of Past, Present, and Future Land Use and Anthropogenic Heat Release Changes on Urban Heat Island Effects in Hanoi, Vietnam: Numerical Experiments with a Regional Climate Model." *Sustainable Cities and Society* 47, no. 101479: 2–9.

Drouin, P. 1938. "L'électrification du Tonkin." *Bulletin économique de l'Indo-Chine* 41, no. 3: 481–89.

Drummond, Lisa. 2004. "The Modern 'Vietnamese Woman': Socialization and Women's Magazines." In *Gender Practices in Contemporary Vietnam*, edited by Lisa Drummond and Helle Rydstrom, 158–78. Singapore: NUS Press; Copenhagen: NIAS Press.

Dutton, Georges. 2007. "Lý Toét in the City: Coming to Terms with the Modern in 1930s Vietnam." *Journal of Vietnamese Studies* 2, no. 1: 80–108.

Earl, Catherine. 2013. "Research Note: On the Energy Footprint of a Vietnamese Middle-Class Household." *Pacific Geographies* 39: 17–21.

Earl, Catherine. 2014. *Vietnam's New Middle Classes: Gender, Career, City.* Copenhagen: NIAS Press.

Elsaesser, Thomas. 2006. "The Camera in the Kitchen: Grete Schütte-Lihotsky and Domestic Modernity." In *Practicing Modernity: Female Creativity in the Weimar Republic*, edited by Christiane Schönfeld, 27–49. Würzburg, Germany: Königshausen & Neumann.

Endres, Kirsten W. 2019. *Market Frictions. Trade and Urbanization at the Vietnam-China Border.* New York: Berghahn.

Eriksen, Thomas Hylland. 2016. *Overheating: An Anthropology of Accelerated Change.* London: Pluto Press.

Feeny, Simon, Trong-Anh Trinh, and Anna Zhu. 2021. "Temperature Shocks and Energy Poverty: Findings from Vietnam." *Energy Economics* 99: 1–15.

Fischer, Edward F. 2014. *The Good Life: Aspiration, Dignity, and the Anthropology of Well-being.* Stanford: Stanford University Press.

Giang, Quốc Hoàng. 2019. "Những chiếc tủ lạnh đã 'tiến hóa' cùng cuộc sống người Việt thế nào?" ("How Have Refrigerators 'Evolved' With the Life of the Vietnamese?"). *Baomoi.com*, June 1. https://baomoi.com/nhung-chiec-tu-lanh-da-tien-hoa-cung-cuoc-song-nguoi-viet-the-nao/c/30937103.epi.

Gough, Kathleen. 1990. *Political Economy in Vietnam.* Berkeley, CA: Folklore Institute.

Gregory, Chris. 2018. Introduction to *The Quest for The Good Life in Precarious Times: Ethnographic Perspectives on the Domestic Moral Economy*, edited by Chris Gregory and Jon Altman, 1–10. Acton, Australia: ANU Press.

Griffith, Thomas E. 1994. *Strategic Attack of National Electrical Systems.* MS thesis, Air University Press, Maxwell Air Force Base, Alabama. https://media.defense.gov/2017/Dec/29/2001861964/-1/-1/0/T_GRIFFITH_STRATEGIC_ATTACK.PDF.

GSO (General Statistics Office). 2016. *Result of the Vietnam Household Living Standards Survey 2016.* Hanoi: Statistical Publishing House. https://www.gso.gov.vn/en/data-and-statistics/2019/03/result-of-the-vietnam-household-living-standards-survey-2016/.

Ha-Duong, Minh. 2021. "Subjective Satisfaction and Objective Electricity Poverty Reduction in Vietnam, 2008–2018." *Fulbright Review of Economics and Policy* 1, no. 1: 43–60.

Hansen, Arve, Kenneth Bo Nielsen, and Harold Wilhite. 2016. "Staying Cool, Looking Good, Moving Around: Consumption, Sustainability and the 'Rise of the South.'" *Forum for Development Studies* 43, no. 1: 5–25.

Harms, Erik. 2009. "Vietnam's Civilizing Process and the Retreat from the Street: A Turtle's Eye View from Ho Chi Minh City." *City and Society* 21, no. 2: 182–206.

Hasenoehrl, Ute. 2018. "Rural Electrification in the British Empire." *History of Retailing and Consumption* 4, no. 1: 10–27.

Headrick, Daniel R. 1988. *The Tentacles of Progress: Technology Transfer in the Age of Imperialism, 1850–1940.* New York: Oxford University Press.

Hoai, Thu. 2019. "Vietnam Electricity Prices Go up after Two Years." *VNExpress Online,* March 20. https://e.vnexpress.net/news/business/economy/vietnam-electricity-prices-go-up-after-two-years-3897362.html.

Hughes, Thomas P. 1983. *Networks of Power: Electrification in Western Society, 1880–1930.* Baltimore: John Hopkins University Press.

Larkin, Brian. 2008. *Signal and Noise: Media, Infrastructure, and Urban Culture in Nigeria.* Durham: Duke University Press.

Lê, Bảo. 2020. "Nghịch cảnh mùa nắng nóng, có điều hòa vẫn không dám dung" ("Having an Air Conditioner in the Hot Season but Not Daring to Use It"). *GiadinhNet,* July 7. https://giadinh.net.vn/nghich-canh-mua-nang-nong-co-dieu-hoa-van-khong-dam-dung-17220070617174 6705.htm.

L'éveil économique de l'Indochine. 1918. "L'éclairage électrique dans la brousse." July 21, p. 9.

Le, Vinh Tien, and Adrian Pitts. 2019. "A Survey on Electrical Appliance Use and Energy Consumption in Vietnamese Households: Case Study of Tuy Hoa City." *Energy and Buildings* 197: 229–41.

Leshkowich, Ann Marie. 2012. "Finances, Family, Fashion, Fitness, and . . . Freedom? The Changing Lives of Urban Middle-Class Vietnamese Women." In *Gender Practices in Contemporary Vietnam*, edited by Lisa Drummond and Helle Rydstrom, 95–114. Copenhagen: NIAS Press.

Miller, Daniel. 2001. "Behind Closed Doors." In *Home Possessions. Material Culture Behind Closed Doors*, edited by Daniel Miller, 1–19. New York: Berg.

Morris, Stephen G. 2012. "The Science of Happiness: A Cross-Cultural Perspective." In *Happiness across Cultures. Views of Happiness and Quality of Life in Non-Western Cultures*, edited by Helaine Selin and Gareth Davey, 435–50. Dordrecht, the Netherlands: Springer.

Morris-Suzuki, Tessa. 1994. *The Technological Transformation of Japan: From the Seventeenth to the Twenty-First Century*. Cambridge: Cambridge University Press.

Neefjes, Koos, and Dang Thi Thu Hoai. 2017. *Towards a Socially Just Energy Transition in Viet Nam: Challenges and Opportunities*. Hanoi: Friedrich Ebert Stiftung. https://library.fes.de/pdf-files/bueros/vietnam/13684.pdf.

Nguyen, Lilly U. 2016. "Infrastructural Action in Vietnam: Inverting the Techno-Politics of Hacking in the Global South." *New Media and Society* 18, no. 4: 637–52.

Nguyen, Minh T. N. 2015. *Vietnam's Socialist Servants: Domesticity, Class, Gender, and Identity*. New York: Routledge.

Nguyen-Thu, Giang. 2019. *Television in Post-reform Vietnam: Nation, Media, Market*. New York: Routledge.

Nye, David E. 1990. *Electrifying America: Social Meanings of a New Technology*. Cambridge, MA: MIT Press.

Reid, Susan E. 2005. "The Khrushchev Kitchen: Domesticating the Scientific-Technological Revolution." *Journal of Contemporary History* 40, no. 2: 289–316.

Reyes, Raquel A. G. 2012. "Modernizing the Manileña: Technologies of Conspicuous Consumption for the Well-to-Do Woman, circa 1880s–1930s." *Modern Asian Studies* 46, no. 1: 193–220.

Rinkinen, Jenny, Elizabeth Shove, and Mattijs Smits. 2019. "Cold Chains in Hanoi and Bangkok: Changing Systems of Provision and Practice." *Journal of Consumer Culture* 19, no. 3: 379–97.

Sahakian, Marlyne. 2014. *Keeping Cool in Southeast Asia. Energy Consumption and Urban Air-Conditioning*. Houndmills, UK: Palgrave Macmillan.

Sands, Gary. 2019. "Growing Environmental Awareness in Vietnam." *Asia Times*, April 28. https://asiatimes.com/2019/04/growing-environmental-awareness-in-vietnam/.

Schlecker, Markus. 2011. "That Has Been! Technology Keepsakes from the Pre-reform Era and Family Individuation in Late 1990s Hanoi." *Studies in Urban Humanities* 3, no. 2: 123–43.

Schwartz Cowan, Ruth. 1983. *More Work for Mother: The Ironies of Household Technology from the Open Hearth to the Microwave*. New York: Basic.

Schwenkel, Christina. 2019. "The Current Never Stops: Intimacies of Energy Infrastructure in Vietnam." In *The Promise of Infrastructure*, edited by Nikhil Anand, Akhil Gupta, and Hannah Appel, 103–32. Durham, NC: Duke University Press.

Schwenkel, Christina. 2022. "The Things They Carried (and Kept): Revisiting Ostalgie in the Global South." *Comparative Studies in Society and History* 64, no. 2: 478–509.

Scott, Andrew, and Romilly Greenhill. 2014. *Turning the Lights On: Sustainable Energy and Development in Viet Nam*. London: Overseas Development Institute.

Tertrais, Hugues. 2002. "L'électrification de l'Indochine." *Outre-mers* 89: 334–35, 589–600.

Vann, Elizabeth. 2003. "Production Matters: Consumerism and Global Capitalism in Vietnam." In *Anthropological Perspectives on Economic Development and Integration*, edited by Norbert Dannhaeuser and Cynthia Werner, 225–57. Vol. 22 of *Research in Economic Anthropology*, edited by Donald Wood. Bingley, UK: Emerald Group.

Veblen, Thorstein. (1899) 2009. *The Theory of the Leisure Class*. Oxford: Oxford University Press.

Wilhite, Harold. 2008. *Consumption and the Transformation of Everyday Life. A View from South India*. Houndmills, UK: Palgrave Macmillan.

Wilhite, Harold. 2009. "Forum: The Conditioning of Comfort." *Building Research and Information* 37, no. 1: 84–88.

Winter, Tim. 2013. "An Uncomfortable Truth: Air-Conditioning and Sustainability in Asia." *Environment and Planning A: Economy and Space* 45, 517–31.

Winther, Tanja. 2008. *The Impact of Electricity: Development, Desires, and Dilemmas*. New York: Berghahn.

Yoshimi, Shunya. 1999. "'Made in Japan': The Cultural Politics of 'Home Electrification' in Postwar Japan." *Media, Culture and Society* 21: 149–71.

Eating Out in Contemporary Hanoi: Middle-Class Food Practices, Capitalist Transformations, and the Late-Socialist Good Life

Arve Hansen

Food has been at the core of Vietnam's dramatic transformations since the Đổi Mới market reforms were initiated more than three decades ago. The country's shift from a planned economy to the Leninist-capitalist hybrid development model known as a socialist market economy (Bekkevold et al. 2020) has seen the country move from a food importer to a major agricultural exporter. Furthermore, the amount and type of food eaten has changed significantly, with the average citizen eating more food in general and the diet including significantly more fat, sugar, and animal-based proteins, partly due to a dramatic increase in the prevalence of eating out (Hansen 2018).

Vietnam's capitalist transformations have involved increasing incomes and the rapid expansion of the urban middle classes. There have been radical changes in access to consumer goods, as well as changes to what are

positions 32:1 DOI 10.1215/10679847-10889947

considered correct and proper forms of consumption (Endres, this issue; Hansen 2022, 2020). The literature focuses on two main aspects of how the new middle classes deal with food: one is food anxiety, an omnipresent issue and concern in contemporary Vietnam (Ehlert and Faltmann 2019); the other, the changing meanings of food in Vietnam, including the role of gender and how food, and particularly eating out, is central to new forms of middle-class life (Ehlert 2016; Earl 2014).

This article takes two different but interlinked approaches to understand the boom in eating out in Hanoi in the context of the late-socialist good life (see Nguyen, Wilcox, and Lin, this issue). Inspired by social practice theory, it mainly focuses on how eating away from home has become embedded in everyday practices under late socialism through particular geographies of food, first through street food and later through a range of new food spaces. Rather than the many, and very real, problematic aspects of food in Vietnam today, the first parts of the article go beyond "the suffering subject" to investigate food as part of "how people . . . strive to create the good in their lives" (Robbins 2013: 457). This is an important perspective from which to understand changing food practices and the role of food in contemporary Vietnam. However, the foodscapes of the socialist market economy are built on specific forms of exploitation that make food cheap. The final part of the article focuses on these by zooming in on the structural conditions within which food practices take place as, to use Ortner's (2016) vocabulary, the study of the good life is combined with acknowledgment of its "dark" sides.

The article proceeds as follows: first, the theoretical framework and the methodology are introduced. Then, after briefly presenting the context of Vietnam's food transformations, it considers middle-class eating-out practices in contemporary Hanoi, starting in the streets and then moving indoors into the many new food spaces in the city. Finally, it discusses the structural conditions that make cheap food possible.

Food, Capitalism, and Ethnography

Food being a necessity, most food consumption is mundane and ordinary. But food is also pleasurable, and eating good food, perhaps particularly at restaurants (Warde and Martens 2000), is for many a central part of living a good life. The theoretical point of departure for this article is food as practice, focusing on mundane, shared, and routinized types of behavior, rather than the choices of individual consumers or food as a cultural marker (Warde 2016). In particular, the article draws on theorizing on the relationship between built infrastructure and everyday food practices (see Hansen and Jakobsen 2020). It combines a practice approach with the geographical concept of foodscapes to illuminate the "processes, politics, spaces, and places . . . embedded and produced in and through the provisioning of food" (Goodman, Maye, and Holloway 2010: 1783) to study both the visible and the hidden geographies of consumption. I pay particular attention to an understudied field within the highly influential practice turn in consumption research, focusing on the political-economic context in which the boom in eating out is taking place (Hansen 2023). I am interested in the constrained agency of the "aspiring subject as shaping and being shaped by the political economy of late socialism" (Nguyen, Wilcox, and Lin, this issue), but also the largely hidden geographies that enable middle-class practices. In other words, I study the geographies of practices and the junctions between practice and foodscapes, as well as the material and social relations that make consumption possible. I understand these relations as enabled by industrialized animal slaughter and a labor regime produced through compressed capitalist transformations (D'Costa 2014). While the former has been explored more in detail elsewhere (see Hansen 2018, 2021a; Hansen and Jakobsen 2020), the latter perhaps warrants more explanation.

According to Anthony D'Costa (2014), capitalism in Asia sees the historical processes of capitalist development take part simultaneously. In other words, it is compressed, with primitive accumulation, petty commodity production, and a small mature capitalist sector coexisting. From this perspective, contemporary Asian capitalism does not involve catching up with mature capitalist countries, a transitional phase, or replication of trajectories seen elsewhere. Rather, these are new and uneven patterns of development led by particular forms of integration with global capitalism that result in the creation and sustainment of low-salaried and precarious forms of employment. Technological complexity and the availability of foreign direct investment allow leapfrogging over stages previously seen as necessary, so there is neither mass employment as found in classic capitalist trajectories, nor generalized income growth, but rather "the mobilization of vast numbers of unskilled and semi-skilled migrant workers in . . . the informal sector" (322). Vietnam's development trajectory has undeniably succeeded in improving living standards but largely fits within this story. While an expanding industrial sector has played an important role in making Vietnam's economy one of the fastest growing in the world over the past three decades (Bekkevold et al. 2020), the country's stalled and partial industrialization has created a considerable amount of precarious employment (Masina and Cerimele 2018). The labor of the precariat created by compressed capitalism in turn creates the foundation for contemporary urban foodscapes and enables the food practices discussed in this article.

The article draws directly on three periods of fieldwork in Hanoi: March to May and October 2017, March to April 2018, and seven months in 2013. During these periods I stayed in the Truc Bach area between Hanoi's old quarter and the wealthy and expat-dense West Lake. I use this area's changing foodscapes as the starting point for the article, although I conducted interviews and observations in many parts of the city. During the most recent rounds of fieldwork, I carried out twenty-five interviews with members of middle-class households and twenty-five with a variety of actors in the food system, including food system experts, government officials, restaurant owners, market vendors, specialty food producers, farmers, and abattoir managers. Approximately half of the interviews were conducted in English and the rest in Vietnamese, with an assistant translator.

In addition to the interviews, the study rests on an ethnographically inspired approach to food practices and foodscapes. This meant engaging directly in Hanoian everyday food practices such as shopping at traditional markets, minimarts, and supermarkets, and eating at a wide variety of food spaces, particularly those frequented by the middle classes. I draw on ten years of working in and on Vietnam for both short and long periods, with food always a core interest. A very large number of food conversations, frequent lunches and dinners at office canteens and in the homes of people in several parts of the country, and an estimated two thousand restaurant and street food meals all over Vietnam inform this research.

Eating Out in Hanoi

"In Hai Phong, people around my age have to go home to eat. You can't eat out. In Hanoi, people don't need to go home to eat at all. They don't go home for any of the three meals of the day" (Nhung, interview by author, March 2017, translated from Vietnamese). Nhung, a dance instructor in her late twenties, had moved to Hanoi from the coastal city of Hai Phong a few years before I met her for an interview about household food practices. In our conversation she quickly pointed toward Hanoians' inclination to eat outside the home. Simultaneously a passion, a matter of convenience, an activity that both passes and saves time, and a gender-unequal practice that frequently causes marital disagreements, Hanoians, and particularly male Hanoians, often eat out.

I knew this well from my own experience: I usually ate three meals away from home a day when living in Hanoi. Still, I was sometimes taken by surprise by some of my interviewees' reported frequency of eating out; for instance the retired woman selling *trà đá* (ice tea) in a narrow alley in Dong Da district who told me that her family normally ate out fifteen times a week.[1] Interestingly, such stories were often combined with narratives about Vietnamese food culture that were oriented toward the home and the family, generally presenting eating out as a relativly new practice. It has certainly become considerably more prominent over the past two decades. According to the Vietnam General Statistics Office's most recent Household Living Standards Survey, urban households' average spending on meals outside of the home increased almost sevenfold between 2006 and 2018. This includes a significant increase in the percentage of total expenditure on the consumption of meals away from home across income groups, although unsurprisingly the urban and the well-off eat out significantly more than other groups (GSO 2019; see also Hansen 2018).

The high incidence of eating out is closely connected to availability. Anyone who has visited Hanoi can testify to the centrality of food on its streetscapes. The typical smells and scents of contemporary Hanoi consist of a combination of fresh herbs, cooking oil, fish sauce, and fried meat, sprinkled with the ever-present whiff of exhaust fumes from millions of motorbikes. Formal and informal markets and a wide range of street kitchens open very early in the morning, and street vendors sell fruit and vegetables from their bicycles. They follow a clear temporal rhythm, streetscapes and foodscapes changing with the time of day, and are at their richest at breakfast and lunchtime and early in the evening. The same spaces can take multiple forms and be run by different people throughout the day serving, for example, *phở* (noodle soup) in the morning, *bún* (rice vermicelli) or *cơm* (rice) dishes for lunch, and *lẩu* (hotpot) for dinner.

Hanoi is home to booming restaurant, food retail, and food delivery industries, including a very large number of eateries. These take many shapes, from small street kitchens to expensive restaurants. Here I separate them into two main categories, restaurant and street food, although the difference between them can be blurred. Many inexpensive street food places are more restaurants than street kitchens, and even some expensive restaurants specialize in serving street food. Nevertheless, like my interviewees, I generally approach street food as a different category of eating out than going to a restaurant (see Hansen, Pitkänen, and Nguyen 2023). While street food has recently become a trend in many cities around the world in the form of often relatively high-priced outlets catering to the middle classes, street food in many Asian cities involves affordable everyday "fast slow food." Although certain places, such as popular *cơm bình dân* spots,[2] offer affordable meals for the working classes, the poorest cannot afford to eat out regularly. It is increasingly becoming a class-divided activity, as new food spaces catering to the well-off are too expensive for most Hanoians. Still, although under ever more pressure from authorities, street food plays a crucial part in Hanoi's foodways and foodscapes.

The Rise and Potential Fall of Street Food

"We're too lazy to have breakfast at home. . . . Never!" I met Dui and Trang at a sidewalk café in one of Hanoi's many leafy avenues. Both young, ambitious government officials typical of the new generation of Communist-Party-connected upper-middle class, they had studied abroad and spoke English fluently. Trang said they had cooked breakfast at home when they were studying in Australia, but not in Hanoi. They preferred to eat out "because it's very cheap and it's easy," she added, laughing (Trang, interview by author, April 2017). Eating out is also a way to make the temporal ends meet in a busy Hanoian day. A defining part of the socialist market economy is time scarcity. Many work long days and are involved in several jobs and leisure activities in addition to family responsibilities and long commutes through traffic jams. Dui and Trang highlighted this, explaining that they led busy lives and ate street food on their way to work to save time.

Eating on the way to work and during the lunch break is the most common way that street food becomes embedded in the rhythm and practices of everyday life in Hanoi. Morning is a busy time for many, particularly those such as Phuoc, a family man in his late thirties, who has to travel a long way to take his children to school. I met him at the Truc Bach branch of the popular coffee chain Cộng Cà Phê early one morning. Sipping a *den dá* (iced black coffee), he explained that he usually either goes home for lunch or takes a packed lunch out with him, and the family generally eats dinner at home or at his parents' house. In the morning, however, they always have street food, first for himself, then his children, who would often form part of a common children's practice in Hanoi: eating *bánh mì* (a Vietnamese-style baguette) on the back of a motorbike: "Every morning I eat breakfast out by myself . . . the kids also eat out on the way to school because it takes an hour to get from my house to the school. [The kids eat] *xôi* (sticky rice), *cháo* (congee), *phở*, or *bánh mì*, the easy ones. Or they buy a *bánh mì* and eat it on the way" (Phuoc, interview by author, April 2017).

While on balance the middle classes enjoy street food, opinions differ. As Earl (2014: 145) notes, for some middle-class women in Ho Chi Minh City, "eating on the street was not an option; they were repelled by a perceived lack of hygiene, concerned about a risk of food poisoning, and discouraged due to a feeling of loneliness and social dislocation felt when eating beyond the sphere of kin." My interviewees appeared to see eating street food as an entirely different category of eating that was not comparable to family meals or even to eating in a restaurant; most did not mention street food at first when we discussed their eating-out practices. Eating at street kitchens is a highly regularized action, in other words a social practice, that for my interviewees represented both tasty food and a time-saving convenience, both known to be central to well-being (Guillen-Royo and Wilhite 2015). In quite inconspicuous ways, eating out is both a component and an enabler of the good life, making everyday life less stressful and freeing up time for other activities. For many, street food is a passion. Parts of the upper-middle classes take great pride in their city's street food, for instance Mai, a young, upper-middle-class woman who frequented expat circles and had a European boyfriend. I met her at a high-end French bakery, and she explained that she ate out several times a day. When asked where she preferred to go, before listing food from a large number of countries and different regions of Vietnam, she immedietaly stated "Street food. *Bún*, always my top choice." Many, both young and old, had clear thoughts about the best places to get particular dishes and had their own spots for different meals, as the typical street kitchen offers only one dish. It is common to share new discoveries of eateries with others, and it is common among young members of the middle classes to experiment with new places together with friends. While often failing to live up to the authorities' late-socialist ideals for civilized cities, and subject to considerable consumer skepticism, street food is to many, and in a wide variety of ways, still central to "a life that is worth striving for" (Nguyen, Wilcox, and Lin, this issue).

That said, many weighed the convenience and tastiness of street food versus significant food-safety concerns (see Hansen 2021b), and many, like Phuc, appeared to feel bad about letting their children eat in the streets for this reason. To Huyen, a relatively wealthy young fashion journalist, it was obvious that eating street food was not part of the good life. While she, like many others, expressed general skepticism about hygiene standards in street-food kitchens, she particularly emphasized those serving *cơm bình dân*. She referred to them as *cơm bụi*, a popular derogatory term for these street-side eateries, literally meaning "dusty rice." She complained that her colleagues went to such places just to save a few tens of thousands of VND. She described one such visit:

> It's like thirty thousand per person. But wow, the seller, the man there, he's shouting like this [illustrates in a loud, rude, voice]. Even when he welcomes customers: "You sit here, you sit there." Oh no, I don't want that stress. And then the food! I don't even look at what they cook. I don't even look at the kitchen. But I say I will never, ever come back there. I can spend time outside with my colleagues, but not that way. Because people,

they don't care. It's like a habit. They don't get used to going to restaurants. (Huyen, interview by author, March 2017)

This conversation effectively demonstrates a common position on street food among well-off Hanoians. The middle classes are divided on the topic of eating in the street. Even among the fairly well-off, many regard street food as a way to eat fast, affordable, proper Vietnamese food, and many young urbanites consider eating in the streets a trendy thing to do. But segments of the upper-middle class see street food as unhygienic and unsafe, and clearly against socially learned expectations about proper consumption.

Street food has been instrumental in Hanoi's consumer transformations as a highly accessible way of eating away from home, embedded in the geographies and rhythms of everyday life in the capital. While the street kitchens have a long history (Peters 2012), they experienced a resurgence after Đổi Mới and have since been a central part of the foodscapes of the socialist market economy. The foodscapes are changing rapidly yet again as Vietnam's capitalist transformation continues to mature. Many street kitchens and street vendors have been forced out of business by the city authorities' campaign to clean up the sidewalks (Turner and Ngo 2019). Intended to make sidewalks walkable, it has forced vendors and street kitchens to move inside or to make do with much smaller seating areas, and many move back and forth depending on the presence of the police. This is part of the vision and effort to modernize Hanoi and threatens one of its defining characteristics. Measures introduced to handle the COVID-19 pandemic intensified the pressure on informal food markets and vendors, possibly offering a taste of things to come: only supermarkets and formally registered markets were allowed to remain open, and street vending was banned (Wertheim-Heck 2020). The fact that the street food scene also serves as a major tourist attraction may save it, although possibly in a sanitized, controllable, indoor form, as in Singapore. There are signs of such a change: the city authorities have long intended and attempted to move traditional markets indoors (Atomei 2017), and both large shopping malls and restaurants catering to tourists and the upper classes offer a safe but expensive introduction to street eating. Famous examples include the popular restaurant chain Quán Ăn Ngon (literally "delicious eatery"). It claims to serve thousands of people a day and takes pride in preserving Vietnamese food culture while interestingly advertising busy streets and snack shops as something belonging to the "old Hanoi."[3] The chain is also present in Vincom Royal City, a large semigated community and underground shopping mall a few kilometers from Hanoi's old quarter, which, in addition to an indoor waterfall, boasts its own indoor imitation of the quarter.

Another part of the modernization of Hanoi is its rapid supermarketization (Wertheim-Heck, Raneri, and Oosterveer 2019), including the many minimarts that have popped up like mushrooms in Hanoi's streets over the recent decade. Both are visible in my old neighborhood of Truc Bach, particularly the many new versions of VinMart+, a chain of convenience stores founded by the powerful Vingroup,[4] which in December 2018 opened 238 new branches in a single month nationwide and is the largest of a range of new actors in Hanoi's authorities' plan to rapidly increase the number of the city's convenience stores (*Vietnam Investment Review* 2018). These are examples of relatively new forms of investment in food in the Vietnamese capital. Another is found just up the street, where new middle-class food spaces have emerged, such as Hutong and GoGi House, owned by the Vietnamese company Golden Gate, which owns many of the new chains catering to the middle classes. Global capital is also increasingly present. In my old neighborhood, the famous and highly popular street kitchens and small restaurants serving *phở cuốn* (fresh rice noodle rolls) in Ngu Xa street are now accompanied by a Circle K, which serves as a convenience store, a fast-food spot, and an example of the coexistence of petty trade and large corporations typical of compressed capitalism. A little farther away, new branches of KFC and the Korean fast-food chain Lotteria have opened. Although the iconic *bia hơi* (fresh beer) places are still there with their male crowds, affordable food, and cheap, fresh, light beer, they face competition from big glitzy beer halls serving expensive imported beer. These are just some examples of the ongoing transformation of food geographies in Hanoi and new foodscapes contributing to defining the good life, where the aspirations and new expectations of upper-middle-class Hanoians both shape and are shaped by the political economy of the socialist market economy. Importantly, while these new foodscapes to some extent can be seen as emerging in response to demand from the new middle classes, they also play an instrumental role in "breeding" and shaping this demand (Rinkinen, Shove, and Marsden 2021) as they gradually become embedded in everyday practices and late-socialist normality. This normality includes moving food from the bustle of the streets into air-conditioned spaces.

Eating a Capitalist Transformation

In the state-of-the-art Japanese-owned Aeon shopping mall in Long Bien, customers and visitors can wander in cool, air-conditioned surroundings looking at luxury brands. They can shop at the popular Aeon supermarket, favored by many upper-end Hanoian consumers due to a common association between Japan and high quality. Hanging out in a mall can be part of the good life for some, although it is rarely accounted for as such. Certainly it is part of people's "capacity to aspire" (Appadurai 2013), although for many visitors their aspiration toward the high-end market represents an example of the elusive "fictional expectations" of capitalism (Beckert 2016) rather than actual engagement with the future. Many malls in Hanoi are very popular hangout spots, particularly for young people, often involving socialization in the open spaces without entering the stores. Those who can afford it can patronize the popular modern coffee outlets provided by global, Asian, and Vietnamese corporations. A typical Asian shopping mall has a large food court; the one in the Aeon mall offers a compressed version of the new, more corporate parts of Hanoi's foodscapes. Here are where one finds the American chains KFC, Popeye's, and Dunkin' Donuts, next to other fast-food outlets such as Lotteria and Jollibee. Burgers and other examples of American fast food have grown in popularity, including a chain eatery called Cowboy Jack's that advertises American dining. However, any claims of Westernization are complicated by the fact that Cowboy Jack's is a Vietnamese concept, Lotteria is Korean, and Jollibee, Philippino. Nevertheless, they all represent energy-dense, highly processed "global junk" (Wilk 2018), and are examples of the expansion of corporate capitalism into Hanoians' everyday foodscapes.

Contrary to popular accounts, capitalist food does not necessarily lead to the adoption of a Western diet. Most of the typical Western fast-food concepts have not performed as well as expected in Vietnam, due to both tough competition from street food and a widespread preference for Asian food (Hansen 2021a, 2021b). Asian food concepts and fast-food chains increasingly dominate the food scene. This is the case in the shopping malls around Hanoi, including the Aeon mall, where a variety of Asian food concept outlets are considerably more popular than the Western concepts. Places offering Taiwanese tea, Japanese sushi, Korean chicken dishes and Thai-style curries, and Japanese and Korean barbecue and steak houses are all popular. But as I have observed in other shopping malls around Hanoi, by far the most popular venues are those serving *lẩu* (hotpot), evidence that eating out does not necessarily involve radical changes in food practices. In many cases these restaurants are parts of a chain, such as the popular Kichi Kichi, again, owned by Golden Gate. Another highly popular place is Hong Kong Town,[5] while Hotpot Story, owned by a Vietnamese joint stock company that operates a wide range of restaurant chains, advertises eight different kinds of hotpot from Thailand, Japan, Korea, and China, served with US and Australian beef.

A proper lunch in Vietnam should include rice of some sort, or at the very least rice noodles, and the most successful foreign fast-food chains, such as KFC and Lotteria, have realized this. When a young couple told me they liked going to Lotteria, I was intrigued by the prospect of meeting someone who had started eating hamburgers for lunch. When it turned out that they went for the rice lunch deal, I asked why they went to Lotteria rather than a more traditional Vietnamese place. They both said they were drawn there by the fried chicken, adding, "If you want to eat traditional food you can eat at home" (interview by author, April 2017).

Street food has been instrumental in making eating out a habit, and for many its convenient, affordable, time-saving, nutritious, and tasty food is still part of the good life. With street kitchens now under pressure from both government policy and increased food safety concerns, local and global capital are investing heavily in the Hanoian street scene, seeking to cash in on the citizens' habit of eating out. This is part of the coshaping of the changing expectations of proper consumption taking place through Vietnam's capitalist transformations, and in turn becoming part of the conceptualization of the good life. Many of my interviewees highlighted foreign-influenced food outlets as places to take the family for a meal, often opting for pizza, pasta, or hamburgers to treat their children. These restaurants offer new dining practices that stand out from the mundane and unglamorous street food meals. While many of these middle-class spaces are fairly expensive, some of the new outlets, such as Lotteria, also compete directly with the local street food scene (Lotteria serves a lunch deal for 35,000 VND, similar to the price of a street food meal), the low prices made possible by the specific political economies that make food cheap (see Moore 2015).

The Political Economy of Cheap Food

In capitalist consumer societies, Ulrich Brand and colleagues (2021: 5) argue, "normality is produced . . . by masking the destruction in which it is rooted." Eating out several times a day, as many middle-class households do in Hanoi, is made possible in many ways by larger processes of capitalist economic development. Rural environmental degradation and the suffering of millions of animals to feed the expanding demand for meat are the foundations of the new geographies of urban food consumption (Hansen 2018). Cheap food in contemporary Vietnam is built on intensified agriculture and increasingly on industrialized animal slaughter. For example, cheap chicken meals add to Vietnam's rapidly increasing poultry consumption, met by the rapid industrialization of domestic poultry production and imports of industrial chicken from the US and elsewhere (Hansen 2021a; see also Porter 2019). Both the scaling up of the domestic livestock sector and the importing of cheap meat from distant factory farms embed the Vietnamese food sector, and the Vietnamese good life, in a global meat complex (Jakobsen and Hansen 2020).

The late-socialist good life is fundamentally based on capitalist exploitation through the low incomes of smallholder farmers and the precarious labor of millions of working-class people, often rural migrants (in many cases the same people: see Nguyen, Gillen, and Rigg 2020). In other words, beyond the jobs, incomes, distinctions, and consumer aspirations of the middle classes, contemporary food practices are often enabled by uneven and compressed capitalism (D'Costa 2014). Just as they are the "socialist servants" that enable middle-class lifestyles through domestic service (Nguyen

2015), rural migrants make up a reserve army of informal laborers in Vietnam's foodscapes (see Lincoln 2008; Agergaard and Vu 2011). Importantly,
these marginalized laborers are a highly heterogenous group of people who
possess a certain, yet highly variegated, capacity for "negotiat[ing] over the
power to change their circumstances," mainly through the negotiation of
social relationships (Kawarazuka, Béné, and Prain 2018: 245). Yet their low-
paid and precarious work strengthens inequalities and enables a flourishing
consumer society for both the old and the new versions of fast food. As
discussed, following D'Costa's (2014) explanation of compressed capitalism,
the large informal sector in Asian cities is the outcome of particular versions of contemporary capitalism. The coexistence of mature capitalism and
petty trade is obvious in Hanoi's foodscapes, where big capital is gradually
becoming more powerful in a trade still dominated by a wide variety of
street vendors.

Without the inequalities that contribute to defining the socialist market
economy, it is unlikely that so many middle-class consumers would be able
to eat out several times a day. The social relations that underpin the late-
socialist good-food life are well illustrated by the food-delivery sector, which
has long been growing but saw its reach expand during the strict COVID-19
measures in Hanoi (Nguyen 2020). Large corporations such as Grab have
replaced informal *xe ôm* ("hugging vehicle," a term used for motorbike
taxis) drivers in the delivery sector, the armies of motorbike drivers serving platform capitalism in many ways formalizing the precarity associated
with compressed capitalism and thriving on the neoliberal dream of unor-
ganized and "flexible" workers pitted against one another in a highly com-
petetive market (Hansen, Nguyen, and Luu 2020). These services provide
vital income for many and new forms of consumer convenience. For those
who can afford it, it makes all kinds of food readily available, in turn feeding new expectations of the convenient good life. But in many ways food
delivery in Vietnam represents the epitome of food transformations under
late socialism, with a chain of cheap labor quickly and conveniently bringing affordable food to urban middle-class consumers. In sum, beneath the
diversity of the practices and aspirations that together connect food with
late-socialist ideals of the good life, there is a large and dark foundation of
exploitation of people and animals to provide cheap food and cheap labor.

Conclusion

Eating out is a central food practice for a large proportion of Hanoians thanks to the plethora of street kitchens. While street food remains at the core of Hanoi's foodways and foodscapes, the rich culinary traditions that it represents are under constant threat due to food hygiene scares, new middle-class expectations, and government regulations and planning, as well as new competition in the form of food franchises and the co-option of street food by more upmarket restaurants. Street kitchens struggle to compete with the status and air-conditioning of their more corporate counterparts, whose restaurant chains and new, indoor, modern food spaces advertise different versions of the good-food life that are often closely aligned with middle-class aspirations. While street food retains its reputation as good food, its position as part of the good life is under threat.

This article has analyzed the embeddedness of street food, and increasingly corporate fast food, in everyday life in the socialist market economy through food practices and foodscapes and how these are changing alongside Vietnam's ongoing capitalist transformations. Late-socialist food transformations in Vietnam include the ever-stronger presence of domestic, Asian, and global capital in the food sector, from production to retail. This article has argued that larger processes of capitalist development must be accounted for to understand Hanoian food practices. The political economy of Vietnam's development, with its intensified livestock sector and multitude of precarious workers, is enabling a strong culture of eating out, whether at street kitchens or modern fast-food outlets. These are the exploitative structural conditions underpinning the late-socialist good life and adding to the complexity and contradictions defining the socialist market economy.

Notes

Many thanks to my informants and research assistants, as well as to Jostein Jakobsen, the editors, and the three anonymous reviewers for highly constructive feedback on earlier versions of this article. Special thanks to my friends, and above all Huong, for exploring all corners of the Hanoian food scene with me.

1 I gradually realized that this woman was much better off than her appearance had led me to believe, and that selling tea was an activity she engaged in mainly to pass the time.

2 Literally "popular rice," these buffet-style eateries come in a range of shapes and sizes.

3 Quán Ăn Ngon (website), http://quananngon.com.vn/ (accessed December 8, 2023).

4 Since then, Vingroup has sold its retail subsidiary VinMart to the Masan Group, who in turn has rebranded it as WinMart. See Vietnam News Agency 2022.

5 Aeon Mall (website), https://aeonmall-long-bien-en.com/shop/hong-kong-town/ (December 18, 2018).

References

Agergaard, Jytte, and Vu Thi Thao. 2011. "Mobile, Flexible, and Adaptable: Female Migrants in Hanoi's Informal Sector." *Population, Space and Place* 17, no. 5: 407–20. https://doi.org/10.1002/psp.622.

Appadurai, Arun. 2013. *The Future as Cultural Fact: Essays on the Global Condition*. New York: Verso.

Atomei, Claudia. 2017. "The Sidewalk Diet: Street Markets and Fresh Food Access in Central Hanoi, Vietnam." June 17. https://sidewalkdiet.files.wordpress.com/2017/06/td_claudia_atomei_17june.pdf.

Beckert, Jens. 2016. *Imagined Futures: Fictional Expectations and Capitalist Dynamics*. Cambridge MA: Harvard University Press.

Bekkevold, Jo Inge, Arve Hansen, and Kristen Nordhaug. 2020. "Introducing the Socialist Market Economy." In *The Socialist Market Economy in Asia: Development in China, Vietnam, and Laos*, edited by Arve Hansen, Jo Inge Bekkevold, and Kristen Nordhaug. Singapore: Palgrave.

Brand, Ulrich, Markus Wissen, Zachary Murphy King, Liliane Danso-Dahmen, and Barbara Jungwirth. 2021. *The Imperial Mode of Living: Everyday Life and the Ecological Crisis of Capitalism*. Brooklyn: Verso.

D'Costa, Anthony. 2014. "Compressed Capitalism and Development." *Critical Asian Studies* 46, no. 2: 317–44. https://doi.org/10.1080/14672715.2014.898458.

Earl, Catherine. 2014. *Vietnam's New Middle Classes: Gender, Career, City*. Copenhagen: NIAS Press.

Ehlert, Judith. 2016. "Emerging Consumerism and Eating Out in Ho Chi Minh City, Vietnam: The Social Embeddedness of Food Sharing." In *Food Consumption in the City: Practices and Patterns in Urban Asia and the Pacific*, edited by Marlyne Sahakian, Czarina Saloma, and Suren Erkman, 71–89. London: Routledge.

Ehlert, Judith, and Nora Katharina Faltmann, eds. 2019. *Food Anxiety in Globalising Vietnam*. Singapore: Palgrave Macmillan.

Goodman, Michael K., Damian Maye, and Lewis Holloway. 2010. "Ethical Foodscapes? Premises, Promises, and Possibilities." *Environment and Planning A: Economy and Space* 42, no. 8: 1782–796.

GSO (General Statistics Office). 2019. *Result of the Viet Nam Household Living Standards Survey 2018.* Hanoi: Statistical.

Guillen-Royo, Monica, and Harold Langford Wilhite. 2015. "Wellbeing and Sustainable Consumption." In *Global Handbook of Quality of Life*, edited by Wolfgang Glatzer, Laura Camfield, Valerie Møller, and Mariano Rojas, 301–16. Dordrecht: Springer Netherlands. https://doi.org/10.1007/978-94-017-9178-6_13.

Hansen, Arve. 2018. "Meat Consumption and Capitalist Development: The Meatification of Food Provision and Practice in Vietnam." *Geoforum* 93: 57–68. https://doi.org/10.1016/j.geoforum.2018.05.008.

Hansen, Arve. 2020. "Consumer Socialism: Consumption, Development and the New Middle Classes in China and Vietnam." In *The Socialist Market Economy in Asia: Development in China, Vietnam, and Laos*, edited by Arve Hansen, Jo Inge Bekkevold, and Kristen Nordhaug. Singapore: Palgrave.

Hansen, Arve 2021a. "Eating a Capitalist Transformation: Economic Development, Culinary Hybridisation and Changing Meat Cultures in Vietnam." In *Changing Meat Cultures: Food Practices, Global Capitalism, and the Consumption of Animals*, edited by Arve Hansen, and Karen L. Syse, 99–120. Lanham, MD: Rowman & Littlefield.

Hansen, Arve. 2021b. "Negotiating Unsustainable Food Transformations: Development, Middle Classes and Everyday Food Practices in Vietnam." *European Journal of Development Research*. https://doi.org/10.1057/s41287-021-00429-6.

Hansen, Arve. 2022. *Consumption and Vietnam's New Middle Classes: Societal Transformations and Everyday Life.* Consumption and Public Life. Cham, Switzerland: Palgrave Macmillan.

Hansen, Arve. 2023. "Capitalism, Consumption, and the Transformation of Everyday Life: The Political Economy of Social Practices." In *Consumption, Sustainability and Everyday Life*, edited by Arve Hansen and Kenneth Bo Nielsen, 27–54. Basingstoke, UK: Palgrave Macmillan.

Hansen, Arve, and Jostein Jakobsen. 2020. "Meatification and Everyday Geographies of Consumption in Vietnam and China." *Geografiska Annaler: Series B, Human Geography* 102, no 1: 21–39. https://doi.org/10.1080/04353684.2019.1709217.

Hansen, Arve, Nguyen Tuan Anh, and Luu Khanh Linh. 2020. "Commercialising the *xe om*: Motorbike Taxis, GrabBike, and Shared Mobilities in Hanoi." In *Sharing Mobilities:*

New Perspectives for the Mobile Risk Society, edited by Sven Kesselring, Malene Freudendal-Pedersen, and Dennis Zuev. Milton Park, UK: Routledge.

Hansen, Arve, Outi Pitkänen, and Binh Nguyen. 2023. "Feeding a Tourism Boom: Changing Food Practices and Systems of Provision in Hoi An, Vietnam." *Food, Culture and Society*. https://doi.org/10.1080/15528014.2023.2263986.

Jakobsen, Jostein, and Arve Hansen. 2020. "Geographies of Meatification: An Emerging Asian Meat Complex." *Globalizations* 17, no. 1: 93–109. https://doi.org/10.1080/14747731.2019.1614723.

Kawarazuka, Nozomi, Christophe Béné, and Gordon Prain. 2018. "Adapting to a New Urbanizing Environment: Gendered Strategies of Hanoi's Street Food Vendors." *Environment and Urbanization* 30, no. 1: 233–48. https://doi.org/10.1177/0956247817735482.

Lincoln, Martha. 2008. "Report from the Field: Street Vendors and the Informal Sector in Hanoi." *Dialectical Anthropology* 32, no. 3: 261–65.

Masina, Pietro, and Michela Cerimele. 2018. "Patterns of Industrialisation and the State of Industrial Labour in Post-WTO-Accession Vietnam." *European Journal of East Asian Studies* 17, no 2: 1–36. https://doi.org/10.1163/15700615-01700200.

Moore, Jason. W. 2015. "Cheap Food and Bad Climate." *Critical Historical Studies* 2, no. 1: 1–43.

Nguyen, Minh T. N. 2015. *Vietnam's Socialist Servants: Domesticity, Class, Gender, and Identity*. London: Routledge.

Nguyen, Quy. 2020. "Food Delivery a Mainstay for Vietnamese Urbanites amid Covid-19 Crisis." *VN Express*, May 17. https://e.vnexpress.net/news/business/data-speaks/food-delivery-a-mainstay-for-vietnamese-urbanites-amid-covid-19-crisis-4099471.html.

Nguyen, Tuan Anh, Jamie Gillen, and Jonathan Rigg. 2020. "Economic Transition without Agrarian Transformation: The Pivotal Place of Smallholder Rice Farming in Vietnam's Modernisation." *Journal of Rural Studies* 74: 86–95. https://doi.org/10.1016/j.jrurstud.2019.12.008.

Ortner, Sherry B. 2016. "Dark Anthropology and Its Others: Theory since the Eighties." *HAU: Journal of Ethnographic Theory* 6, no. 1: 47–73.

Peters, Erica J. 2012. *Appetites and Aspirations in Vietnam: Food and Drink in the Long Nineteenth Century*. Lanham, MD: Altamira Press.

Porter, Natalie. 2019. *Viral Economies: Bird Flu Experiments in Vietnam*. Chicago: University of Chicago Press.

Rinkinen, Jenny, Elizabeth Shove, and Greg Marsden. 2021. *Conceptualising Demand: A Distinctive Approach to Consumption and Practice*. New York: Routledge.

Robbins, Joel. 2013. "Beyond the Suffering Subject: Toward an Anthropology of the Good." *Journal of the Royal Anthropological Institute* 19: 447–62.

Turner, Sarah, and Ngô Thúy Hạnh. 2019. "Contesting Socialist State Visions for Modern Mobilities: Informal Motorbike Taxi Drivers' Struggles and Strategies on Hanoi's Streets, Vietnam." *International Development Planning Review* 41, no. 1: 43–61.

Vietnam Investment Review. 2018. "117 VinMart+ Stores to Be Launched Per Day." December 30. https://www.vir.com.vn/117-vinmart-stores-to-be-launched-per-day-64857.html.

Vietnam News Agency. 2022. "VinMart Officially Changes Its Name to WinMart." *VietnamPlus*, January 16. https://link.gov.vn/cD6eXIZl.

Warde, Alan. 2016. *The Practice of Eating*. Cambridge: Polity.

Warde, Alan, and Lydia Martens. 2000. *Eating Out: Social Differentiation, Consumption, and Pleasure*. Cambridge: Cambridge University Press.

Wertheim-Heck, Sigrid C. O. 2020. "The Impact of the COVID-19 Lockdown on the Diets of Hanoi's Urban Poor." IIED blog, April 8. https://www.iied.org/impact-covid-19-lockdown-diets-hanois-urban-poor.

Wertheim-Heck, Sigrid, Jessica E. Raneri, and Peter Oosterveer. 2019. "Food Safety and Nutrition for Low-Income Urbanites: Exploring a Social Justice Dilemma in Consumption Policy." *Environment and Urbanization* 31, no. 2: 397–420. https://doi.org/10.1177/09562 47819858019.

Wilk, Rick. 2018. "Global Junk: Who Is to Blame for the Obesity Epidemic?" *RAE-revista de administração de empresas* 58, no. 3: 332–36.

Not before Twenty-Five: Contesting Marriage and Looking for the Good Life in Contemporary Urban China

Roberta Zavoretti

In post-Mao China, and particularly since the 1990s, visions and articulations of the good life have revolved around the realm of the personal (Farquhar 1996). As the personal replaced Maoist politicization of everyday life, individual desire became something that the state not only allowed but also actively promoted as the lifeblood of the consumer economy, entrepreneurial competition, and national progress in the international arena (Rofel 2007).

The anthropologist Yan Yunxiang (2003) paints a sometimes bleak picture of the consequences of this shift for family life: individualist youngsters who impose unreasonable material demands on their elders, the decline of the time-honored pact of intergenerational care, and the rejection of family responsibility in accordance with the spread of "uncivil individualism." Other authors have looked at the state's efforts to promote personal desire as a governmental technique. From this perspective, although the emergence

positions 32:1 DOI 10.1215/10679847-10889960

of private life does depart from Maoist collectivism, it heralds increasingly effective forms of social control that sustain the political power of the party-state (Chen 2001; Rofel 2007; Zhang and Ong 2008). The desiring subject appears nowadays as a pivotal actor in the flourishing of China's consumer market, the stratification of Chinese society, and the forging of national cultural life (Brownell 1995; Chen 2001; Farquhar 2002; Zhang 2010).

The state-led promotion of desire for a good life is mapped out on a heteronormative gender/sex matrix (Zhang E. 2007; Zhang L. 2010). Visions of the good life are bound to be different for men and women, as men and women are supposed to shoulder different family roles within the exclusive mode of alliance and family making allowed by the state: the heterosexual, monogamous, married couple. Marriage remains the exclusive arena for reproduction both legally and socially, as it is generally assumed that marriage should precede childbirth and that childbirth should happen within marriage. Bearing a child is commonly experienced as the highest duty to the older generation, as offspring ensure family continuity and embody the promise of care for the elderly.

Marriage in China is quasi-universal and is generally followed by childbirth (Davis and Friedman 2014). This nexus recalls Borneman's (1996, 2008) argument about the hegemonic link between the institution of marriage and life-giving kinship, which in turn promises social respectability, wider connections, access to intimacy, and a secure horizon of care provision. Remaining unmarried is hardly a viable option: unmarried young people undergo severe parental pressure to tie the knot and have children at the appropriate age. Lifelong singlehood is associated with shame and is generally feared as the worst possible prospect. Many lifelong bachelors experience their state as a mark of their failure to compete, and lament their inability to access full adulthood through fatherhood, which is essential to become "a real Chinese man" (Greenhalgh 2012, 2014: 360; Zavoretti 2016b). Without a proper family to fend for and a legitimate outlet for their emotional and sexual needs, lifelong bachelors have long been considered a threat to the social order (Greenhalgh 2012, 2014). For over a decade official media and government agencies have promoted debates about *leftover* women and men; single females are in the minority compared to bachelors in China, yet they attract far more public concern (Fincher 2014; Zhang and

Sun 2014). According to the current English version of the All China Women's Federation website: "Left-over woman refers to the women who remain unmarried in their late twenties and beyond. Most of them enjoy high-level education and handsome-paid jobs.... Now a growing number of Chinese professional women delay their marriages and children to achieve career success and they are labeled as left-over women even as young as 27."[1]

Many articles discuss so-called leftover women on the Chinese-language part of the website, affecting various degrees of sympathy or lack thereof. The widespread use of this terminology in the media effectively produces the idea of leftover women as a social group and a problem for society at large. By not marrying, these women appear to defy the imperative to fulfill family obligations and to constitute the root cause of forced bachelorhood for many Chinese men. Unmarried men and women have come to embody the other of respectable, life-giving kinship, sustaining the discourse that produces marriage as an essential building block of the good life. As abject bodies, unmarried people are associated with unfilial behavior, insecurity, poverty, and illness.

While the media and propaganda target a few top-end unmarried women as responsible for declining family values, for most the decision to marry is a carefully calculated compromise that involves personal feelings and family attachments as well as economic projections for themselves, their children, and their parents (Zavoretti 2016a). For women, marriage is the primary channel to gaining home property, as most families with a son will invest in his house rather than in a daughter's. Accordingly, care of the elderly is a pressing concern for those who plan to seal or break a union in a country where medical and elderly care are increasingly mediated by private-sector organizations (Chen 2001; Nguyen and Chen 2017). In post-Mao China, therefore, making a good marriage is pivotal to the achievement of affective, social, and economic security.

While alternative visions of the good life find little space to flourish in urban China, those who postpone or avoid marriage altogether do not always match the stereotypical representation of the bitter spinster or sad bachelor. This article explores how two unmarried women of different ages and social class articulate their own visions of a good life. While both come across as post-Mao desiring subjects who articulate their life paths according to the vocabulary of personal choice, this cannot simply be reduced to the exercise of negative freedom (Illouz 2018). These women are determined to question hegemonic models of relatedness and foster bonds beyond those of the conjugal couple and the patrilineal family. The bonds they privilege, however, remain marginal to state and social recognition, and are therefore unlikely to guarantee substantial future economic security.

Jiangnan, 2018

In September 2018, I traveled across China for several weeks, visiting old friends and informants in Nanjing and Suzhou. Nanjing is the capital of Jiangsu Province, one of the most prosperous provinces, on China's east coast. Although its official population is under ten million, Nanjing's actual population is much larger due to the influx of unregistered migrant labor. Not far to the east of Nanjing, Suzhou is considered one of the most important historical cities in the country. While its town center is famous for having at least partly preserved its low-rise, old-style architecture, its administrative area counts over ten million official residents. During the past twenty years the expansion of neighboring Shanghai has had a strong impact on the city, which, while remaining administratively independent, is largely considered a de facto extension of the metropolis. A high-end cultural center, Suzhou is generally regarded as a prestigious location at the forefront of the government's Spiritual Civilization project.

In the four years following my 2014 fieldwork, the country had undergone visible shifts. The current leadership had largely consolidated its power, for example by including Xi Jinping thought in the Constitution and implementing the country's first comprehensive immigration policy. In large cities, the presence of CCTV and facial recognition technology had become ubiquitous. In this general context of strengthened orthodoxy and increased emphasis on law and order, between 2015 and 2016 the government had dropped the one-child policy, or what remained of it (Denyer and Zhang 2016; Goldman and Boheler 2015).

Since its planning and inception in 1979 and 1980 (Greenhalgh 2014: 365), the one-child policy had been implemented in different phases and to varying degrees across the country. The formal relinquishing of this highly unpopular policy, however, not only marked the government's acknowledgment that the country's demography had substantially changed since the 1980s but also heralded renewed governmental attention to the issue of care. Already married friends in Nanjing were eagerly asking me how Europeans dealt with their pension funds because, they said, they were worried that their future pensions would not allow them a decent old age. Female university students, on the other hand, talked about the newly introduced policy with concern rather than relief. The government, they said, was now encouraging young women to have children as soon as possible and to focus fully on motherhood (Zhang and Sun 2014). Wouldn't this heighten familial pressure on women to become mothers? I took their anxiety seriously; even before the one-child policy was lifted, professional women of my acquaintance had mentioned experiencing strong family pressure to relinquish their jobs and become full-time wives and mothers. Some of those who were not getting pregnant were being pressured by their in-laws to leave their jobs to prove that they were earnestly putting all their efforts into producing offspring.

Desire and Filiality

As soon as I could, I traveled to Nanjing to meet the Zhangs, who had been my neighbors during my first period of ethnographic fieldwork in 2007–8 and had remained key informants during subsequent fieldwork in 2011–12 and 2014. Since then, I had briefly visited them and kept in touch through WeChat. On this occasion, however, I had not informed them that I was in the country. Had I forewarned them of my arrival they would have organized a banquet, but my time in town was too limited to attend formal celebrations. I decided I would just drop by and pay them an unexpected visit. At around 1:00 p.m. I arrived at the apartment compound where I had been living and where the Zhangs still had their home. In 2014 they had lost their food stall when the city government renovated the surrounding alleys in preparation for the Nanjing Youth Olympics. Determined to remain in the neighborhood, the family had had to plan a new business enterprise quickly. A year later they had managed to open a new restaurant, which I found as I approached the west gate of the compound.

The small restaurant looked neat compared to the family's old stall. Lunchtime had passed, but a few customers were still eating at the wooden tables arranged outside the kitchen. My arrival surprised the family. Since Mr. Zhang and his wife, Ma Ying, were busy serving customers, Mr. Zhang invited me to sit down with his daughter Hong for a while. Hong had grown so much since my last visit that upon approaching the restaurant I did not recognize her. She was by now the tallest among us, a twenty-two-year-old young woman. She had always been a cheerful, outgoing girl, and now she had grown into an outspoken young woman. She told me that she had quit her sales job in the food industry because it required too much travel. Her uncles and cousins had moved away, and after multiple attempts her younger brother had been admitted into a local primary school, where he was attending class. I wanted to ask her what had led her to interrupt her studies, but she was quicker to shift the focus of the conversation: "And now I am already twenty-two years old, you know, but I don't think about getting married yet. Even if everybody asks me about this all the time. I mean, why should you get married young? Look at yourself, how old are you now? You're much older than me, and still, you're unmarried (*weihun* 未婚), is that right?" I confirmed this, adding that I, however, did not live there.

> Yes, I imagine abroad one can stay unmarried without experiencing much pressure. The problem is that with the new marriage law, you know about it, right? If a woman gets married—well, suppose she divorces and she had a baby in the meantime—she basically loses everything [*wandanle* 完蛋了]. So why hurry [*ganma name zhao*ji 干嘛那么着急]? It's better to think carefully before marrying. And anyway, you know, boys aren't mature. It's pointless talking about anything serious with them before they turn twenty-five. Therefore I'm not marrying before that age. Sometimes they [indicating her parents in the kitchen] say something to me, but I tell them that it's too early. I prefer to consider things carefully before marrying. Take the problem of elderly care [*yanglao* 养老], for example. Nowadays in China this is a big problem. One cannot make decisions about marriage without thinking about it first.

This unsolicited declaration surprised me. I was particularly impressed by Hong's reference to the recent interpretation of the marriage law, which regulates the division of property in the case of divorce (Davis 2014).[2] Her clear program indicated some thinking behind the matter. On WeChat a few days later, her father shared a news article titled "New Regulations of the Marriage Law: For Women, It's a Deadly Hit, Who Dares to Marry?" 婚姻法新规定:对女人来说, 是致命打击,谁敢结婚 ("*Hunyinfa xinguiding: Dui nüren laishuo, shi zhimingdaji, sheigan jiehun?*").

Unlike the students I could meet on campus, Hong did not have to choose between focusing on marriage or on her studies: university attendance and a high-flying professional career were, at least for the moment, out of her reach. Although as a healthy, intelligent, young woman with a middle-school diploma, she was highly marriageable within her own class, for the moment she saw no advantage in marrying. Her father encouraged her to consider it, but must arguably have shared some of her concerns. Ma Ying seemed less worried about her daughter's reluctance to wed. She had always fostered Hong's independence (Zavoretti 2017: 159), and even in the presence of her husband she kept asserting that her daughter was supposed to choose for herself.

Later that day Mr. Zhang proudly told me that the following year they would all move out of the basement where they were living into a first-floor apartment in the same compound. This enormous improvement was becoming possible thanks to his new side business selling insurance policies. I promised to keep in touch and come back to visit as soon as possible, then took my leave. Mr. Zhang, with whom I had spent countless hours in conversation in the past, had to stay in the store, but Ma Ying and Hong insisted on walking me the few hundred meters to the main road; and as I observed the two women chatting excitedly and moving in synergy, I could not help remembering the complicity I had noticed between mother and daughter in the past. Although Hong was now an adult, her bond with her mother seemed as strong as ever. We gave each other one last hug and I ran across the busy main road, the two women waving to me before going back to their store.

Desire and Social Pressure

Leaving Nanjing for Suzhou, Hong's concerns echoed in my mind during conversations with other women who were very different from her in terms of age, class, and personal history. One of these was Chengyi, whom I met through a common friend while we were having dinner at a small restaurant run by Mrs. Lin, Chengyi's mother. The middle-aged Mrs. Lin enjoyed wearing makeup and sported shoulder-length hair. After serving us she apologized for the limited choice: at that time in the evening, roughly 8:30 p.m., most of her ingredients were gone, and she was preparing to clean the kitchen and close the restaurant. Although this was supposed to be a busy neighborhood, it appeared significantly quieter than Nanjing city center, where people fill small restaurants until late.

While we were eating, the owner's daughter walked in with two large Labradors on a leash. Mrs. Lin's daughter Chengyi was tall, had vivid eyes, and smiled broadly. Mrs. Lin disappeared into the kitchen again to prepare something for Chengyi, who explained that she had spent the afternoon practicing rock climbing. She showed us pictures she had taken during the training: her trainer, she said, was not young but was still in perfect physical condition. Chengyi, her long, strong legs bare beneath her shorts, looked quite athletic herself. She kept her thick hair long and had arranged it in waves. Her mother brought her some red bean *zhou* (粥), and she dug into it with an appetite.

Chengyi was thirty-eight years old and self-employed as a piano teacher. She hailed from Xi'an, but had moved to Suzhou during her late twenties, and her mother had recently joined her. She often traveled abroad and had spent some time visiting her last boyfriend in Europe. Although the relationship had ended a couple of years earlier, Chengyi still kept her two Labradors as a memory of this bond and had bought a car to take them around. After living in Suzhou for many years she relied on a close circle of mostly female friends in town. She was close to Lisa, another unmarried woman of her age, who in her twenties had given birth to a son after a brief relationship with a Westerner and was raising the child alone. Besides her relatively unusual family arrangement, Lisa was not conforming to the lifestyle expected for a woman of her age in many other ways. She had a lively social life, a long-distance relationship with an absent foreign boyfriend, and spent her free evenings with Chengyi in the city's bars and dance clubs. Her appearance reminded me of the punk youths of the 1990s, a style that is less than fashionable in present-day urban China.

One evening after eating dinner at a friend's place, Chengyi and I left the others for a private conversation. Chengyi told me that she had spent her childhood in the care of her maternal grandmother in a village just outside Xi'an. Her parents had separated when she was a toddler, and she had no memory of her father. Her mother, she said, was not cut out to look after children, and soon delegated the care and supervision of her daughter to her own mother. Chengyi's grandmother had a stern personality and had raised her austerely, but Chengyi remembered her with respect, especially because she had encouraged her to study music. Her account then shifted to her most important relationship, with a man she had met when she was twenty-six. He was from a prosperous Suzhou family and had intended to marry her, but when he introduced her to his parents she failed to make a good impression:

> His parents despised me because of my family background. I didn't have a father; my mother had never remarried and didn't have an official profession. I could make a good income from my teaching, but I was self-employed. They didn't like that either—you know Chinese people always prefer a steady profession. Therefore they said they would agree to the marriage if I gave up my job. They would look for a steadier job for me through their contacts. But I didn't want to abandon my piano teaching, and I declined the offer. It was at that point that I moved to Suzhou. I thought that if I moved they would eventually understand that I was serious about their son and accept me. I thought "They're old people; I can do more to soften their hearts and win them over." I settled in Suzhou to be closer to them, but it didn't work.... Things with my boyfriend kept going, however, and I was willing to wait.

Chengyi was not in a hurry to marry and have children. She said she had never been particularly eager to be a mother, and she already dealt with children all the time in her job. The relationship, however, finished a year and a half later. One day her boyfriend, while visiting her, had left his computer unattended for a while and she sat down to use it. As soon as the screen saver faded she saw the image of a birth certificate naming him as the father. Chengyi could not believe her eyes and immediately confronted him. He admitted that after his parents had refused her as a daughter-in-law he had agreed to marry another woman. All of this had happened soon after she moved to Suzhou. I wondered how he could have arranged and entered into a marriage without any sign of change, and asked her whether she had noticed anything strange during that period. She answered that she had been very busy moving house and resuming work and had not suspected anything because he was visiting her regularly. Besides, Chengyi was not a local and had little contact with his relatives and friends.

Chengyi had to threaten to visit the man's wife to make him accept that their relationship was over. After this experience, she was inclined to think that all men were unreliable. "If men are not trustworthy," I asked her, "how is it possible to build a family with them?"

> What can I say?! I still believe in—love—I still believe in that. But marriage—I can't believe in it. Take all these women who are cheated on by their husbands and don't leave them—why don't they leave? Because they're worried about other people's judgment. I have a friend who recently discovered that her husband has a lover. When I suggested that she may divorce him she replied that she couldn't because "everyone thinks they're the perfect couple"! Right, even if they hadn't had sex in months. Think about that! Doesn't she have any demands [*yaoqiu* 要求] to make of her husband? Because I would have!

Most of her acquaintances, she lamented, were excessively preoccupied with other people's gazes. She thought they spent too much on designer clothes just to be admired, and questioned why they posted countless pictures on social media. While Chengyi came across as a desiring subject, she claimed the right to explore avenues of fulfillment that departed from the trope of the affluent heteronormative married couple. She could exercise this degree of autonomy thanks to her profession, which earned her enough money to live and to support her aging mother. Chengyi worked long hours and weekends with no sick leave or paid holidays. However, instead of complaining about this, she protested about the social pressure she experienced:

> When people find out I'm still not married at thirty-eight, I can tell from their faces that they're looking down on me [*kanbuqi wo* 看不起我]. But I walk on with my head held high! I could give you so many examples; a few

months ago, for instance, I was at the gym. I realized that one of the trainers was looking at me. When I finished my training he approached me and chatted me up. He was all smiles, but I could already tell what was going to happen. As soon as I told him I was thirty-eight [with a cynical laugh] he didn't know what to say. You had to see his face, you could tell he was thinking, "Thirty-eight"? Give me a discount [*pianyi yi dian* 便宜一点]!'

The Unmarried as Abject

Chengyi is an educated and solvent woman. After her boyfriend's family had rejected her, she moved to another city to win them over, only to find herself in the position of a mistress. In present-day China, being recognized as the mistress of a married man attracts strong social stigma. While the adulterous party is considered at fault (*guocuo fang* 过错方) in legal proceedings, outside the court the third party (*disanzhe* 第三者) is often blamed more violently than the unfaithful married person. Mistresses may be accused of using their charms to access the man's financial resources and of ruining his family's happiness, and in the worst cases they may be subjected to serious physical harassment. Discussions about declining family values associate unmarried and divorced people, and particularly women, with greediness, sexual promiscuity, and lack of responsibility in ways that echo the moral panic described by ethnographers of contemporary Japan (Alexy 2020). While these fears are often framed in terms of the real or imagined gaze of others, they also dovetail with a largely shared expectation that the government should play an active role in promoting marriage (Zhang and Sun 2014).

The anthropologist John Borneman (1996) argues that marriage constitutes an exclusionary mechanism of productive social control. While in the US, as in China, marriage is regularly associated with birth and the giving of life, Borneman contends that its efficacy as an exclusionary institution rests on its connection with death. As marriage defines the limits of acceptable and life-giving kinship, it rests on the exclusion of those who cannot enter a socially and legally sanctioned alliance, who become abject bodies. The abject are constituted as incapable of producing legitimate offspring and durable social bonds, as carriers of disease (Borneman refers here to the AIDS crisis), and as a threat to the moral and social order. While Borneman's argument builds on psychoanalytical theory (Kristeva 1980), it also echoes Mary Douglas's *Purity and Danger* (1966) insofar as it departs from the merely symbolic understanding of abjection and uses it to deconstruct kinship and the social order.[3]

In contemporary China, marriage is pivotal to the reproduction of the kinship system and class structure, as well as hegemonic visions of the good life. Visions of marriage-centered bliss need to be sustained by a discursive other to gain some stability of meaning. These discursive others are the divorced, as well as those labeled "leftovers" by state institutions and the media: the spinster and the childless bachelor. Ironically, while these people are cast as superfluous, their presence as abject beings underpins the stability of hegemonic visions of the good life and the institutions that populate such visions.

Unmarried queer people may share this experience of abjection, as they often undergo strong pressure to marry at the age deemed appropriate (Engebretsen 2014; Yip 2007, 2012). Ethnographers highlight the affective dimension of their struggles: informants face the impossible dilemma of choosing between preserving their relationship with their kin by entering heterosexual marriage and remaining single in the hope of saving their relationship with a partner and/or the queer community. The otherness of their lives is not only based on sexual preference, but also on their (un)readiness to embrace a specific and gender-coded way of making family. Elisabeth Engebretsen (2014) describes how lesbian women who enter a heterosexual "contract marriage" (and hence motherhood) must face expectations surrounding the role of wife and mother, eventually losing much of their previous autonomy. Gay men entering such marriages are in a better position to negotiate access to personal time and space, and therefore to maintain extramarital intimate relationships. This scenario directly mirrors Chengyi's engagement to a man who had enough social, symbolic, and material capital to marry behind her back, highlighting the fundamental difference that gender makes in the conditions of access to hegemonic constellations of kinship.

Abjection not only occurs at an ideological or affective level; it has a material dimension as well. Unmarried women are unlikely to access homeownership, a fundamental channel to middle-classness and long-term economic stability (Fincher 2014; Zavoretti 2016a; Zhang 2010). The state-led privatization of housing provision has posited the heteronormative, marriage-based family as the ideal unit of consumption.[4] Accordingly, most families assume patrilocality to be a premise of a good marriage and therefore invest preferentially in housing for sons rather than daughters (Zavoretti 2016a). Housing is seen as an inherently male asset that men should secure to gain both solid status in society and the upper hand in the marriage market (Zavoretti 2016a, 2016b; Zhang 2010; Zhang and Sun 2014). At the same time, while some single daughters may rely on their parents' economic support to buy property, their newly attained economic security may limit their potential pool of spouses. Housing is one of the thorniest issues in both marriage negotiations (Zavoretti 2016a) and divorce cases (Davis 2010). Buying a house without parental support or as a single earner is a privilege that few people can afford.

Finally, the law and bureaucracy implicitly take patrilocality for granted as a condition of marriage, and childbearing as the direct consequence of the latter (Croll 1981). The law stipulating equal rights for legitimate and illegitimate children was drafted in the aftermath of the Liberation to grant rights to children born to concubines. Over seventy years after the imposition of monogamy, however, a baby born out of wedlock may encounter challenges in his or her relationship with the state, starting from the moment of residence registration (Australian Refugee Review Tribunal 2007; Branigan 2014; Zhang Y. 2015). Motherhood outside wedlock is gaining visibility but remains rare and carries a social stigma even in large cities, similar to what Ekaterina Hertog (2009) describes in Japan.

Chengyi is acutely aware that she is highly unlikely ever to become a homeowner. Her choices may have serious repercussions not only on her well-being but also on the life of her aging mother, who has no housing of her own and cannot access a husband's property or income. Hong, conversely, attempts to postpone marriage precisely on the basis of her allegiance to her own kin. A working-class young woman of rural origin, she lives with her parents in a cramped basement and helps them with their business, hoping to provide them with security in their old age. To her, the enterprise of marriage is a risky business that she prefers to delay. Hong does not draw on the vocabulary of "speaking bitterness" (*suku* 诉苦)[5] and self-sacrifice to legitimate her stand. A bad marriage or divorce would strongly jeopardize the stability and continuity she desires for herself and her family, and her decision to wait simply accords with this. Hong mocks the pressure she receives from her father and other relatives, who in turn will have to provide a substantial sum for her brother's marriage. As an affectionate father, on the other hand, Mr. Zhang is keen to see his daughter in a respectable and financially solid alliance that may lead to conventional and proper motherhood. To him, marriage is the only possible shelter from the "leftover" labeling and social censorship experienced by women like Chengyi.

Exclusion or Negative Choice

In present-day China, state and market policies cast marriage as a fundamental milestone on the path to the good life. However, while this social contract regulates, privileges, and protects those who enter it, it also works as a matrix of "exclusion, abjection, and closure" (Borneman 1996: 228) from social respectability and economic security. Besides remaining dependent on the state's evaluation of their reproductive capability, women like Chengyi and Hong are exposed to a negative public gaze. Women who avoid or delay marriage are often said to have a "strong character" (*xinge qiang* 性格强), a euphemism that indicates a lack of feminine docility and ultimately links declining reproductive desirability with moral deficiency.

In *La fin de l'amour* (*The End of Love*) the sociologist Eva Illouz (2018) looks at the decline of long-term romantic relationships and married partnerships in Israel and Europe through a study of what she calls *negative relations*. Connecting the rise of consumer society, twentieth-century sexual liberation, and economic precarity, Illouz argues that the emotional horizon of her informants is dominated by negative choice: a rejection of or withdrawal from commitment, attachment, or relationships in the name of freedom and personal fulfillment (33). Her study suggests that although the rise of the desiring subject may enable social actors to search for alternatives to oppressive familial bonds, it may also throw them into a state of emotional precarity and anomie.

Illouz's study resonates in many ways with the cases presented here, yet Chengyi and Hong do not come across as examples of anomie. They do not reject marriage altogether, and they certainly do not strive to overcome personal and affective relations in general. Unlike women who find autonomy later in their marriage and life cycle (Zeamer 2013), they refuse a match under conditions that most other women are ready to accept. By questioning the necessity of marrying, they reclaim the freedom to nurture bonds of care, albeit in constellations that cannot be assimilated into the conjugal family or the patriline in present-day China. These women's choices are not a negative but a positive effort toward a more secure affective horizon in the context of social and economic precarity. By claiming their right to explore alternative paths to the good life, women such as Chengyi and Hong contest the centrality of marriage and childbearing in a woman's life cycle, and with it the kinship and social order resting on this institution of inclusion and exclusion.

Conclusion

The bonds that Hong and Chengyi privilege revolve around their own kin, especially female kin, and include close homosocial friendships as a source of continued care provision (Friedman 2009). Despite being neglected in kinship studies, these bonds occupy a substantial place in women's everyday lives and imaginations of the future (Evans 2007; Friedman 2009; Judd 1989). Nonpatrilineal bonds, however, lack the social and legal recognition required to endow them with moral and economic value, and therefore fail to confer social respectability and upward mobility.

The importance that Chengyi and Hong accord to nonpatrilineal and nonmarital bonds challenge the assumption that a woman's most important life project must be marriage and childbearing. This principle is not only articulated through law, market policies, patriarchal customs, and the abandonment of the one-child policy; it is also fostered by media portrayal of specific lifestyles as the natural destiny of all Chinese citizens. Take for example the popular TV series *Ode to Joy* (seasons 1 and 2), in which five young women from different backgrounds become friends. They are all visibly in need of male help; even the main lead, a strong and successful executive, eventually emerges as psychologically fragile due to her mother's uncertain mental health. The three female leads have difficult relationships with their kin, who are unsupportive, manipulative, or surrounded by disquieting mysteries. The boyfriends, however, are tall professionals dressed in suits and ties who drive cars, invite women out for expensive dinners, and buy them designer bags. Female friendship, which the show supposedly celebrates, merely assists the main characters as they build what *really* matters: the prized relationship with a male partner and his materially prosperous kin. This is the one "happy object" (Ahmed 2010) that young women desperately need to get closer to the trope of the good life.

This assumption implicitly grounds the official discourse of leftover women that portrays unmarried status as the most undesirable condition. However, many solvent and educated women reclaim their right to pursue happiness without marrying. Chengyi questions the assumption at the basis of the leftover-woman narrative: on the one hand, she acknowledges that marriage could improve her economic position in a society where older men control most of the wealth, while on the other, she reappropriates the right to live according to simple standards in order to enjoy a personal freedom that she could not have as a married mother. Similarly, Hong does not seem concerned about being "left over." After spending her childhood and youth in scarcity, she feels burdened by the responsibility of caring for her parents and supporting a much younger brother. A bad marriage followed by divorce would not only put her in a precarious situation, it would also prevent her from assisting her own kin in the not-so-distant future.

Mirroring the characters in *Ode to Joy* (seasons 1 and 2), both Chengyi and Hong emerge as desiring subjects who claim the right to choose. Unlike in the fictional show, however, the care responsibilities that these women will face in both the near and distant future prompt them to question the "utopia of permanence" promised by the ideology of marriage (Borneman 2008: 33). Chengyi and Hong's reclamation of personal desire does not identify them as uncivil individualists (Yan 2003), nor can it be reduced to what Illouz (2018) calls negative choice. Both women's visions of the good life are fundamentally rooted in the relations they entertain and nourish both emotionally and, through their own work, economically. Women like these not only defy the imperative of competing for the best husband, they also stand critically vis-à-vis a state that strives to control and direct their care and reproductive labor. The fostering of nonpatrilineal bonds appears as a tactical reappropriation of the right to look for a different way to a good life.

Notes

1 All China's Women Federation (website), http://www.womenofchina.cn/womenofchina/html1/culture/hot_words/16/5651-1.htm (accessed January 2, 2020).

2 According to the recent interpretation of the Marriage Law, in case of divorce the property acquired on the occasion of marriage remains with the part that brought it to the marriage, rather than being equally divided between the spouses, implying that a married woman would have no right to a house bought by her husband's family previous to the marriage.

3 In the third chapter of *Pouvoirs de l'horreur* (*The Powers of Horror*), Kristeva (1980) largely draws on Mary Douglas's ([1966] 1984) work to highlight how anthropological analysis of abjection and taboos complete psychoanalytical inquiry on the same topic.

4 I am not implying that housing distribution under Mao necessarily followed more inclusive visions of family making. The hegemonic character of the patrilocal, heteronormative family in Maoist China implied that housing distribution would follow the same matrix and would moreover play a fundamental role in marriage negotiations (Croll 1981; Davis 2002). However, ethnographers and sociologists have documented the increasing gender-based inequality in access to secure housing since the privatization of the housing market (Davis 2002, 2010: Zhang 2010). Li Zhang's ethnography further highlights how the emergence of the housing market in China rests on a strong synergy between state and market.

5 After 1949, workers were encouraged to frame their pre-Liberation stories as "speaking bitterness." This practice allowed them to see themselves as victims of feudal exploitation and to find a new role as socialist subjects (Rofel 1999).

References

Ahmed, Sarah. 2010. *The Promise of Happiness*. Durham, NC: Duke University Press.

Alexy, Allison. 2020. *Intimate Disconnections: Divorce and the Romance of Independence in Contemporary Japan*. Chicago: University of Chicago Press.

Australian Refugee Review Tribunal. 2007. Research response N.CHN31644.24.07.2007.

Borneman, John. 1996. "Until Death Do Us Part: Marriage/Death in Anthropological Discourse." *American Ethnologist* 23, no. 2: 215–35.

Borneman, John. 2008. "Marriage Today." *American Ethnologist* 32, no. 1: 30–33.

Branigan, Tania. 2014. "For Chinese Women, Unmarried Motherhood Remains the Final Taboo." *Guardian*, January 20.

Brownell, Susan. 1995. *Training the Body for China: Sports in the Moral Order of the People's Republic*. Chicago: University of Chicago Press.

Chen, Nancy. 2001. "Health, Wealth, and the Good Life." In *China Urban: Ethnographies of Contemporary Culture*, edited by Nancy N. Chen, Constance D. Clark, Suzanne Z. Gottschang, and Lyn Jeffery, 165–82. Durham, NC: Duke University Press.

Croll, Elisabeth. 1981. *The Politics of Marriage in Contemporary China*. Cambridge: Cambridge University Press.

Davis, Deborah S. 2002. "When a House Becomes His Home." In *Unofficial China: Popular Thought and Culture in the People's Republic*, edited by P. Link, R. Madsen, and P. G. Pickowicz. Boulder, CO: Westview Press.

Davis, Deborah S. 2010. "Who Gets the House? Renegotiating Property Rights in Postsocialist Urban China." *Modern China* 10, no. 10: 1–30.

Davis, Deborah S. 2014. "On the Limits of Personal Autonomy: PRC Laws and the Institution of Marriage." In *Wives, Husbands, and Lovers*, edited by Deborah S. Davis and Sara L. Friedman, 41–61. Stanford, CA: Stanford University Press.

Davis, Deborah S., and Sara L. Friedman. 2014. "Deinstitutionalizing Marriage and Sexuality." In *Wives, Husbands, and Lovers*, edited by Deborah S. Davis and Sara Friedman, 1–40. Stanford, CA: Stanford University Press.

Denyer, Simon, and Congcong Zhang. 2016. "China Drops One Child Policy, But One Is Plenty Says Tiger Mom." *Washington Post*, October 16. https://www.washingtonpost.com/world/asia_pacific/china-drops-one-child-policy-but- exhausted-tiger-moms-say-one-is-plenty/2016/10/14/336f1890–8ae7–11e6–8a68- b4ce96c78e04_story.html.

Douglas, Mary. (1966) 1984. *Purity and Danger. An Analysis of the Concepts of Pollution and Taboos*. New York: Routledge.

Engebretsen, Elisabeth L. 2014. *Queer Women in Urban China: An Ethnography*. New York: Routledge.

Evans, Harriet. 2007. *The Subject of Gender: Daughters and Mothers in Urban China*. Lanham, MD: Rowman and Littlefield.

Farquhar, Judith. 1996. "Market Magic: Getting Rich and Getting Personal in Medicine after Mao." *American Ethnologist* 23, no. 2: 239–57.

Farquhar, Judith. 2002. *Appetites: Food and Sex in Post-socialist China*. Durham, NC: Duke University Press.

Fincher, Leta H. 2014. *Left-Over Women: The Resurgence of Gender Inequality in China*. London: Zed.

Friedman, Sara L. 2009. "The Ties that Bind: Female Homosociality and the Production of Intimacy in Rural China." In *Chinese Kinship: Contemporary Anthropological Perspectives*, edited by S. Brandtstädter and G. D. Santos, 95–111. New York: Routledge.

Goldman, Russell, and Patrick Boheler. 2015. "China's One-Child Policy." *New York Times*, October 29. https://www.nytimes.com/interactive/2015/10/29/world/asia/china-one-child-policy -timeline.html.

Greenhalgh, Susan. 2012. "Patriarchal Demographics? China's Sex Ratio Reconsidered." *Population and Development Review* 38: 30–149.

Greenhalgh, Susan. 2014. "'Bare Sticks' and Other Dangers to the Social Body: Assembling Fatherhood in China." In *Globalized Fatherhood*, edited by Marcia C. Inhorn, Wendy Chavkin, and Jose-Alberto Navarro, 359–81. New York: Berghahn.

Hertog, Ekaterina. 2009. *Tough Choices: Bearing an Illegitimate Child in Japan*. Stanford, CA: Stanford University Press.

Illouz, Eva. 2018. *La fin de l'amour: Enquête sur le désarroi contemporain* (*The End of Love: A Sociology of Negative Relations*). Paris: Seuil.

Judd, Ellen. 1989. "Niangjia: Chinese Women and Their Natal Families." *Journal of Asian Studies* 48, no. 3: 525–44.

Kristeva, Julia. 1980. *Pouvoirs de l'horreur* (*Powers of Horror*). Paris: Seuil.

Nguyen, Minh T. N., and Meixuan Chen. 2017. "The Caring State? On Rural Welfare Governance in Post-reform Vietnam and China." *Ethics and Social Welfare* 11, no. 3: 230–47.

Rofel, Lisa. 1999. *Other Modernities: Gendered Yearnings in China after Socialism*. Berkeley: University of California Press.

Rofel, Lisa. 2007. *Desiring China: Experiments in Neoliberalism, Sexuality, and Public Culture*. Durham, NC: Duke University Press.

Yan, Yunxiang. 2003. *Private Life under Socialism: Love, Intimacy, and Family Change in a Chinese Village, 1949–1999*. Stanford, CA: Stanford University Press.

Yip, Lucetta L. K. 2007. "Noras on the Road: Family and Marriage of Lesbian Women in Shanghai." *Journal of Lesbian Studies* 10, nos. 3–4: 87–103.

Yip, Lucetta L. K. 2012. *Shanghai Lalas: Female Tongzhi Communities and Politics in Urban China*. Hong Kong: Hong Kong University Press.

Zavoretti, Roberta. 2016a. "Being the Right Woman for Mr. Right: Marriage and Household Politics in Present-Day Nanjing." In *Transforming Patriarchy: Chinese Families in the*

Twenty-First Century, edited by Gonçalo Santos and Stevan Harrell. Seattle: University of Washington Press.

Zavoretti, Roberta. 2016b. "Is It Better to Cry in a BMW or to Laugh on a Bicycle? Marriage, 'Financial Performance Anxiety,' and the Production of Class in Nanjing." *Modern Asian Studies* 50, no. 4: 1190–219.

Zavoretti, Roberta. 2017. *Rural Origins, City Lives: Making Class and Place in Contemporary China*. Seattle: University of Washington Press.

Zeamer, Emily. 2013. "Single Woman." In *Figures of Southeast Asian Modernity*, edited by Joshua Barker, Erik Harms, and Johan Lindquist, 121–23. Honolulu: University of Hawai'i Press.

Zhang, Everett. 2007. "The Birth of Nanke (Men's Medicine) in China: The Making of the Subject of Desire." *American Ethnologist* 34, no. 3: 491–508.

Zhang, Jun, and Peidong Sun. 2014. "When Are You Going to Get Married?" In *Wives, Husbands, and Lovers*, edited by Deborah S. Davis and Sara L. Friedman, 118–46. Stanford, CA: Stanford University Press.

Zhang, Li. 2010. *In Search of Paradise: Middle-Class Living in a Chinese Metropolis*. Ithaca, NY: Cornell University Press.

Zhang, Li, and Aiwha Ong. 2008. *Privatizing China: Socialism from Afar*. Ithaca, NY: Cornell University Press.

Zhang, Yiqian. 2015. "China's Unwed Couples Grapple with Restrictions on Having Babies." *Global Times*, August 7. http://www.globaltimes.cn/content/931023.shtml.

Dancing and Rapping the Good Life:
Sharing Aspirations and Values in Vietnamese Hip-Hop

Sandra Kurfürst

Hip-hop is all about aspirations. It is ultimately linked to the good life, as it is used as a medium of social commentary against the status quo (Lee 2010). As a "global signifier for many forms of marginalizations" (Osumare 2001: 173), hip-hop renders the marginal positioning of individuals and groups in the city and society at large visible and audible, while its bodily sensations attract more and more people into this art form. An art and cultural form that travels globally, its uptake differs according to locality. In Vietnam the uptake of hip-hop is closely linked to the country's integration into the world economy following decades of war and isolation. Rap and breaking (break-dancing), and later other dance styles, all emically summarized under the term *văn hoá hip hop* (hip-hop culture), appeared in Vietnam in the 1990s shortly after the introduction of the Đổi Mới economic reform program. As the government actively pursued the country's integration into the world

positions 32:1 DOI 10.1215/10679847-10889981

economy, cultural commodities from other parts of the world were able to enter the country. Students were suddenly allowed to study abroad, notably in nonsocialist countries, resulting in the circulation of hip-hop practitioners, knowledge, and storage devices such as audio cassettes, video cassettes, and photos. However, as the anthropologist Brian Larkin (2013) reminds us, the circulation of cultural commodities requires more than technological infrastructure. Looking at meaning making in the local context, at which objects and subjects enter through circulation, he suggests examining practices of uptake and rejection. Uptake is always driven by desire. Circulation then involves "complex acts of identification and translation," as well as commensuration, as these images move across cultural differences (Larkin 2013: 241, 245). As a result, the uptake of hip-hop in Vietnam was and still is mediated not only by technical means such as mixtapes, video cassettes, and recently social media, but also by individuals' desire and willingness to adopt new cultural practices.

The female rapper Suboi recalls how she used to listen to different types of music such as pop, rock, blues, and jazz as a teenager, but ended up making hip-hop music because "This is, you know, the music of rebellious people . . . I need that in my life" (interview, Viet Talk 2015). In a similar vein, Phương Silver Monkey, an icon (đại) of hip-hop dance in Vietnam, says, "Hip-hop is very free. In hip-hop music you can easily create with all the skills you have. . . . In this music, you're free to develop yourself" (Hanyi 2015; my translation). In other words, in hip-hop culture late-socialist youth are able to carve out their own spaces as they seek economic independence from their parents and withdraw from societal expectations.

In his account of young people's navigation through a precarious urban environment, AbdouMaliq Simone (2019) outlines the practices of crafting, harvesting, and detachment as determinants of their agency. Crafting is a specific stylized performance created to attract the "attention of some and the dis-attention of others" (28): "In crafting, there is the recognition of a sought-for instrumentality, of the ability to accomplish something through composition, through piecing together different styles, influences, and skills to gain access to specific opportunities" (30). Harvesting relates to appropriating resources offered by the urban environment to build a livelihood, for instance by putting materials, cultural memories, and solidarities to work for personal goals. Detachment is the active withdrawal of young people, increasingly aware of their expendability, from the expectations of others (28–29).

Local, Socialist, and Hip-Hop Norms

Many young people practicing hip-hop argue with their parents about the purposefulness of their desires to dance or make rap music, raising the question of what constitutes a good person under late socialism. In Vietnam, as in China, the marriage of economic liberalism and political authoritarianism places contradictory demands on the individual, creating an ambiguous moral landscape that late-socialist citizens, in particular young people, have to navigate. The party-state propagates self-entrepreneurship and the private accumulation of wealth while becoming a moral person who is loyal to the nation and the community (Schwenkel and Leshkowich 2012; Zhang 2018). The result is an "ethic of striving" that demands that one rises to the top, with failure to do so seen as not having tried hard enough or responsibly enough (Nguyen 2019: 172). Yet simultaneously individuals accumulating personal wealth and power are expected to share with and take care of others and the community. As Li Zhang (2012: 663) summarizes, "The search for a private self and the good life is still deeply entangled with larger social relationships, moral concerns, and traditional cultural practices." In this regard, hip-hop, promoting the values of authenticity, competitiveness, strength, and collectivity (Berggren 2014; Lee 2010; Liu 2010), adds yet another layer to the already complex politics of aspiration arising from the realities of people negotiating various value frameworks to create meaning in their lives (Nguyen, Wilcox, and Lin, this issue). Against this background, hip-hop practitioners literally move between different value regimes, becoming translators between different social worlds. On the one hand they strive to make a successful career in the highly competitive cultural industry or in their office jobs; on the other, they embody the translocal values of support and fierceness shared by hip-hop artists around the world. Young women particularly need to navigate different social roles and social expectations; in fact, the convergence of local, artistic, socialist, and neoliberal values becomes most explicit with respect to normative ideas of gender.

Although the predominance of Confucianist-informed gender norms has been challenged (Hakkarainen 2018), they seem to provide a blueprint against which femininity is assessed. Both state propaganda and private advertisements draw on norms of femininity such as the Four Virtues (*tứ đức*) (Leshkowich 2008) that determine *công* (women's labor), *dung* (appearance), *ngôn* (speech), and *hạnh* (conduct). Women should be skilled at cooking and housekeeping (labor), be physically attractive to please their husbands (appearance), adopt a humble and submissive communicative repertoire and voice (speech), and finally embody female integrity, presenting obedience to their seniors and husbands (conduct) (Khuat, Le, and Nguyen 2009; Ngo 2004). As I will show, the idea of voice and women's speech is relevant to the evaluation of female rap in East Asian contexts. Nguyen (2015: 153) points out the prevailing ideology of women's domesticity with the underlying notions of caring and providing for the family as the good wife and mother. Yet the young women presented in this article have acquired skills and knowledge that they want to put to work on their own terms, shifting the focus of care from family and kin to relationships with their peers.

Aihwa Ong (2008) introduces the term *self-fashioning* to capture the individualizing logic of young professionals in Shanghai. Much like Simone's crafting, self-fashioning involves "the astute defining and mixing of different knowledge and the capacity to convert information from one zone into a new value in another" (187). Apart from crafting their lives to support themselves economically, the female rappers and dancers use hip-hop as a creative vehicle to achieve their own aspirations and freedom from social expectations and gender norms. The following analysis is based on narrative interviews with rappers and dancers in Hanoi, Ho Chi Minh City, and Ninh Binh, as well as go-alongs (Kusenbach 2003) in public spaces and studios in Hanoi. The interviews with rappers are complemented by analysis of rap lyrics and videos.

Self-fashioning in Viet Rap

Rap has been termed an "outlaw expression" (Bradley 2009: 88). It is a means of speaking up and challenging the status quo. In Vietnam, local artists and fans refer to the music genre as *Viet rap*. Since its beginnings in the

1990s, rap has been associated with violence and unruly behavior, one reason being that battles between male rappers frequently used to become violent; another is the use of foul language, references to violence, and sexual insults. This is why rap is often subject to state censorship (Margara 2014; Norton 2015).

Nevertheless, a few rappers, including Đen Vâu, Lil Knight, Young UNO, Binz, and Suboi, have risen to the top in recent years. Using creative wordplay and verbal art, they evade censorship, rapping about issues that are pertinent to contemporary Vietnamese youth. Much like their East Asian counterparts, their lyrics address social issues such as family, filial piety, love, and education (Lee 2010; Liu 2010). Although Viet rap is increasingly being co-opted by media corporations, the topics rappers address resonate with young Vietnamese, and particularly urban middle-class youth, who follow rap stars on Facebook and Instagram and watch TV shows such as *King of Rap Vietnam*. Viet rappers who brag about money, wealth, sexuality, and violence are referred to as *underground*, with a general distinction between underground and overground artists (Norton 2015).

Against this background it is rather surprising that two of Vietnam's most famous artists in the hip-hop music business are female. Suboi is a twenty-nine-year-old female MC from Ho Chi Minh City.[1] Her stage name, Suboi, already transgresses the traditional binary gender categories, combining her nickname "Su" given to her by her family with "boi," coined by her friends due to her tomboy nature. Suboi raps in both Vietnamese and English and claims to be influenced by Eminem; Kendrick Lamar; Will Smith; Erykah Badouh; and, closer to home, Lê Hữu Hà, a Vietnamese musician, and Elvis Phương, a former star on *Paris by Night*, a popular Vietnamese variety show that has aired in several countries overseas.

Suboi started out singing in a rock band in high school when she was fifteen or sixteen years old. After graduating she became a solo rapper, initially producing tracks herself by downloading beats, writing lyrics, and rapping. When she turned nineteen, she signed with Music Faces, a Vietnamese music label promoting Vietnamese artists (interview, Viet Talk 2015). Working with the Dutch producer Grem Linh, she released her first album *Walk/ Bước* in 2010, and in 2012 she founded her own company, Suboi Entertainment. Two years later in 2014, she released her second studio album, *Run*, this time with the title only in English. The transition from *Walk* to *Run* symbolizes the dynamics of her professional career and personal development. By starting her own label she has become an entrepreneur, giving her the freedom to choose her own staff and write her own lyrics.

Nonetheless, Suboi reflects on the hardships of her choice. For instance, on the last track, "Away," from her 2014 album, she raps about her struggles early in her career and how other people's opinions and judgments did not prevent her moving forward.[2] In the hook she sings, "Let's get away together. Let's get away to a place. Let's get away. I wanna get away get—get—get away." After releasing this second album she took a break from show business, struggling to continue, but decided to keep writing and making her own music (Viet Talk 2015).

In a similar vein the Hanoian artist Kimmese, born in 1991, accomplished the transition from teenage girl star to mature singer and rapper. When I met her for the first time during a noisy walk-and-talk in the Ancient Quarter one Saturday evening in late October 2018, she explained how hip-hop had become her aspiration in life. She had first encountered it at the age of twelve. In a neighborhood where people struggled financially, she would save all her breakfast money to buy hip-hop CDs on her way home from school. When she watched her first US hip-hop video CD with clips from artists such as Wyclef Jean, 50 Cent, and Usher, she thought "Yeah, I want that. It was like an addiction to me at that time" (interview, October 2018). At the age of fourteen, a Vietnamese music label signed her as a singer in a girl band. Despite being signed by a label and producing pop music, she tried to remain true to herself as a rapper. In his analysis of South Korean rap, Lee (2010: 156) describes how authenticity, the value of keeping it real, is "closely tied to maintaining artistic integrity and not succumbing to commercialism or pressure from competitors and fans."

Kimmese recalls how her first contract allowed her to write three songs of her own. She decided to make them rap tracks. In the first, she defends herself against accusations of going mainstream and not having her own style. She asks, "How can you know me so well, how could you know what I want, what I need, and what I'm doing?" With this she criticizes the evaluation of her personhood by others, especially in her fragile status as a teenager. She adds that she was tired of being told what to do and how to be by others. So, instead of people judging one another, she suggests that they get along together. "Why don't we just get along . . . ? Why [do] we just like turn around and like be, like an enemy, when we have the same love: it's hip-hop, you know" (interview, October 2018). However, studio postproduction turned her self-written rap track into a commercial music product, undermining its idiosyncrasies.

After releasing her first pop album as Kim in 2012, which was well-received in Vietnam, she left the record label and decided to return to her passion for hip-hop music. Like the dynamization of the album titles being indexical of Suboi's career path, she took an alternative stage name after leaving the music label, finally calling herself Kimmese. Under her new name she recorded a track with Justatee, a major artist collaborating with male Viet rappers such as Lil Knight, Đen Vâu, and recently the female artist Tiên Tiên, from Ho Chi Minh City. The track was produced by Touliver, Vietnam's top hip-hop producer. Kimmese has collaborated with both ever since.

In summary, both women entrepreneurs engage in self-fashioning. According to Ong (2008: 187), self-fashioning is an important part of becoming a successful player in the fast-changing late-socialist market. Both Suboi and Kimmese put the skills they acquired in their early careers to work in their own interests, leaving the music labels under whose contracts they had started their musical careers. In this way they have evaded the music industry by founding their own company or becoming an independent artist, doing everything on their own. Suboi founded her own music label, giving her the freedom to choose her preferred producers, directors, and managers, and finally to become a rap mogul herself. Kimmese, in contrast, has acquired the skills and social capital necessary to accomplish the different stages of the music production process by herself. Bringing together the skills she has acquired and the relationships she has made over the years enables her to access specific opportunities (Simone 2019) in hip-hop music. Both women have succeeded in making a name for themselves in the Vietnamese music business.

Gender Fluidity

The genre of rap music is usually male-dominated, in terms of both the main artists and the language norms. Berggren (2014: 233) points out that the genre's conventions of *dissing* and *battling* are full of tokens of masculinity such as aggression, competitiveness, and references to heterosexual sex. In Ci's (2014: 36) words, the representation of the self in rap can be characterized as "wealth-chasing and pleasure-seeking" male subjects. However, the female artists presented above fashion themselves as pleasure-seeking and self-determining but nevertheless caring subjects. In the track "Away" (2010), Suboi appeals to her audience to stop dissing, rapping "So don't, don't bring your black stains onto other people's clothes. And don't, don't talk with each other pouring offensive words into each other's ears. And don't, don't tell stories that destroy others' reputations" (verse 1, lines 6–8, translated from Vietnamese). In rap battles, the pragmatic function of dissing is exactly to insult and destroy the opponent's reputation. However, Suboi uses the negative imperative *đừng* (don't) to express her disregard for such derogatory practices. Like Kimmese in her first self-written track, Suboi pleads for harmony, asking her peers to leave her alone and stop judging and harassing others.

By renouncing dissing, these women stand out from their (underground) male counterparts, who frequently make use of foul language and sexual insults. Notably, homophobic insults serve to substantiate their heteronormative masculinity. The two female rappers, by contrast, fashion themselves as ethical citizens in an increasingly competitive socialist market economy, reactivating "collectivist ideas of social life through the idiom of care" (Nguyen, Wilcox, and Lin, this issue). At one moment they adhere to normative ideas of femininity, assuming the expected position of a caretaker, watching out for others and adhering to the gender norm of *ngon*, using a humble voice and polite speech; in the next, they employ a different linguistic repertoire, raising their voices again to crisscross stereotypes of gendered language use.

In her single "Người ta hiểu" ("They understand"), released in 2017 and addressing her personal struggle against following the conventional path of a young, urban, middle-class Vietnamese woman, Suboi raps, "If you got guts, step up and pull the trigger, instead of standing there saying nothing. I step out from a small alley with big guts" (verse 1, lines 12–13, translated from Vietnamese). Linguistically, her choice of more direct, even aggressive, language matches the message she aims to convey. To emphasize that she is liberating herself from social expectations, the hook repeats: "Whether they understand or not, my life is still like this, whether they understand or not." In this track she also makes use of the stylistic device of braggadocio. More than just bragging, braggadocio assists by making the MC larger than life. By narrating the story of her life, the MC elevates herself above all others (Bradley 2009). Suboi uses masculine metaphors to demonstrate her superiority: "If they are b-boys, I am Easy Roc. If they are rockers, I am the Chili Peppers. If they are riders, hi! I am Schumacher."

First, she explicitly references hip-hop, comparing herself to Easy Roc, a b-boy in the globally renowned US Rock Steady Crew. Second, having been a singer in a rock band, she acknowledges the success of the Red Hot Chili Peppers, an all-male rock band. Third, and finally, she represents herself as Michael Schumacher, the Formula One world champion. By taking the positions of outstanding male figures in global popular culture and sport, she produces an image of the self that evades binary gender categorization. The linguistic anthropologist Shigeko Okamoto (1995) argues that in Japan, where the idea of "women's speech" or woman's language also prevails, women make strategic language choices to communicate images and pragmatic meanings of self. Based on her work, Ian Condry (2006: 179) concludes that female rappers use supposedly vulgar, and therefore masculine, language to construct their performative personae.

In fact, rappers can have multiple selves. What mediates "between the 'I' of the rapper and the 'I' of the character" is the *I* of the first-person narrator (Cecil Brown, quoted in Bradley 2009: 165). Kimmese and Suboi both use the personal pronoun *tôi* (I) in their lyrics. This is a strategic linguistic choice, as expressing the *I* correctly in Vietnamese is no small matter. Self-reference and second-person address are always based on the asymmetric relationship determined by social status, gender, and age, and mirror the hierarchical social system. Consequently Vietnamese interlocutors have to choose from among a broad spectrum of terms for *I* and *you*, according to the interactional situation. Most common is the use of kin terms, regardless of the speaker's and addressee's genealogical relatedness (Luong 1990; Thompson 1965). While pairs of proper pronouns such as *tôi* and *bạn* exist for *I* and *you*, they are rarely used colloquially except in very specific interactions. *Tôi* is used to express social distance, for example, when dealing with people in authority or those whom one does not know at all. It is very offensive if used inappropriately, e.g., to someone higher in social status or age. With the increase in mass media, the use of *tôi* and *bạn* (you; or, plural, *các bạn*) has become more common in public broadcasting. Nonetheless, young women's use of the first-person pronoun *tôi* in Vietnamese popular culture, especially in music, is rare. Female Vietnamese singers frequently refer to themselves as *em* (younger sister), as in most (love) songs an imagined *anh* (older brother) is present.

By employing the gender-neutral first-person pronoun *tôi*, Suboi and Kimmese perform selves that do not submit to any gendered or otherwise hierarchical social relationship. In her self-reference, Suboi alternates between *tôi*, Suboi, and her nickname, Su. Only when she (re)situates herself in her relationship with her father or mother does she use the relevant kin terms, referring to herself as *con* (child). Her track "Đời" ("Life") (2016) narrates the story of when her father lost his job, her family almost lost their house, and her father tried to commit suicide, taking up the intimate consequences of socioeconomic transformation that many people in contemporary Vietnam face and which are rarely spoken about in public. This personal life story not only demonstrates the downside of economic development but also unsettles gender roles, as her father, as head of the household, is at least temporarily unable to provide for his family.

In conclusion, young women employ rap as a vehicle to speak up against social expectations and normative ideas of gender. With their wordplay, conscious use of *tôi* as self-reference, and choice of metaphors, female rappers become gender-fluid, reworking gendered identities. Their gender performance is also an inspiration to their fans, resulting in a public debate about the (in)commensurability of hip-hop and being female in Vietnam.

Dancing the Good Life

But it's really good when you join the dancing, because I see it makes us younger and see everything brighter than normal people. I see that now. Like positive thinking.

—(Nguyệt, female hip-hop dancer from Hanoi)

Twenty-seven-year-old Nguyệt, a renowned dancer from Hanoi, realizes her vision of the good life together with her husband Bi Max, a b-boy from Quảng Trị Province in Central Vietnam. They met at a hip-hop battle event and married in January 2018. Together they overcome gendered expectations about spousal mobility (Kurfürst 2021). Since the Vietnamese wife is commonly associated with the outside of the family and is then integrated into the realm of the inside through marriage, she is expected to move in with her husband's family after marriage. The husband, by contrast, is considered in charge of inside kin relations (Brandtstädter 2008; Nguyen 2019). However, rather than Nguyệt moving in with Max, Max decided to quit his job as a car mechanic in Central Vietnam, where his family lives, and move to Hanoi to live and dance with his spouse. They are members of the same hip-hop dance crew and teach a dance class together. Although they work as instructors in different dance studios around the city, Nguyệt is the family's main provider. She says, "I have a class [that I teach], but since I have family now I think that I have to do more to earn money. So, I work for a fashion company—sportswear—yes, a sportswear company. But it's online, so my time is flexible" (interview, October 2018). Pluralizing her sources of income (Simone 2019), she still has enough time to practice and enter international dance competitions in Southeast Asia. Nguyệt makes it clear that she chose a partner from the world of dancing because he can understand her lifestyle (Kurfürst 2021). As a dancer, she often has to stay out late because crew practice only starts in the evening, usually after 8 p.m., a fact that her parents, particularly her father, disapprove of, and she has to travel a lot. When I met her she was also thinking about having children, although some years in the future rather than immediately, as expected of a Vietnamese woman in her late twenties. On the one hand she liberates herself from the force of domesticity (Nguyen 2019), traveling abroad alone, staying out late at night, and not moving in with her husband's family; while on the other, she acknowledges her responsibility as a family provider, the household member with a stable income in contrast to that of her husband, a freelancer.

Nguyệt holds her own dance class once a week in the park surrounding the Lenin Monument in Hanoi, thereby harvesting the urban environment (Simone 2019) as she uses the materiality and accessibility of public space to create a public domain for hip-hop culture in the capital. Together with other dancers, she makes the physical practices visible and accountable in the city. Dance techniques render the body legible in a shared idiom, offering possibilities for imagining new ways of being oneself as well as being with others (Hamera 2007). As a collective meeting on a regular basis, they share the meaning of hip-hop culture by helping and talking to one another, being connected, and *chơi với nhau* (playing together) (interviews, October 2018), thereby shifting the collective pole of the good life from the family to their community of peers.

Vy, a female dancer in her twenties from Ho Chi Minh City, explained that in general people in Vietnam know little about hip-hop and associate it with negatives such as young people coming home late at night, people living on the streets, and unemployment. What is more, the parents of dancers seem to fear that their children's desire to dance might interfere with their studies. Dancing appears to be seen as useless, as it does not provide a job or a steady income (interviews, October/November 2018). Vy elucidates, saying that graduating from university while also dancing allowed her to prove that she was still a "good" person, and that she was able to earn money from dancing by working as a dance instructor and winning cash prizes in dance competitions (Kurfürst 2021). Vy's self-assessment of what it means to be a "good" person demonstrates her agency. According to Sherry B. Ortner (2006), agency presupposes awareness and self-reflexivity concerning the circumstances in which the subject finds herself. While she was seeking the personal happiness embodied in dancing, she acted within the moral constraints imposed on her by social expectations of her economic success and moral conduct as a daughter. In fact, she acted against the circumstances she found herself in, as she made enough money from dancing to become independent of her family's resources. Yet as dancing is a precarious undertaking, she also has stable employment in quality assurance. In fact, all of the female dancers participating in this research hold a bachelor's degree and are urban and middle-class. They decouple themselves from "a fixed set of aspirations and development trajectories" (Simone 2019: 27), by taking employment based on their university education and combining it with teaching dance. Simultaneously, they decouple themselves from gendered aspirations, contesting the imperative of marriage (see Zavoretti, this issue), looking for a partner who will support and care about their personal aspiration to a dancing life more than for a provider for the family.

Thanh Phương's parents were not happy about her dedicating her free time to dance hip-hop. Thanh Phương is thirty years old, unmarried, and childless, and lives with and takes care of her parents. With a degree from the University of Law in Hanoi, she works in marketing for a large Vietnamese real-estate company, where she was recently promoted to team leader. Explaining how she manages to maintain a dancing life while holding down a time-consuming and responsible job, she differentiates between "knowledge from school," and the sensory knowledge she gains from dancing and traveling. She explains that "normal" people working in the office would usually apply the knowledge acquired at school. She considers such knowledge boring, and puts everything she feels and sees around her into her job. As she works in marketing, she researches what people like and what makes them happy. She says that dancing allows her to maintain a more vibrant and creative mind than those of other people (Kurfürst 2021). She concludes that without hip-hop, she would not be able to work in her current position: "I love my job and I love dancing, too. So I wanna mix this like I can use my knowledge for dancing. So I can help more people" (interview, October 2018). Thanh Phương is able to navigate and capitalize on her knowledge of and reference to the different value regimes of late socialism (see Nguyen, Wilcox, and Lin, this issue). According to Ong (2008: 187), self-fashioning implies not only "fine-tuning oneself but also steering oneself through diverse networks of knowledge and value." Thanh Phương engages in self-fashioning when she puts money from her full-time job aside and uses her skills to generate sponsors to raise money to organize a local hip-hop event. She hopes to have her own studio in the future, and plans to rent a building from the real-estate company she works for, which will give her a discount.

Conclusion

Ong (2008: 195) uses the metaphor "dancing across the fault lines" to describe Chinese professional women's maneuvering of Chinese socialism and Orientalist capitalism and their position in the late-socialist economy. The young women from Hanoi and Ho Chi Minh City introduced in this article literally dance and rap across the fault lines. Kimmese, Suboi, Vy, Thanh Phương, and Nguyệt are female entrepreneurs who combine the skills and knowledge acquired from school, university, and employment with their verbal and somatic skills and knowledge to advance their personal, economic, and social interests. Their practices of crafting and harvesting (Simone 2019) convert their different kinds of knowledge and their cultural and social capital as members of the urban middle class into economic capital. According to Ong (2008: 187), self-fashioning is the steering of oneself through diverse networks of knowledge and across multiple regimes of value, thereby generating opportunities for strategy and play. The young women presented above are all making strategic decisions to foster their careers while remaining true to themselves. Suboi and Kimmese left the music labels with which they had started their careers to become self-made entrepreneurs, while Thanh Phương decided on a career in marketing to finance her future dance studio. Vy detaches herself from the economic resources of her family by financing her trips abroad to dance competitions herself, proving her moral strength by graduating from university and acquiring stable employment. Play, in this regard, refers to their trying out of creative practices and new ways of being together, as in dance.

Although increasingly co-opted by media corporations, hip-hop continues to transgress social norms in the way that the women dance and rap across the binary gender poles. They detach themselves from social expectations as they delay or reject marriage, or look for a partner who will support their aspirations in life. Despite social pressure, they decide for themselves on the right time to have children. In this way, each of the women becomes "a translator of values, a mediator among the surfeit of forms of knowledge" that circulates in contemporary Vietnam (Ong 2008: 186). Engaging in the cultural practice of rap, they mediate between the global art form and local meanings by addressing their own positioning as young women in both the rap game and Vietnamese society. The ethical work that the female artists perform on themselves also has an impact on the public among their urban middle-class fans and in the national media discussing the (in)commensurability of notions of femininity with hip-hop culture. By combining the use of the gender-neutral first-person pronoun *tôi* with male metaphors, they evade the hierarchical social order and rework gendered identities. Bringing home achievements such as cash prizes and awards from dance competitions and combining these with conventional jobs, female dancers succeed in gaining recognition from their parents for what they love most. Even in their pursuit of what seem to be individualized goals and desires, they invest in the common project of living well together (Nguyen, Wilcox, and Lin, this issue). Young dancers make their bodily practices visible and accountable when practicing and teaching dance classes in public spaces. Harvesting the physical environment of the city, they aim to communicate a positive image of hip-hop culture, building on values such as sharing and contributing to the community, paving the way for future generations to indulge in their passion for dance.

Notes

1 *MC* means "Master of Ceremony" and is another term for rapper.
2 I am grateful to Dr. Phuong Glaser, who assisted me with the translation of Suboi's lyrics.

References

Berggren, Kalle. 2014. "Hip Hop Feminism in Sweden: Intersectionality, Feminist Critique and Female Masculinity." *European Journal of Women's Studies* 21, no. 3: 233–50.

Bradley, Adam. 2009. *Book of Rhymes: The Poetics of Hip Hop*. New York: Basic Civitas.

Brandtstädter, Susanne. 2008. "The Gender of Work and the Production of Kinship Value in Taiwan." In *Chinese Kinship*, edited by Susanne Brandtstädter and Goncalo D. Santos, 168–92. Abingdon, UK: Routledge.

Ci, Jiwei. 2014. *Moral China in the Age of Reform*. New York: Cambridge University Press.

Condry, Ian. 2006. *Hip-hop Japan: Rap and the Paths of Cultural Globalization*. Durham, NC: Duke University Press.

Hakkarainen, Minna. 2018. "Rereading Confucianism: A Feminist Gender Project." In *Myth Busting Vietnam*, edited by Catherine Earl and Adam Fforde, 45–65. Copenhagen: NIAS Press.

Hamera, Judith. 2007. *Dancing Communities: Performance, Difference, and Connection in the Global City*. New York: Palgrave Macmillian.

Hanyi, Linh. 2014. "Phương Silver Monkey, 'Nhiệt' và tình yêu hip hop" ("Phương Silver Monkey, 'Fire,' and the Love for Hip-Hop"). Đẹp, May 26. https://dep.com.vn/phuong-silver-monkey-nhiet-va-tinh-yeu-hip-hop/.

Khuat, Thu Hong, Le Bach Duong, and Nguyen Ngoc Huong. 2009. *Easy to Joke about, But Hard to Talk About: Sexuality in Contemporary Vietnam*. Hanoi: Knowledge.

Kurfürst, Sandra. 2021. *Dancing Youth: Hip Hop and Gender in Late Socialist Vietnam*. Bielefeld, Germany: Transcript.

Kusenbach, Margarethe. 2003. "Street Phenomenology. The Go-Along as Ethnographic Research Tool." *Ethnography* 4, no. 3: 455–85.

Larkin, Brian. 2013. "Making Equivalence Happen: Commensuration and the Architecture of Circulation." In *Images That Move*, edited by Patricia Spyer and Mary Margaret Steedly, 237–56. Santa Fe, NM: SAR Press.

Lee, Jamie Shinhee. 2010. "Globalizing Keepin' It Real: South Korean Hip-Hop Playas." In *The Languages of Global Hip-Hop*, edited by Marina Terkourafi, 139–62. New York: Continuum International.

Leshkowich, Ann Marie. 2008. "Working out Culture: Gender, Body, and Commodification in a Ho Chi Minh City Health Club." *Urban Anthropology* 37, no. 1: 49–87.

Liu, Xuexin. 2010. "Across the Borders: Hip Hop's Influence on Chinese Youth Culture." *Southeast Review of Asian Studies*, no. 32: 146–53.

Luong, Hy V. 1990. *Discursive Practices and Linguistic Meanings: The Vietnamese System of Person Reference*. Amsterdam: John Benjamins.

Margara, Andreas. 2014. "Hip Hop in Vietnam." *taz*, January 6. https://taz.de/Hip-Hop-in-Vietnam/!130265/.

Ngo, Binh T. N. 2004. "The Confucian Four Feminine Virtues." In *Gender Practices in Contemporary Vietnam*, edited by Helle Rydstrom and Lisa Drummond, 47–73. Copenhagen: NIAS Press.

Nguyen, Minh T. N. 2015. *Vietnam's Socialist Servants: Domesticity, Class, Gender, and Identity*. New York: Routledge.

Nguyen, Minh T. N. 2019. *Waste and Wealth: An Ethnography of Labor, Value, and Morality in a Vietnamese Recycling Economy*. New York: Oxford University Press.

Norton, Barley. 2015. "Music and Censorship in Vietnam Since 1954." In *The Oxford Handbook of Music Censorship*, edited by Patricia Hall, 303–30. New York: Oxford University Press.

Okamoto, Shigeko. 1995. "'Tasteless' Japanese: Less 'Feminine' Speech among Young Japanese Women." In *Gender Articulated: Language and the Socially Constructed Self*, edited by Kira Hall and Mary Bucholtz, 297–325. New York: Routledge.

Ong, Aihwa. 2008. "Self-fashioning Shanghainese: Dancing across Spheres of Value." In *Privatizing China: Socialism from Afar*, edited by Aihwa Ong and Li Zhang, 182–96. Ithaca, NY: Cornell University Press.

Ortner, Sherry B. 2006. *Anthropology and Social Theory: Culture, Power, and the Acting Subject*. Durham NC: Duke University Press.

Osumare, Halifu. 2001. "Beat Streets in the Global Hood: Connective Marginalities in the Hip Hop Globe." *Journal of American and Comparative Cultures*, no. 2: 171–81.

Schwenkel, Christina, and Ann Marie Leshkowich. 2012. "How Is Neoliberalism Good to Think Vietnam? How Is Vietnam Good to Think Neoliberalism?" *positions: east asia cultures critique* 20, no. 2: 379–401.

Simone, AbdouMaliq. 2019. "Precarious Detachment: Youth and Modes of Operating in Hyderabad and Jakarta." In *The Routledge Handbook of Anthropology and the City*, edited by Setha Low, 27–40. London: Routledge.

Thompson, Laurence C. 1965. *A Vietnamese Reference Grammar*. Seattle: University of Washington Press.

Viet Talk. 2015. "Viet Entertainment Talk Suboi and Linda D." *YouTube*, March 30. https://www.youtube.com/watch?v=B4RXLKPvEV4.

Zhang, Li. 2012. "Afterword: Flexible Postsocialist Assemblages from the Margin." *positions: asia critique* 20, no. 2: 659–67.

Zhang, Li. 2018. "Cultivating the Therapeutic Self in China." *Medical Anthropology* 37, no. 1: 45–58.

Philanthropy Fever from Below: On the Possibilities of a Good Life in Late-Socialist China

Jiazhi Fengjiang

Everyday life in late-socialist China is characterized by hypermobility (e.g., Chu 2010; Xiang 2021b) and growing socioeconomic stratification, together with the diversification of desires (Rofel 1999) and moral frameworks (Kleinman et al. 2011; Stafford 2013; Steinmüller 2013), haunted by the Maoist socialist legacy and conditioned by the global neoliberal order (e.g., Rojas and Litzinger 2016; Zhang and Ong 2008). This article explores the possibilities open to ordinary people for shaping a good life, despite and within the restrictions imposed by their limited power or wealth.[1] For ordinary people in late-socialist China, the good life seems to be shaped by aspirations to upward mobility and the "politics of destination" (e.g., Chu 2010; Coates 2019; Xiang 2021b). Mobilities, in their multiple forms, have become a powerful and insightful lens for understanding the pursuit of a good life in late-socialist China. Xiang's (2021b: 236) description of a hummingbird

positions 32:1 DOI 10.1215/10679847-10889997

in suspension (*xuanfu*) is a telling metaphor for the modern yet unsettling aspiring subject: it "struggles hard but moves nowhere, yet it is incapable of landing." The lens of mobilities provides invaluable insights into the broader political economy of China's late-socialist transformations.

However, the good life that people pursue through the lens of mobilities is confined to a singular kind: in the future and the elsewhere, it is oriented toward one's own well-being and the well-being of the next generations (e.g., Coates 2019; Xiang 2021a). What other possibilities do ordinary people have for shaping a good life that is worth the effort (Nguyen, Wilcox, and Lin, this issue)? For instance, how do we account for the ordinary people whose aspirations afford much weight to the well-being of people beyond their own family, and to their immediate local environment? This article argues that the lens of grassroots philanthropy (a direct translation of the local term *caogen gongyi* 草根公益) helps us rethink the possibilities of the good life for ordinary people in plural forms in the context of late-socialist China.[2]

Over the past decade many ordinary people in China have been caught up in "philanthropy fever" (*gongyi re*), which has emerged from the grassroots. They organize diverse forms of charity, philanthropy, and volunteerism, some of which are increasingly monitored and supported by the state. This article uses the term *philanthropy* to gloss the various concepts and practices seen in the Chinese context that are mainly expressed by the local terms *cishan* 慈善 (compassion or charity), *gongyi* 公益 (common good), and *zuohaoshi* 做好事 (doing good deeds). Although these words have different genealogies and different meanings and connotations for different people, most in China use them interchangeably according to context.[3] They constitute a wide range of social acts that benefit others beyond the immediate family, including individuals, communities, and a notion of *shehui* 社会 (society).

While youth volunteerism (Spires 2018), community volunteerism (Luova 2011), religious charity (Weller et al. 2017), and celebrity philanthropy (Jeffreys 2015) have received ample media and scholarly attention, this article focuses on ordinary people who are committed to mobilizing resources and promoting philanthropy as a lifestyle for everyone, across all socioeconomic strata. It draws from my long-term ethnographic fieldwork on the emergence of grassroots philanthropy in Haicheng County in Wenzhou, southeast China, from 2015 to 2017, supplemented with short field trips in 2018,

2019, 2020, and 2022.[4] In Wenzhou the most popular forms of grassroots philanthropy are offering material and other aid to children, elderly people, and the disabled; conducting search and rescue and other aid missions in response to emergencies such as disasters and the recent COVID-19 epidemic; and environmental and wildlife protection projects. I was puzzled during my first fieldwork period to discover that the majority of the founders and organizers of gongyi projects and organizations in Wenzhou are ordinary people in their thirties and forties whose livelihoods have been strongly affected by recent national and local economic restructurings.

For example, Hu Ming, the founder and manager of an organization offering aid to juvenile delinquents, was a small mobile-phone vendor at a local shopping mall whose business had greatly decreased, and who had a young primary-school-age daughter to raise; and Old Wang, the founder and manager of an organization offering aid to rural children and elderly people, was a laid-off state enterprise worker. Despite their relatively precarious ability to provide for their families, people like Hu Ming and Old Wang were committed to mobilizing and managing resources for philanthropic organizations, calling themselves *caogen gongyiren* 草根公益人 (grassroots philanthropists). The term *caogen* 草根(grassroots) denotes not only their commitment to local as opposed to transnational affairs such as those described by Weller et al. (2017), but also their low socioeconomic standing in contrast to the conventional Euro-American association of philanthropy with big donations and philanthropists with wealth and power. As I have elaborated elsewhere (Fengjiang 2022), many grassroots philanthropists have found their labor marginalized by economic restructuring and are anxious to use the time this has made available as a resource with which to restructure their lives and find a way to make a living that they consider worth the effort.

This article shows how care for the well-being of others beyond the immediate family and of the environment offers opportunities for many ordinary people with limited resources to engage socially and politically in ways that are central to their experience of a good life in contemporary China. Unlike better-off philanthropists and volunteers, whose philanthropic activities tend to enhance their status and dominance, the ordinary people presented in this article experience major tensions between providing for their family and caring for others in society, between ensuring the material conditions of the good life and being able to live the ethical life of a person who is contributing to society and is recognized as such. Many ordinary people find pursuing the good life in this way extremely labor-intensive and emotionally draining. While philanthropic engagement does not bring them substantial or sustainable material returns, their creative imaginations and public actions open up possibilities for valorizing their lives in social arenas, despite and within the prevailing economic valorization of the good life.

The Rise of Grassroots Philanthropy in China

The rise of ordinary citizens' participation in charitable and volunteer projects as founders, managers, volunteers, and donors in China is attracting growing social sciences research and triggering heated public debate. One widespread assumption is that people are engaging in more charity and volunteer work today as a countervailing response to both the perceived moral crisis in contemporary China and the retreat of socialist welfare programs that has accompanied the country's economic reforms toward marketization since the 1980s. Briefly, there has been ongoing popular discourse about a moral decline or moral crisis since the economic reforms toward marketization and privatization in the 1980s (Yan 2021). Some scholars attribute the causes of the present moral-crisis discourse to the thirty-year Maoist revolution. It is suggested that the Maoist socialist engineering of morality abolished "stranger sociality" (Lee 2014: 24), contributing to the "rise of the uncivil individual" without a self-motivated "commitment to civic duty" (Yan 2003: 262), as people have developed a hostile attitude to strangers outside of their own social networks (Yan 2009: 19).

In contrast, other anthropological findings in both rural and urban contexts suggest that the perceived moral crisis does not necessarily reflect actual moral decay but rather heightened moral sensibility and moral ambiguity. These authors (e.g., Brandtstädter 2011; Brandtstädter and Steinmüller 2017; Kleinman et al. 2011; Steinmüller 2013) suggest that this is a typical modern problem in which individuals in China have to negotiate different moralities, including those of the capitalist market and the socialist state, and local ideas about community, fairness, justice, and good governance.

For instance, Ning and Palmer (2020) report that long-term educational volunteers are caught in a "moral breakdown" between the socialist ethics of altruistic sacrifice and neoliberal utilitarianism, leading them to downplay their public engagement. However, similar to peasant lawyers' main concern with "concrete social good" as the outcome of their actions (Brandtstädter 2021: 187), the anxiety among my interlocutors is not so much about moral arbitrariness or crisis related to the diversification of moral frameworks as it is about a tendency to normalize certain moral values, such as notions of interpersonal moral obligations and reciprocity, communal obligations and service, which, as ethnographies widely find, mark the continuity of certain aspects of traditional values (e.g., Oxfeld 2010; Stafford 2013; Zavoretti 2017).

In the context of this debate on moral life in late-socialist China, some argue that people's fear of living with risk and lack of a moral compass has translated into new forms of political and moral action that foster change in state-society relations. They see the growth in volunteerism and charity as evidence of a new kind of ethic. For instance, William Jankowiak (2004: 204) suggests that the increased mobility of the post-Mao market economy has facilitated "a kind of mobility of the mind," whereby people's ability to empathize with strangers beyond their own social circles is growing, resulting in an expanded "moral horizon" and the emergence of different forms of civic activism and philanthropy. Some anthropologists suggest that volunteers embody a new kind of "modern, entrepreneurial, and responsible selves" (Fleischer 2011: 300), a new notion of "universal goodness" (Weller et al. 2017: 2), a new and "generalized notion of compassion and charity" (Yan 2011: 66), and enhanced "public morality" (Yan 2021: 120). Similarly, and building on their insights, my research suggests seemingly novel forms of ethics and associational lives as the products of a particular political-economic moment.

Another body of work on the recent rise of youth volunteerism (e.g., Spires 2018) and community volunteerism (e.g., Luova 2011) in urban China offers insights into the role of the party-state in mobilizing grassroots resources and shaping the "moral subject" in the form of "neosocialist governmentality" (Palmer and Winiger 2019) and the "politics of compassion" (Zhan 2020). Indeed, the state has always promoted moral exemplars in different political projects in Chinese society (Bakken 2000; Hershatter 2000;

Lee 2014: 19–28). The various state-led moralization campaigns are based on traditional belief in the power of example, or what Bakken (2000: 9) calls "the Chinese cultural undercurrent of exemplarity." Lei Feng, who was a soldier in the People's Liberation Army, has been a prominent official moral exemplar since the Maoist era, raised up as the ultimate symbol of a good person who selflessly dedicated all his surplus labor to serving the people. Since the 2000s, Lei Feng and many new living moral exemplars among the ordinary population have regained a public presence nationwide through a series of heightened government campaigns promoting the development of a spiritual civilization, similar to Vietnam's socialization policy (Nguyen 2018).

Admittedly, government-directed volunteerism and campaigns encouraging the spirit of volunteerism are on the rise in urban areas, and while the party-state has played a role in legitimizing and regulating grassroots action, it is often grassroots actors who actively appropriate government campaigns to mobilize resources and legitimacy for their self-organized projects. In fact, the lack of government interventions and connections are often at the center of the complaints of grassroots organization managers. While some grassroots philanthropists in Wenzhou explicitly draw from socialist ideals of altruistic service and public engagement informed by Maoist revolutionary traditions and modern notions of gongyi and *gongmin shehui* 公民社会 (civil society), most draw from multiple vernacular cultural sources, including Daoist-Buddhist-infused idioms of *gongde* 公德 (public virtue), cosmopolitan notions of *da ai* 大爱 (universal goodness), *renqingwei* 人情味 (empathy), and Christian-infused notions of *aixin* 爱心 (love), as well as traditional moral values such as social obligation and reciprocity (Fengjiang 2019, 2023).

Rather than analyzing empirical materials within the framework of governmentality or individual morality, this article foregrounds the moral agency, political imagination, and social organization of ordinary people in their engagement with social projects. It takes a bottom-up ethnographic perspective that approaches their desire to form voluntary associations, mobilize grassroots resources for people in need, seek resources and support from the government, and participate in local government rather than being subject to techniques of governance. This approach draws inspiration from recent lines of anthropological enquiry into the political economy of everyday life (Adebanwi 2017; Narotzky and Besnier 2014), and in particular, into how "life acquires value within, but also despite, the prevailing economic systems of valuation" (Adebanwi 2017: 5). Their attention to a thick ethnographic description of people's creativity, resilience, and imagination in making a life that is worth the effort reveals multiple possibilities for human life within, and enabled by, the limits of a given economy conditioned by neoliberal capitalism, even from the most marginal positions.

My research suggests that the contemporary rise of grassroots philanthropy in southeast China should be contextualized within two major social and economic processes. The post-Mao national and local restructurings of the economy have caused many ordinary people, particularly men working in the private sector, to seek a career that provides recognition and purpose (Fengjiang 2022). They seek voluntary associations, explore opportunities, and navigate risks to operate philanthropic projects in a legal grey zone before the state relaxes its registration of social organizations. In Haicheng, two pioneering volunteering organizations offer operational models and have stimulated the growth of local grassroots philanthropic projects and organizations since the 2000s. One of these is an environmental wildlife protection organization founded by a sixteen-year-old student, Zhang Tianshuai, in 2000 and officially registered in 2003. Tianshuai did not go to college and has remained the full-time manager of his organization since its establishment. The other is a countywide volunteer search and rescue organization founded in 2007. As a devastating local typhoon approached Haicheng, Song Jiang, a taxi driver, joined a local journalist, Liang Sicheng, to mobilize a team of 128 taxi drivers, creating the first volunteer grassroots search and rescue team in the county in support of the local government's disaster relief effort. As a pioneer, Liang Sicheng negotiated with the local government and received an unprecedented amount of government and private financial support. In 2008 the two managed to register as a philanthropic social organization under the name United Rescue. They rapidly established branches with volunteer teams in local towns and expanded their services to include a wide range of charitable and volunteering projects including search and rescue, environmental protection, children's education, care of the elderly, and care of people with AIDS. Many of the early volunteers later formed their own organizations.

Since around 2013 the state has been increasingly opening up an intermediary space from which it can draw from the surplus energy of ordinary people to participate in both state and non-state welfare provision. The entry requirements are undemanding enough for ordinary people of relatively low social standing to participate. Even in the late 1990s, regardless of the discussion flourishing in the media and among scholars about civil-society and public-private cooperation in the provision of welfare (Metzger 2001; White, Howell, and Shang 1996), state policy on the grassroots provision of social services remained unclear. It was not until 2013 that the State Council issued guidelines for local governments purchasing public services from private companies and social organizations (Zhu 2013). The central government aimed to build an effective legal framework and purchasing system for the philanthropic sector by 2020 (Zhu 2013). Since 2013, many existing organizations in Haicheng have been able to register themselves officially with few restrictions. The number of organizations registered as *gongyi cishan lei shehui zuzhi* 公益慈善类社会组织 (philanthropic-type social organizations) in Haicheng County increased rapidly from three prior to 2013 to fifty in 2015.

As I argue elsewhere (Fengjiang 2022), the rise of grassroots philanthropy is a response not only to changing moral lives but also, and perhaps more importantly, to changing and complex political-economic developments. Committed volunteers who persist in the managing and organizing of volunteer and charity projects find that institutionalized grassroots philanthropy offers them the possibility of a career in a time of economic restructuring that is worth the effort. Their anxieties and aspirations are simultaneously about making a living and about living a life that is worthwhile. The good life to which they aspire comprises two intertwining yet often conflicting care projects: care for the family, and care for others in one's social and ecological environment. The following section explores the journeys of volunteers turned grassroots philanthropists who aspire to integrate philanthropic projects into their careers.

Grassroots Philanthropy as a Possible Arena for Self-realization

Most grassroots philanthropists started their journey with the initial idea of spending their time meaningfully but with no specific ideas about whom they will serve, or how to serve as a volunteer. Most developed aspirations to integrate their grassroots philanthropy into a possible career through participating in volunteer activities for existing organizations and copying such models when setting up their own teams and organizations. Such trajectories are reflected in the high degree of homogeneity of the organizational structures and activities of the growing body of philanthropic organizations and networks in Haicheng County. They have a shifting reserve of volunteers ready to put on the uniforms of various governmental or nongovernmental organizations and carry out all kinds of work, subject to the source of their sponsorship. Without their volunteer uniforms these grassroots philanthropists and volunteers are self-employed social media journalists, taxi or truck drivers, laid-off employees of state-owned enterprises, temporary contract workers for government institutions, salespeople, traders, and entrepreneurs who run and work at their own household and small enterprises, stores, restaurants, and cafes. To varying extents, these types of work rely on long-term local and translocal social relationships and performance of credibility.

Song Jiang's case illustrates the typical journey of a volunteer turned grassroots philanthropist. He was born in the early 1970s in a rural village in Jiangsu province and moved to Haicheng County in the late 1990s, where he worked in a factory warehouse for two years before starting to drive a taxi with a relative. He married a woman from his home village, and they had two sons. Apart from being a taxi driver, a remarkable element in his narrative about himself is his determination to defend the weak and help the needy, which has earned him the title Hero of the Greenwood (*lulin haohan*) in his social circle and his hometown. This title, originally given to those who mobilize collectively against violence imposed by the ruling government, has been popularized to refer to a righteous person who fights against violence in defense of the weak, who values brotherhood, and yet is not necessarily antagonistic to the ruling government. Song Jiang's masculine appearance suits this appellation: he is tall and robust, with dark skin. When he was young, he almost lost his life fighting village gangs that bullied powerless villagers. He was an activist who had successfully protested against the township government's land grab in his home village and confronted government officials in his hometown. During his time as a taxi driver in Haicheng, he helped homeless elderly people without household registration (*hukou*) to acquire a legal identity and shelter, fought criminals, rescued people in danger, and performed numerous other heroic acts.

In 2007, by now an experienced taxi driver, Song Jiang helped Liang Sicheng by mobilizing his taxi-driver coworkers as volunteers prior to the arrival of a dangerous typhoon. A photograph shows him carrying an elderly person through a flood on his back, on a voluntary mission to transfer affected villagers to safe sites. The photograph went viral and appeared in various official reports for several years afterward, representing the local humanitarian scene. Since then Song Jiang has been a regular figure in the media in both his hometown in Jiangsu and in Haicheng County in Zhejiang, which he now calls his "second hometown," despite maintaining his rural hukou in his actual hometown of Jiangsu. Official recognition in the form of awards from various levels of government arrive one after another every year, a few of which include Top Ten Exemplary Taxi Driver; Good Person at the Home Prefecture, Home Provincial, and National Levels; [Top] Ten Most Touching Wenzhou Persons; Most Beautiful Volunteer; Warmest New Resident; Rescuing People in Danger; and Living Lei Feng. His morality is described as "beautiful," "warm," "courageous," and "good." The central government recently awarded him the Serving the People badge, the highest official recognition so far, and he wears the little red badge on his neat black suit when participating in gongyi-related events. He carefully keeps a thick scrapbook of all the newspaper clippings and social media reports about his good deeds.

This unexpected fame has had a strong impact on Song Jiang's aspirations to a new working life more dignified than that of a taxi driver, an occupation that is often disrespected by locals. Song Jiang, like others of his generation, was much influenced as a child by state-led socialist exemplary campaigns. The iconic image of Lei Feng, the selfless and courageous soldier, with the slogan "Serving the People," and the socialist ideals of altruistic service and public engagement that accompany the figure were important sources for Song Jiang in his construction of a synthetic identity. Once the modern term *gongyi* became popular he adopted it in the rearticulation of his aspirations for a good life. This rearticulation has also meant that Song Jiang is no longer a lonely Hero of the Greenwood but an organization manager with concerns about a larger community beyond his immediate family. He quickly picked up the Wenzhou government's official discourse that replaced the terms *floating population* and *migrant workers* with *new residents*, and started to mobilize more new residents as his volunteers to promote what he termed a "new moral climate" in town. He has since carried out many projects, delivering gifts and free medical and legal aid to poor elderly villagers, street cleaners, and other marginalized migrant workers in town. Now gongyi feeds his dreams (*mengxiang*) while driving the taxi feeds his family.

Song Jiang's path might be seen as unique in the context of the prevailing portrayal of peasants-turned-migrant-workers trapped in a state of hypermobility in the quest for upward mobility (cf. Xiang 2021a, 2021b). The trajectories of ordinary people turned grassroots philanthropists are indeed diverse, and while those with migrant status are still in the minority, a substantial number of volunteers for local gongyi projects are migrants who have kept their rural hometown hukou but have been living with their families and raising their children in Haicheng for years, or even decades. Their migrant status creates additional challenges for new resident grassroots philanthropists without Haicheng hukou who are seeking to officially register their organizations and compete with organizations established by locals, and to secure governmental purchases of the social services. When United Rescue became famous across Wenzhou, the earliest volunteer members, who were primarily migrants, were soon taken over by local volunteers who started organizing many other projects. Only Chen Junxian, a migrant taxi driver, remained a leader of teams of mostly local volunteers at United Rescue. As the head of the earliest team, Song Jiang broke away from United Rescue to establish his own organization, New Residents' Pride. However, lacking *guanxi* (social connections) with government officers, he found the registration process prolonged and painstaking. He was only able to register New Residents' Pride in 2015 after renting an apartment as office space, a requirement that does not usually apply to organizations founded by locals. Song Jiang had to pay a yearly rent of 17,000 yuan for the apartment, which has three office rooms, a kitchen, a bathroom, and a living room.[5] Volunteers donated three desks, three computers, and a tea table, and occasionally came to help him with the office work and drink tea together. Despite being largely empty, the physical space of this office sustained Song Jiang's gongyi aspirations, and he hoped to be able to fill it with staff one day.

I have described the diverse journeys of grassroots philanthropists in Haicheng elsewhere (Fengjiang 2019). Whether migrant or local, they share the officially recognized language of *gongyi cishan*, and the relatively minimal administrative obstacles to volunteering for and organizing philanthropic projects offer them possibilities for self-realization in social arenas despite their relatively marginal socioeconomic standing in local society. Partly due to the diverse forms of economic and social marginalization they encounter, volunteer projects targeting local and migrant children and the elderly offer rare opportunities to participate in local affairs and gain a sense of social participation and recognition that they otherwise lack. Although they usually do volunteer work on an ad hoc basis, some committed volunteers aspire to integrate grassroots philanthropy into their careers, and thus support both their families and their organizations.

Grassroots Philanthropy as a Laborious and Emotionally Draining Career

The journey from volunteering to managing projects of their own offers grassroots philanthropists a sense of public engagement and the possibility of a more meaningful and valuable career. However, for many ordinary people with limited power or wealth, juggling family and philanthropy is laborious and wrought with struggle and familial tension. Many grassroots philanthropists managing their own organizations and projects struggle with periods when they are emotionally drained and torn between quitting and persisting. The pressure to provide for and support the family is always at the center of their struggle to balance their engagement with philanthropy. Their lives often include disputes with their parents, wives, or husbands, divorce, lonely emotional breakdowns, and debt. Debt and risks are particularly acute for those engaged in business projects. Ordinary people in Haicheng commonly engage in multiple business projects while also moonlighting in part-time wage labor: undertaking multiple and diverse economic projects is a common livelihood strategy in China (Smart and Smart 2005). Under growing economic and social pressure, many of these grassroots philanthropists shift back and forth between managing their organizations full-time, managing them part-time, and stopping activity altogether for a while. During my long-term fieldwork period I often heard grassroots philanthropists planning to quit managing their organizations so that they might return to life as a "normal person." They often claimed that they were almost at the limit of coping with the pressure, but clung to the hope that trying one more time, getting to know one more supportive government officer, might lead to things working out. Some have been able to push on toward making a career out of managing their organization, while others are still in an anxious and ambiguous state but continue to aspire to more without a clear immediate target.

After registering his organization in 2015, Song Jiang had to devote more time to his gongyi work and lived a double life as a grassroots philanthropist and taxi driver. Having previously driven the taxi during the day, he changed his schedule so that he could spend the days in his office until 4 p.m. and then take the night shift in his taxi. Despite the long hours, he originally found his double life fulfilling and meaningful, and said that he was genuinely happy. However, he started to feel increasing economic pressure when the local taxi industry was hit hard by the rise of underregulated ride-hailing services such as DiDi (a Chinese counterpart of Uber) and *weidi* (electric two-wheelers). Although the exploitative elements of the taxi industry have been in the spotlight for many years and the nationwide taxi-driver strikes in 2008 and 2011 raised agendas for reform in the National People's Congress, many taxi drivers could not afford to wait for the long-overdue structural changes to the industry and left for other work. While waiting for the taxi industry to recover from its crisis, Song Jiang had to work longer hours to earn enough to support his family.

In mid-2016 he was hospitalized with an acute infection after working continuous day and night shifts to catch up on his earnings. Neglecting his health in this way, he finally reached a breaking point, and conceded that "this is a deadly game." Later that year after driving taxis for eighteen years, he quit. He received 50,000 yuan in refunded taxi rental fees and planned to start a new business project similar to a social enterprise, which would incorporate gongyi as its purpose. He was thrilled when he finally became a full-time organization manager sitting in an office planning projects. However, the need to earn money created ongoing stress. He had paid 20,000 yuan in advance for the annual rent of office space and supplies for his projects. The promised sponsorship from state enterprises and government offices for his projects for local rural elderly people and left-behind children often failed to materialize. He tried many ideas for business projects with businesspeople who had befriended him when they joined his projects as volunteers. For a time he was committed to the idea of setting up an online media company, a percentage of whose profit would contribute to the cost of his gongyi projects and salaries for his staff. He wrote a ten-page project description and discussed it with me at length. The original plan was to have ten company shareholders: a local businessman who had been his friend for a decade, a local Daoist monk who had made donations to his organization, and eight of his migrant taxi-driver friends. As the "elder brother" among his taxi driver friends, he hoped that a collaborative project would uplift the group, who were all facing the same precarious economic conditions and seeking an alternative to driving taxis. However, he realized that his "Hero of the Greenwood" mentality did not fit him at this stage in his life. Song Jiang gradually discovered that his taxi-driver friends were increasingly demanding gifts and awards as remuneration for volunteering their services, and that while they came to him with penalties imposed by the police for evidence of their volunteer work, which often helped them negotiate a lower penalty, they were becoming less willing to participate in his social enterprise project.

Close to the Chinese New Year of 2017, with increasing debt and his social enterprise project stagnating, Song Jiang was preparing to leave for his hometown. It was the first Chinese New Year that he would spend there for twenty years. He told me about his deep denial on realizing that there was a wide moral gap between earning money from waged labor and making a profit from business projects. He asked me, "Where else can I go, and what else can I do? I'd be better off living in wartime so I could die a dignified death." Meanwhile his persistence at gongyi with little income and growing debt had alienated his wife, who asked for a divorce. He had a tough choice to make after the New Year trip: get a divorce, or return to driving a taxi. At the end of the day-long conversation with me, he expressed some optimism: "Now I'm in a wild forest where there are wolves and tigers. I am the human. I need to survive. So I need to fight. I need to become a hunter. I must defeat them for my survival."

Several days later Song Jiang told me that the director of the Haicheng publicity department had visited him at his office and unexpectedly promised to appoint him as a delegate of the county's People's Political Consultative Conference (PPCC, Renmin Zhengxie). The local PPCC is a consultative body that garners public opinion and advises the local party-state on building good governance (see Yan 2011), and each term of office lasts for five years. This offer gave Song Jiang new hope for his gongyi career. In March 2017 he returned to driving taxis, mostly at night. His appointment as a local PPCC delegate (from 2017 to 2022) was subsequently reported in his hometown media as an honorable achievement and an advance in the political participation of Haicheng's new residents. He enthusiastically sent me reports he had written on the working conditions of migrant taxi drivers pressured by unregulated ride-railing and the discrimination they faced: "This society is complicated. Although my organization will cease to exist one day due to my limited capability, I have at least done something in my lifetime. It is good to not have any regrets. It is good to leave behind some memories and hope."

Song Jiang's journey reflects the aspirations, anxieties, and struggles of many grassroots philanthropists in Wenzhou. Gongyi seem to offer an inclusive avenue for public engagement for ordinary people that may enhance their political and social participation. In fact, in a place that remains a "big society, small government," ordinary citizens across the Wenzhou region have a long history of participating in various aspects of local social governance. When the state started to promote social management (*shehui guanli*) (Pieke 2012), it also reevaluated the role of supervision by public opinion (*yulun jiandu*) (Chen 2017). Quite a few grassroots philanthropists have served as volunteer citizen-supervisors in the Wenzhou's Public Oversight Group since 2010, and some still are doing so, reporting social issues and social problems that the local government has failed to address. Some have been able to gain a sense of higher justice (Brandtstädter 2021) and have created resonance with the emerging "new publics" constituted by "stranger relationality" (Brandtstädter 2017). Moreover, in 2015 the Party started to "explore consultations carried out by social organizations" (Communist

Party of China 2015). A number of local grassroots philanthropists have, like Song Jiang, been appointed as members of the local PPCC, several to the Standing Committee of the municipal or provincial People's Congress (Renmin Daibiao Dahui). While some volunteers may strategize volunteering work as a means of becoming a member of the Communist Party, many organization founders and managers are not Communist Party members, and their leadership in officially recognized philanthropic projects gives them an opportunity to claim their local expertise and engage in institutionalized political participation through these official consultative bodies. Once their grassroots organization gains a certain amount of municipal or provincial recognition, some organization managers are also able to gain negotiating power with the local government and affect policy (see also Shieh 2009; Zhou 2015). In fact, during the collective drafting of the first Charity Law of the People's Republic of China by academics, lawyers, and philanthropic pioneers in 2015, a few grassroots philanthropists in Wenzhou with national reputations were invited to make suggestions about the draft before it was finalized and handed to the State Council's Legislative Affairs Office for review and consideration.

On the other hand, however, there remain many hurdles for grassroots philanthropists, especially those who are migrant workers and entrepreneurs, to achieve their desired impact on governmental policy and governance. When I returned to the field in late 2022, the overflowing optimism about their growing political roles among my interlocutors waned. Song Jiang failed to continue his term of office in the local PPCC for the coming five years, as did several other interlocutors. The fame and recognition gained by grassroots philanthropists via social media or official channels do not always translate into better government support, better business opportunities, or family and social support. Like Song Jiang, ordinary people who commit to gongyi with scarce resources often state that they are exhausted, and that it is time to quit. Having experimented with different degrees of engagement with their philanthropic projects, varied funding channels, and collaboration models with governmental departments, many remain structurally trapped in philanthropy fever, but have not yet managed to make it work for them as a sustainable professional pursuit and identity.

Conclusion

In late-socialist China, ordinary people's aspirations to a good life are conditioned by multiple political and economic processes. This article has explored these aspirations through the lens of grassroots philanthropy. Drawing on multiple cultural sources such as socialist ideals of public engagement, various vernacular notions of public virtue and charity, and modern notions of gongyi and civil society, some aspire to engage in grassroots philanthropy as part of creating a good life for themselves that is worth the effort. Organizing charitable and volunteer activities offers opportunities to gain a sense of social and political participation that is central to their experience of a good life. Some of those whose livelihoods were badly affected by China's economic restructuring and slowdowns, and who sense stagnation in socioeconomic mobilities, find temporary refuge in grassroots philanthropy, mobilizing resources to deliver care to the local people and their environment.

At the same time, growing political space for social management (Pieke 2012), particularly in relation to welfare, education, and development, together with the evolving legal frameworks for charity, bring ordinary people recognition for their social organizations and projects. While to a certain extent the growing space for welfare-oriented philanthropic organizations offers possibilities for ordinary people to valorize their lives in the social arena despite the prevailing economic valorization, the pervasive moralism in public and social life in contemporary politics has a cost (see also Zhan 2020). For many ordinary people with limited resources, the question of whether grassroots philanthropy is a worthy career endeavor remains contested in their social circles and families. Many feel ambivalent about the awards and recognition they have received from government and social organizations. The deepening inequalities of late socialism mean that certain groups are more disadvantaged than others in their pursuit of a career with social objectives (Bruckermann, this issue; Nguyen 2018; Nguyen, Wilcox, and Lin, this issue). Many grassroots philanthropists juggle providing for their family and caring for people in society. The new social management government seems to offer ordinary people the hope of public engagement as contributing members of society, and yet provides them with insufficient institutional and material support.

In late-socialist Chinese society, which is conceived by many scholars as heavily organized by the party-state, I suggest that ethnographic attention to voluntary associations, mutual aid, and self-organizations allows us to envision different possibilities for how lives are governed from below. As Roberta Zavoretti's (2017) ethnography on rural-born migrant workers in urban China and her article on the meaning of family and marriage (this issue) show, ordinary people's aspirations and predicaments are diverse and shifting: they are not "a passive, irrational mass that is compelled to seek idealized (capitalist) modernity" (Zavoretti 2017: 8). This article aims to open up discussion about the different possibilities for a good life in late-socialist China. Thick ethnographic descriptions of the dynamism in grassroots political imagination, resilience, and moral agency would enable us to see and envision alternative and diverse politics that transcend the dominant "politics of destination" that shapes ordinary people's "cruel optimism" in their pursuit of a good life (cf. Coates 2019; Xiang 2021a).

Notes

My unreserved gratitude goes to my research interlocutors. Many thanks to Charles Stafford, Hans Steinmüller, Ka Kin Cheuk, Zhang Li, Jonathan Mair, Stephan Feuchtwang, Minh T. N. Nguyen, Phill Wilcox, Jake Lin, Roberta Zavoretti, Susanne Brandstädter, William Jankowiak, Zhan Yang, and Xu Jing whose insightful comments have been invaluable to composing my arguments. I thank the participants and discussants at the Bielefeld University conference for their critical input and encouragement on earlier drafts of this article. Lastly, special thanks go to the journal editors and the three anonymous reviewers for their generous input and constructive criticism. A follow-up field trip in 2022 was generously supported by the Royal Society of Edinburgh Personal Research Fellowship.

1 By *ordinary people*, I am broadly referring to those whose decision-making is restricted by their limited possession of wealth or power (see also Narotzky and Beisnier 2014: S4).

2 It should be noted that the English term *grassroots philanthropy* often refers to philanthropy "*by* and *from* the grassroots," which is set against ideas of "top down or elite driven funding" (Ruesga 2011: 457). I use the term *philanthropy* more broadly to apply to more than funding in the Chinese case.

3 Compared to the synonymous terms *cishan*, *yixing*, or *shanju*, which have a long history in China (Smith 2009), the term *gongyi* is modern, first appearing in late nineteenth-century China (Chen 2003; Wu 2018). Some Chinese scholars and NGO professionals have tried to differentiate *cishan* and *gongyi*, suggesting that the former represents individual acts driven by

spontaneous charitable impulses and the latter denotes rational long-term projects aimed at social change. Such distinctions refer to the third or voluntary sector in Western Europe and North America. However, local people in China usually make no distinction between the two terms and often conflate them to mean care for individuals and for the collective good.

4   Names of places, organizations, and people have been changed to protect the confidentiality of the research participants.

5   In November 2015, the value of the Chinese yuan was approximately 6.36 yuan per US dollar.

References

Adebanwi, Wale. 2017. "Approaching the Political Economy of Everyday Life: An Introduction." In *Political Economy of Everyday Life in Africa: Beyond the Margins*, edited by Wale Adebanwi, 1–33. London: Boydell and Brewer.

Bakken, Børge. 2000. *The Exemplary Society: Human Improvement, Social Control, and the Dangers of Modernity in China*. New York: Oxford University Press.

Brandtstädter, Susanne. 2017. "Introduction: Judging the State in Contemporary China." In Susanne Brandtstädter and Hans Steinmüller 2017: 1–17.

Brandtstädter, Susanne. 2021. "Rising from the Ordinary: Virtue, the Justice Motif, and Moral Change." *Anthropological Theory* 21, no. 2: 180–205.

Brandtstädter, Susanne, and Hans Steinmüller, eds. 2017. *Popular Politics and the Quest for Justice in Contemporary China*. London: Routledge.

Chen, Dan. 2017. "'Supervision by Public Opinion' or by Government Officials? Media Criticism and Central-Local Government Relations in China." *Modern China* 43, no. 6: 620–45.

Chen, Jo-Shui. 2003. "Conceptions of Gong: A Typological and Holistic Approach to the Chinese Version of 'Public.'" *Journal for Philosophical Study of Public Affairs* 7: 87–144.

Chu, Julie Y. 2010. *Cosmologies of Credit: Transnational Mobility and the Politics of Destination in China*. Durham, NC: Duke University Press.

Coates, Jamie. 2019. "The Cruel Optimism of Mobility: Aspiration, Belonging, and the 'Good Life' among Transnational Chinese Migrants in Tokyo." *positions: asia critique* 27, no. 3: 469–97.

Communist Party of China. 2015. "Guanyu jiaqiang shehuizhuyi xieshang minzhujianshe de yijian" 关于加强社会主义协商民主建设的意见 ("Suggestions on Strengthening Socialist Consultative Democracy"), September 2. http://www.gov.cn/xinwen/2015-02/09/content_2816784.htm.

Fengjiang, Jiazhi. 2019. *Grassroots Philanthropy in China: Work, Ethics, and Social Change.* London School of Economics PhD diss.

Fengjiang, Jiazhi. 2022. "Remaking the Value of Work: The Emergence of Grassroots Philanthropy in China." *American Ethnologist* 49, no. 4: 536–48.

Fengjiang, Jiazhi. 2023. "The Desire to Help: Vernacular Humanitarian Imaginaries in China." *Social Anthropology* 31, no. 1. https://doi.org/10.3167/saas.2023.310104.

Fleischer, Friederike. 2011. "Technology of Self, Technology of Power: Volunteering as Encounter in Guangzhou, China." *Ethnos* 76, no. 3: 300–325.

Hershatter, Gail. 2000. "Local Meanings of Gender and Work in Rural Shaanxi in the 1950s." In *Redrawing Boundaries: Gender, Households, and Work in China*, edited by Barbara Entwisle and Gail E. Henderson, 79–96. Berkeley: University of California Press

Jankowiak, William. 2004. "Market Reforms, Nationalism and the Expansion of Urban China's Moral Horizon." *Urban Anthropology* 33, no. 2: 167–210.

Jeffreys, Elaine. 2015. "Celebrity Philanthropy in Mainland China." *Asian Studies Review* 39, no. 4: 571–88.

Kleinman, Arthur, Yunxiang Yan, Jing Jun, Sing Lee, Everett Zhang, Tianshu Pan, Fei Wu, and Jinhua Guo. 2011. *Deep China: The Moral Life of the Person: What Anthropology and Psychiatry Tell Us about China Today.* Berkeley: University of California Press.

Lee, Haiyan. 2014. *The Stranger and the Chinese Moral Imagination.* Stanford, CA: Stanford University Press.

Luova, Outi. 2011. "Community Volunteers' Associations in Contemporary Tianjin: Multipurpose Partners of the Party–State." *Journal of Contemporary China* 20, no. 72: 773–94.

Metzger, Thomas. 2001. "The Western Concept of Civil Society in the Context of Chinese History." In *Civil Society: History and Possibilities*, edited by Sudipta Kaviraj and Sunil Khilnani, 204–31. Cambridge: Cambridge University Press.

Narotzky, Susana, and Niko Besnier. 2014. "Crisis, Value, and Hope: Rethinking the Economy: An Introduction to Supplement 9." *Current Anthropology* 55, S9: S4–S16.

Nguyen, Minh T. N. 2018. "Vietnam's 'Socialization' Policy and the Moral Subject in a Privatizing Economy." *Economy and Society* 47, no 4: 627–47.

Ning, Rundong, and David A. Palmer. 2020. "Ethics of the Heart: Moral Breakdown and the Aporia of Chinese Volunteers." *Current Anthropology* 61, no. 4: 395–417.

Oxfeld, Ellen. 2010. *Drink Water, But Remember the Source: Moral Discourse in a Chinese Village.* Berkeley: University of California Press.

Palmer, David A., and Fabian Winiger. 2019. "Neo-socialist Governmentality: Managing Freedom in the People's Republic of China." *Economy and Society* 48, no. 4: 554–78.

Pieke, Frank N. 2012. "The Communist Party and Social Management in China." *China Information* 26, no. 2: 149–65.

Rofel, Lisa. 1999. *Other Modernities: Gendered Yearnings in China after Socialism.* Berkeley: University of California Press.

Rojas, Carlos, and Ralph A. Litzinger, eds. 2016. *Ghost Protocol: Development and Displacement in Global China.* Durham, NC: Duke University Press.

Ruesga, G. Albert. 2011. "Civil Society and Grassroots Philanthropy." In *Oxford Handbook of Civil Society*, edited by Michael Edwards, 455–67. Oxford: Oxford University Press.

Shieh, S. 2009. "Beyond Corporatism and Civil Society: Three Modes of State-NGO Interaction in China." In *State and Society Responses to Social Welfare Needs in China*, edited by J. Shwartz and S. Shieh, 22–41, New York: Routledge.

Smart, Alan, and Josephine Smart, eds. 2005. *Petty Capitalists and Globalization: Flexibility, Entrepreneurship, and Economic Development.* Albany: State University of New York Press.

Smith, Joanna Handlin. 2009. *The Art of Doing Good: Charity in Late Ming China.* Berkeley: University of California Press.

Spires, Anthony. 2018. "Chinese Youth and Alternative Narratives of Volunteering." *China Information* 32, no. 2: 203–23.

Stafford, Charles, ed. 2013. *Ordinary Ethics in China.* London: Bloomsbury.

Steinmüller, Hans. 2013. *Community of Complicity: Everyday Ethics in Rural China.* New York: Berghahn.

Weller, Robert P., Julia Huang, Keping Wu, and Lizhu Fan. 2017. *Religion and Charity: The Social Life of Goodness in Chinese Societies.* Cambridge: Cambridge University Press.

White, Gordon, Jude A. Howell, and Xiaoyuan Shang. 1996. *In Search of Civil Society: Market Reform and Social Change in Contemporary China.* Oxford: Oxford University Press.

Wu, Huanyu. 2018. "Zhongguo jindai 'gongyi' deguannian shengcheng" 中国近代"公益"的观念生成 ("The Development of the 'Gongyi' Concept in Modern China"). *Shehui* 6, no. 38: 180–215.

Xiang, Biao. 2021a. "Production-Driven Labor Migration from China." *Georgetown Journal of Asian Studies* 7: 34–43.

Xiang, Biao, ed. 2021b. "Suspension: Complexed Developments and Hypermobility in and from China." Special issue, *Pacific Affairs* 94, no. 2: 233–50.

Yan, Xiaojun. 2011. "Regime Inclusion and the Resilience of Authoritarianism: The Local People's Political Consultative Conference in Post-Mao Chinese Politics." *China Journal* 66: 53–75.

Yan, Yunxiang. 2003. *Private Life under Socialism: Love, Intimacy, and Family Change in a Chinese Village, 1949–1999.* Stanford, CA: Stanford University Press.

Yan, Yunxiang. 2009. "The Good Samaritan's New Trouble: A Study of the Changing Moral Landscape in Contemporary China." *Social Anthropology* 17, no. 1: 9–24.

Yan, Yunxiang. 2011. "Changing Moral Landscape." In *Deep China: The Moral Life of the Person: What Anthropology and Psychiatry Tell Us about China Today*, edited by Arthur Kleinman, Yunxiang Yan, Jing Jun, Sing Lee, Everett Zhang, Tianshu Pan, Fei Wu, and Jinhua Guo, 36–77. Berkeley: University of California Press.

Yan, Yunxiang. 2021. "The Politics of Moral Crisis in Contemporary China." *China Journal* 85: 96–120.

Zavoretti, Roberta. 2017. *Rural Origins, City Lives: Class and Place in Contemporary China*. Seattle: University of Washington Press.

Zhan, Yang. 2020. "The Moralization of Philanthropy in China: NGOs, Voluntarism, and the Reconfiguration of Social Responsibility." *China Information* 34, no 1: 68–87.

Zhang, Li, and Aihwa Ong, eds. 2008. *Privatizing China: Socialism from Afar*. Ithaca, NY: Cornell University Press.

Zhou, Huiquan. 2015. "Mapping the Level of Development of Grassroots NPOs in China." *Voluntas* 27, no. 5: 2199–228.

Zhu, Ningzhu. 2013. "China Issues Guidance for Government Purchases of Services." *Xinhuanet*, September 30. http://news.xinhuanet.com/english/china/2013-09/30/c_132764453.htm.

The Good Life as the Green Life: Digital Environmentalism and Ecological Consciousness in China

Charlotte Bruckermann

Introduction: Carbon in the Sky

> All this low carbon *goupi* 狗屁 [bullshit]—it's all up there in the sky, but here we have our feet on the ground—we face real problems.
> —Bingwen, e-commerce shop manager

Bingwen scoffed as he rolled his eyes. He lifted his gaze from the computer screen and gazed across the shop he managed, a subsidiary of one of the largest e-commerce platforms in China. In the spring of 2019 Bingwen was in his late twenties and an only child. Although he studied finance at a first-tier city university, he subsequently completed a short training course with an e-commerce giant before returning to his hometown of Minqin in the deserts of northern Gansu's Wuwei Prefecture. The sandstorms of his childhood had by then subsided in severity and frequency, but Bingwen viv-

positions 32:1   DOI 10.1215/10679847-10890010

idly remembered billowing ochre clouds darkening the sky with suspended particles, swallowing up all daylight and necessitating electric lighting in the middle of the day. The yellow winds tore the roofs from rural homes, causing environmental refugees to seek shelter behind solid concrete walls in the city, an urban island in the midst of the dunes.

The "real problems" Bingwen referred to were not the encroaching desert but economic woes. This shop is part of the e-commerce boom that has swept across China in the last decade, boosting domestic consumption in the wake of the uncertainties of the global financial crisis after 2009. In parallel, Minqin became a premier site for afforestation projects as Beijing pinpointed the area as a source of sandstorms that could reach as far as the capital. Subsequently the area became emblematic for its contribution to nationwide environmental duress, and was subject to a flagship campaign targeting airborne particulate matter including sand and pollution (Zee 2017, 2021).

In contrast to this university graduate, many rural women in the Wuwei area earned their livelihoods from afforestation work, often in grueling conditions and with low pay. Bingwen nonetheless insisted that afforestation has become more manageable, comparing its work shifts to office hours. According to Bingwen, these shifts leave workers time to raise children, cook food, and lead a fulfilling life. He also considered that afforestation work is unconnected to environmental concerns, instead simply offering a good way to make a living in the countryside. Many such incongruous assumptions about environmental work circulated among rural and urban residents, who faced very different challenges in both their immediate environment and their future position in China's green transformation.

The afforestation work in Gansu's deserts reveals the emerging costs of the good life as a green life, a transformation that both deepens rural-urban inequalities and fosters diverging ecological aspirations through environmental projects. Although early market reforms in the late twentieth century conjured a *Zhongguo meng* 中国梦 (Chinese dream) built on rising consumption and prosperous lifestyles, popular imaginaries in the twenty-first century increasingly call for *shengtai yishi* 生态意识 (ecological consciousness) to realize state promises of a coming *shengtai wenming* 生态文明 (ecological civilization). This emerging neosocialist subjectivity extolls the virtues of labor contributing to building a greener future that includes both urban and rural lives. Yet this shared discourse of reciprocal exchange between city and countryside masks the fact that rural citizens bear both the brunt of environmental degradation and greater responsibility for its reparation.

Ecological Consciousness between City and Countryside

The Chinese Dream imagines the future nation as a *xiaokang shehui* 小康社会 (moderately prosperous society). This governmental goal can be traced to the market reforms initiated by the post-Maoist Reform-era leader, Deng Xiaoping, with the aim of fostering well-being. Yet beyond fulfilling consumer demands, future visions for Chinese society increasingly mobilize green aspirations and a population characterized by *shengtai yishi* 生态意识 (ecological consciousness). The current president, Xi Jinping, has even promised to shift developmental trajectories from a classic industrial economy to a *shengtai wenming* 生态文明 (ecological civilization) as part of the economic rebalancing efforts that began in the late 2000s under President Hu Jintao (Hansen, Li, and Svarverud 2018).

These ecological priorities and environmental practices in the People's Republic of China build on a long history of spiritual civilization discourse and its institutions, which provide temporal depth to the contemporary configuration of neosocialist governmentality (Palmer and Winger 2019). Realizing China's green dream involves commitment to environmental projects through work and labor, simultaneously building on the Maoist legacies of sacrifice and heroism (see Pieke 2018) and invoking an internalizing discourse of the self in governmental policy (see Zhang 2017). Therefore, the past melding of technocratic Leninism and revolutionary volunteerism has not been fully replaced by a totalizing neoliberal trajectory in the present; rather, current configurations instantiate a particular genealogy of willing subjects contributing to national development and collective rejuvenation under Party guidance (Palmer and Winger 2019).

When chasms appear between personal desires and ambitions and the Party's mapping of collective ambition for the future of Chinese civilization, these can nonetheless result in cynicism and criticism of conventional, ritu-

alized state propaganda (Palmer and Winger 2019). Most individuals, organizations, and corporations seeking transformation and change engage in
nonconfrontational activism in online and offline spheres of action, involving
the tactful negotiation of legitimacy and authority without outright opposition (Wang 2019). As environmental concerns, anxieties, and even protests,
including against airborne pollution, become increasingly commonplace, it
no longer suffices for the state to merely deliver economic growth through
spectacular increases in GDP; it must also demonstrate concern about the
environment to appease its citizens' demands for a happier, healthier, and
greener future (Ding 2020).

Although China's environmental policies cover both urban metropoles
and rural peripheries, the inequalities between the two mark the actual ecological work of bringing about China's green transformation. The burden of
China's green transformation falls disproportionately to its rural population.
This is due to the historical outsourcing of environmental degradation and
industrial pollution to the countryside, on the one hand, and rural areas
bearing future environmental responsibility through the provision of sustainable resources and green compensation zones, on the other (Lord 2020).
Although sketching how urban centers and rural peripheries are positioned
differently in terms of China's environmental policy and ecological action is
necessarily reductive, it is also illuminating.

For urbanites, many recommendations for the green life and ecological
consciousness that are widely circulated in the mainstream media focus
on lifestyle and consumption, particularly nutrition and diet, and connect
affluent, health-conscious lifestyle choices with green living. Across urban
China there is a plethora of green-city campaigns, smart grids, and recycling
drives, often initiated by provincial, regional, or municipal governments to
meet central state targets (Hoffman 2011). Urbanites may find the lack of
clean air, open spaces, or quiet places for respite detrimental to living standards, with pollution restricting good health and exercise, and massive high-
rise housing areas and working conditions leaving them feeling alienated
(Zhang 2010). City dwellers participate in recycling efforts, green energy
campaigns, and public transport use in attempts to become more sustainable
consumers (Hansen, Li, and Svarverud 2018). However, rather than make
deep-seated changes in their lives, many rely on top-down state initiatives

for ecological redress, with recent surveys revealing the popular notion that the state, rather than its citizens, is responsible for cleaning up the environment (Wang 2017).

Many rural residents have experienced resource scarcity all their lives, and while some aspire to consume as urbanites do, or at least to improve their livelihoods through economic opportunities, many simultaneously confront pollution and degradation in their everyday life (Lora-Wainwright 2013). They experience landscape degradation, the loss of livelihoods and resources, and their environs being used as sites for outsourced industrial pollution in immediate and direct ways (Lord 2020). These conditions often motivate local calls to action, and sometimes even personal engagement with environmental reparation, from cleanup drives to ecological restoration. Central and local state bureaus pour huge financial resources into rural policies on direct environmental intervention, thereby interlinking ecological improvement and rural employment (Bruckermann 2020). In the countryside, residents frequently frame their commitment to ecological restoration as a matter of human survival and national improvement. However, more systemic problems with environmental degradation, such as laxity on the part of the law and other forms of protection that are in the hands of the authorities, often remain unaddressed (Lord 2020).

Encompassing both the countryside and the cities, the political conception of governance and policy directed at bringing about ecological civilization proposes a techno-social utopia (Hansen, Li, and Svarverud 2018) foregrounding ecological preservation and restoration while also prioritizing economic growth (Schmitt 2018). During fieldwork in both rural and urban areas, typical responses to direct questions about ecological civilization as a state-led vision for the future included some criticism, cynicism, and even eye-rolling, while ecological consciousness enjoyed a more positive valence as something to strive toward, and worth exhibiting personally through performative and visible labor.

The public's acceptance of directing not just one's behavior but also one's subjective consciousness to a shared project may constitute a dimension of China's desire to create an exemplary society (Bakken 2000). This takes on particular forms, including holding up model workers and model projects for emulation, especially in technocratic experiments sanctioned, and even fostered, by the state (Bakken 2000). Despite this orientation toward moral exemplars, grassroots philanthropy oriented at *zuo gongyi* 做公益 (contributing to public welfare) is considered an authentic expression of the self in China (Fengjiang, this issue). Yet Chinese citizens also enact and perform subjectivity in ways that take up ideological party-state concepts, such as by conforming to *suzhi* 素质 (human quality) discourse (Anagnost 2004; Kipnis 2007). This plays on subtle subversions, such as those based on "cultural intimacy" (Herzfeld 2005; Steinmüller 2013) and multiplicity of the self (Liu 2002; Tan 2016), as citizens may even satirize their own position in the state project, for instance in the *diduan renkou* 低端人口 (low-quality population) discourse of recent years (Bruckermann 2019).

While consciousness discourse could imply the rise of an individualized and self-oriented disposition rather than commitment to larger social projects, this does not do justice to the concept in neosocialist contexts. Specifically, in China and Vietnam, conceptions of consciousness emerge in subjectivities and institutions that mesh with new forms of socialization (Nguyen 2018), civility (Harms 2016), and community (Brandtstädter 2003; Zhang 2010). These may be rooted in the collective past yet champion consideration and care for others and the environment as part of the personal, private, and political endeavor for the future (Fengjiang, this issue; Nguyen, Wilcox, and Lin, this issue; Bruckermann 2023).

Specifically focusing on the intersection between civilized and sustainable consciousness in urban Ho Chi Minh City, Erik Harms (2014) uncovers a shared logic of deferring immediate personal desire in favor of collective and future-oriented goals. This conceptualization often stands in contradiction to actual practice on the ground, as privileged residents translate urban consciousness into individualized and resource-intensive lifestyles that exclude or even displace those more vulnerable to dispossession for development (Harms 2014). Confronting resource extraction and degraded environments across the Laotian landscape, urban and academic middle classes engage in moral nostalgia as they yearn for a more sustainable past, while rural residents evoke the spirits of the forest for moral orientation (Kleinod-Freudenberg and Chanthavong, this issue).

In the People's Republic of China, and particularly in the tree-planting projects in the deserts of Gansu Province we turn to next, the good life as a green life is promoted, envisioned, discussed, and enacted as urbanites and rural citizens come together to care for the environment. While the Chinese Dream relies on the cheap labor of rural migrants engaged in manufacturing, the notion of the green life instantiates a rural-urban spatial order in which urbanites visit the countryside, where residents are exploited as producers of the green life. Echoing ecotourism trends more generally (Park 2014), this type of inversion forms part of a discourse of restoring damaged selves under strain from shifting moralities and living under new pressures in alienating urban contexts, as citizens strive for green lifestyles (Zhang 2010) and experience therapeutic governance (Zhang 2017). As urban professionals engage in ethical consumption via digital infrastructure in cities and ecotourism in the countryside, their activities nonetheless reproduce a spatial order that prioritizes consumption. The interaction among government rhetoric, urban consumption, and rural production of the green life brings issues of scale into play as local desertification interlinks with global climate change.

In the Eye of the Storm

Beyond government policy and urban consumers, Minqin County is particularly noteworthy as the epicenter of a region where, according to a cadre at the local forestry bureau, "everybody is engaged in constructing ecological civilization and has attained ecological consciousness as a result of environmental hardship." The prefecture of Wuwei in central Gansu is bordered by Inner Mongolia to the north and Qinghai to the south. The region is on the ancient northern Silk Road and is now heralded as an illustrious milestone on China's One Belt One Road development strategy stringing together Eurasia. Its arid climate leads to a net water loss between precipitation and evaporation despite biting winters, while summers on the plateau are scorching. Nonetheless, farmers coax vegetables, melons, and corn from the silty soil and raise livestock that roam across the plains, while some locales even provide conditions for vineyards to flourish. Two deserts, the Tengger and Badain Jaran, threaten to engulf housing and land, despite being separated by China's largest desert reservoir, Hongyashan, since 1958.

The whole Wuwei region is plagued by sandstorms, a dustbowl in which large amounts of particulate matter regularly swirl through the atmosphere and sometimes cause sandstorms further afield. Rows of hardy pine and poplar trees flank the new roads crisscrossing the prefecture and help to safeguard this flagship infrastructure from the golden sand dunes that shift under the relentless sun. The border zones between the oases and the desert have become an expanding target area for *zhisha zaolin* 治沙造林 (sand control afforestation) (see Zee 2021). These are overseen by a variety of local actors, most prominently forestry and environmental bureaus but also scientific projects, forestry farms, corporate social responsibility programs, volunteer associations, and even some citizen activists.

The region has gained prominence via a cautionary campaign that casts the area as an example of the vagaries of both desertification and climate change, for which it now serves as an experimental model in scientific and political circles (Zee 2021, 2017). Jerry Zee (2017) evocatively traces how the constant threat of *shahai* 沙海 (the sand ocean) surrounding Minqin enfolds earthly and political horizons into temporalities as shifting as the sand. Past sandstorms and the anticipated desertification create a sense of impending environmental collapse and planetary crisis. As personal, scientific, and even state projects engage with a looming sense of doom, the stakes in the region reach beyond aspirations of *fazhan* 发展 (development) to the very politics of *cunzai* 存在 (existence) (Zee 2021: 113). In addition to the scientific projects and government campaigns Zee describes, the deserts surrounding Minqin have become the unlikely stage for corporations, especially the two heavyweights of the Chinese tech sector, Tencent and Alibaba, competing to fight desertification. As part of the corporate digital landscape and a recipient of central state forestry funds, afforestation has become a major employment sector in Wuwei.

The fight against the desert takes the form of planting shrubs and trees to fix the shifting sandbanks (Zee 2021, 2017). In a sequence of arduous tasks, workers lay out grids for stabilizing fixtures across the sand dunes, using anything from nylon mesh and woven straw to chemical fixes. They then dig holes and plant small seedlings of hardy desert bushes and trees. Buckets of water are handed along human chains before being poured onto the new transplants to help them secure their rhizomic hold in the granular surface. Despite these human efforts, seedling survival rate is often very low, as they depend on factors beyond the planters' control, such as rainfall, wind, and extreme temperatures.

Most of the manual workers at the state-owned forestry farms and forestry bureau projects I encountered are middle-aged women, often with out-migrated children in urban centers and husbands who sell their industrial and manual labor far from the desert. A local foreman with forestry training usually directs operations, driving a vehicle with supplies and water along the working routes. The harsh conditions in the dunes make the rest periods particularly welcome, and in the midday break the women share steamed buns, often drenched in the juice of fresh watermelon, a local specialty in the summer planting season. On cooler days some women even dance in the dunes to pop music blasting from their mobile phones.

Beyond these formal labor arrangements, the Wuwei region also boasts various volunteering and grassroots projects for antidesert afforestation. Most of these local projects bring in helpers from nearby urban centers where they work in the same organization or institution. As such, they take part in the afforestation activities as part of an office outing. Their engagement with the environment is therefore typically not purely motivated by personal voluntarism or individual altruism, but also enmeshed with aspirations for professional reputation and corporate bonding arranged by their employer. Nonetheless, some urban volunteers describe their ancestral ties to the land or concern for future generations as the reason for their participation. In addition to these afforestation projects with regional networks, a small handful of farmers have also taken antidesertification measures into their own hands. Despite the differences in motivation across projects and participants, some of the dynamics driving afforestation in the region are shared, especially in terms of the vision of mutual labor to create an ecologically healthy future.

Reciprocal Restoration of Environmental Imbalances

The pressure of the cities is severe, you can tell that their life is missing something. I don't know what, but with every year there are more political cadres and company leaders coming to the countryside to *huifu jiankang* 恢复健康 (restore their health).
—Taobing, regular tree planting volunteer on his brother-in-law's afforestation project

This empathy with urban visitors was echoed throughout the Wuwei deserts by rural citizens interacting with visiting tree planters. Zhang Laomo, who is celebrated as a model worker, was discussing the large number of urbanites pouring into the desert to plant trees in recent years, including for his grassroots project in Wuwei, when his brother-in-law, Taobing, interrupted with the above explanation of this phenomenon. Taobing compared the various afforestation movements in the region to the rise of *nongjiale* 农家乐 (rural family guesthouse tourism) that has gained popularity throughout the country in recent decades. He pointed out that the pressures of urban life lead to many *xinli wenti* 心理问题 (psychological problems), some of which can be balanced by sojourns in the countryside, visiting ancestral homes, seeing rural relatives, doing manual work, and caring for the environment. Despite the pathologizing and psychologizing of the effects of city life on urbanites, a mixture of pity, admiration, and gratitude permeated these characterizations of urban counterparts.

For both urbanites and rural citizens, these tree-planting movements complicate narratives of a sequential turn from collectivist ethics to individualist motivations. Via apps such as those of the Zhengjiu Minqin Zhiyuanzhe Xiehui 拯救民勤志愿者协会 (Save Minqin Volunteers Association) or Mayi Senlin 蚂蚁森林 (Alipay's Ant Forest), users plant virtual trees individually, and they also express gratitude to rural workers who plant the actual trees collectively. Moreover, if workplaces organize the tree-planting as volunteering events for their employees, their activities are group oriented, with collective action ordered through institutional affiliation. When rural workers plant the trees, whether as production teams organized by state bureaus or by green foundations, they too plant them as a group, and emphasize the social and ecological aspects of their work.

Zhang Laomo, the model worker mentioned above, runs a grassroots afforestation project drawing on workers from his entire village and former brigade for cooperation. The Zhang family also hosts urbanites on tree-planting drives, for which employees of various companies, corporations, and bureaus clamber out of their buses, clasping broad-brimmed hats and wearing black sunglasses as they brace themselves for the hard work of afforestation. They pay a set price for the seedlings and commit to a short stint of manual labor. In return, they receive elaborate photo sessions for their employers, a set of invigorating speeches celebrating their environmental prowess, and a lavish homecooked banquet prepared by the extended Zhang family, served in the afternoon with a hearty helping of sorghum wine.

At one such event in May 2019, most of these afforestation volunteers spoke of their motivation in terms of the workplaces they represented, an ethos amplified by the content of the speeches given at the outset of the event and the banquet that followed it. The main themes of the speeches were cooperation between the urban association and the rural desert residents, with the association leaders voicing their gratitude for the opportunity to plant trees and thanking the Zhang family for all their sacrifices to realize this ecological civilization project. The corporate dynamic was reinforced by banners, flags, and photographs taken on the hillside before and after the event, documenting the environmental consciousness expressed at the site.

Many of the employees were driven not so much by individual commitment as by feelings of corporate responsibility and pride in their company. Others were persuaded by the restorative powers of tree planting for body, psyche, and landscape, possibly as part of the rise of therapeutic and psychological activities in recent years. Work completed with or for others holds significant weight in China (Potter and Potter 1990), where a long history of work for kin and family meets identification with the socialist workplace to make labor a means of forging belonging, intimacy, and connection (Bruckermann 2019).

Besides these personal and corporate motivations, tree planting is a responsibility for Chinese citizens and part of a national discourse. In 1915, shortly after the end of the Qing dynasty, the Republican president Sun Yatsen initiated a national tree-planting initiative. This was reinforced by Mao Zedong's 1956 Lüse Zuguo 绿色祖国 (Green Ancestral Land) campaign, although this failed to prevent the disastrous consequences of grain production policies for forest coverage during the Mao years. In 1982 the Implementation Measures of the State Council on Launching a National Voluntary Tree Planting Campaign made every citizen responsible for planting three to five trees each year, a mobilization Deng Xiaoping launched by planting a tree on Yuquan Mountain in Beijing. Since 2018 even Alipay's Ant Forest has provided official government afforestation certification to app users whose virtual trees have been planted in the desert, so that they can fulfill their target quota. Although the app's tree-planting activities may seem quintessentially individual, the extension of digital activities in the city to the green labor in the countryside afforestation projects tells a different story.

Long-Distance Environmentalism in the Digital Age

In August 2016, Alipay introduced carbon accounts for each of its 450 million users. Complementing their conventional cash and credit accounts, the new carbon accounts track consumers' carbon usage through the mini-app Mayi Senlin 蚂蚁森林 (Ant Forest) and reward green consumption habits with tree-planting credits of equivalent carbon value.[1] Three years later, Alipay boasted that about half of its nearly one billion users had clicked into the Ant Forest system, planting 100 million trees with their energy points and covering 933 square kilometers in northern and northwestern China with green flora. The Communist Party and fintech aficionados have praised Alipay for this effort, and it has even attracted a high-profile collaboration with the UNEP on greening financial technologies. Although the app promises to offset the destructive tendencies of economic growth, it simultaneously allows users to absolve themselves of responsibility for their carbon footprint through the touch of a smartphone button, thereby potentially increasing consumption by rendering it guilt-free for urban consumers.

To entertain some of its more die-hard fans, in March 2017 Ant Forest livestreamed a visit to one of its afforestation projects, a Tengger desert site where gusts of wind buffeted the small shrubs in the sand as the sun beat down from above. Ant Forest had called for participation from users to volunteer in the afforestation drive by applying online, but only eight individuals won golden tickets to actually attend the event on World Forest Day. It was an awkward affair, including scenes with the handful of volunteers ineptly posturing for interviews and aimlessly wandering around with shovels while anonymous local workers did the planting in the background. A scientist was onsite to explain what was going on to the heavily made-up moderator, who struggled to be heard above the gale-force winds sweeping across the dunes.

In the comments section below the video, fans expressed their gratitude to one particular *shushu* 叔叔 (uncle), the main interlocutor for subsequent exchanges, eagerly commenting on his transformation into a *wenming nonmin* 文明农民 (civilized peasant). The onsite presenter introduced this man as Uncle Tan, not only repeatedly drawing attention to how laborious his afforestation work was but also echoing viewers' patronizing comments about his cute smile and sweet temperament. The moderator's gratitude was similar to that of many app users. Their comments expressed their appreciation and admiration of Tan and his coworkers for undergoing the strenuous labor to help them plant "their" trees from the comfort of their homes.

A fairly typical comment read, "I am very busy every day at my office job in the city, and I cannot go out to the green areas myself. I am deeply grateful for the arduous labor of Uncle Tan, which allows me to plant trees in the desert from my desk." The engagement of urban digital e-tree planters with rural onsite afforestation workers exhibited a certain reflexivity, and even cynicism, among city dwellers obsessed with peripheral, long-distance environmentalism. Although they articulated their respect and the value of rural labor, particularly that of the afforestation workers planting trees for them in the countryside under harsh conditions, the app users both recognized and appropriated the rural workers' labor. Moreover, this seems to have had consequences for Uncle Tan's self-presentation. Under his fans' watchful gaze and streaming commentary, over the following three months he underwent a transformation in terms of dress and comportment, over time becoming a cleaned-up blue-collar worker, much to the satisfaction of urban green consumers, who complimented him on his clean shirts even as he continued to shovel sand in the desert for them.

Notably, rural afforestation workers in Wuwei with less immediate interaction with visiting urbanites than, for instance, the Zhang family or the Save Minqin organization, were more skeptical of urban visitors to the desert. As an afforestation worker with a deep commitment to antidesertification campaigns, Jin, Zhang's wife, described how she had grown up as one of nine children. Her family waged an ongoing battle with the desert, so she began planting trees in the dunes from a young age, summarizing how, "for the visitors, planting the trees is an entertaining activity, but for me, fighting the desert is my life." When I then commented on the environmental sustainability of their life in the countryside compared to that of their urban visitors, and asked whether their practices were closer to ecological civilization, Zhang replied that this was not so much a *shenghuo fangshi* 生活方式 (way of life or lifestyle) as simply the *nongmin shenghuo* 农民生活 (peasant livelihood).

Another villager, Leila, who participated in the Zhang family's afforestation drives on a regular basis, was in her mid-forties. She originated from a faraway township, but had married into the village two decades ago. Her husband worked as a day laborer in Wuwei City, often earning up to 200 RMB a day on construction sites. While Leila rarely earned more than 100 RMB planting trees in the dunes, she was very happy with the work. Having given birth to her second son at the age of forty-one and with no family in the area, she found working close to home *fangbian* 方便 (convenient) and at times *youyisi* 有意思 (meaningful) and even *haowan* 好玩 (fun).

As Leila pointed out, the grueling work was broken up by the shared lunches of steamed buns and watermelon, and the street-dance routines that they rehearsed on the dunes during the day and performed in the village alleys at night. More important, she insisted, was the fact that *zhisha* 治沙 (controlling the sand) is the only way to defend the place she now calls home from being swallowed by the desert. When asked about the visitors, she pointed out that many of the urbanites were more interested in taking photographs in the sand and enjoying the dunes. She somberly lamented the inequality of their divergent lifeworlds, as the visitors had no need to be paid for their labor and often even paid to participate, and once the work was done they had the luxury of leaving the desert to return to their comfortable urban apartments. However, as an avid user of WeChat who frequently posted clips, memes, and photos on her account, Leila also empathized with urbanites' desire to share their afforestation activities on social networks. With a cheeky smile, she summarized conspiratorially, "Playing in the desert just looks so *haokan* 好看 [really good]!"

E-tree Planting Goes Offline

On Labor Day 2019, approximately thirty Tencent employees flew to the desert area from Beijing and Hangzhou to participate in a weeklong tree-planting drive. I was planting trees with a small number of urban family volunteers when they arrived at the site, clad in outdoor gear and full of energy for a few hours' work before nightfall. They had volunteered internally through their company and were thrilled to be there, looking forward to a week spent working in the golden sands during the day and camping in tents under the desert stars at night. They described it as a welcome break from office life in front of their computers. Discussing their upcoming *laodong* 劳动 (hard physical labor), they joked about going back in time to finally participate in a *shengchandui* 生产队 (production team), explicitly using the Maoist term for this labor unit, and, furthermore, about going to the countryside to learn from the peasants, again using the Maoist phrase for the educated youth who worked in the countryside during the Shangshan Xiaxiang 上山下乡 (Up to the Mountains and Down to the Countryside Movement).

One Tencent software developer, Xiaogang, a Guangdong native in his early thirties, framed the experience as part of pursuing his hobbies, exclaiming that his motivation was to enjoy nature, thereby embedding afforestation work into his leisure time. He explained that in the office he sat at a computer all day, and he saw this as a great opportunity to get outside and work with friends and colleagues, summarizing that "for somebody who loves nature and exercise, this is perfect!" In the following days, evidence of their trip circulated on social media, including images of the volunteers standing on top of pickups donning shovels, their tents glowing beneath the star-studded sky, and posing with the Tencent and Chinese flags in the dunes. Much like Alipay's livestream event described above, the rivaling Hangzhou tech company of Tencent thereby competed for online visibility of their Corporate Social Responsibility campaigns in afforesting the desert by disseminating volunteering activities.

The Tencent trip was hosted by the NGO Save Minqin, an organization founded by a pair of dynamic classmates in 2006 after graduating from Lanzhou University. While Han Jierong took over the innovative digital side of operations, his classmate Ma Junhe returned to Minqin to learn, experiment with, and implement antidesertification schemes involving volunteering, donation-based afforestation, poverty alleviation projects, and even a digital tree-planting system that has won several innovation awards. Their organization, in cooperation with collective land leased from village committees, has reforested a huge area, partly through the work of urban volunteers but also by hiring temporary workers from the villages for 5,000 to 6,000 RMB per month, with only a handful of permanent workers. Discussing local motivation for afforestation, Ma told me that this work is not so much oriented toward *gongyi* 公益 (public good) as many news articles about him state, insisting that it is a matter of survival, and that if residents do not plant trees they will be left *wujia kegui* 无家可归 (without a home to return to).

In sum, a variety of ecological commitments and moral motivations drew participants to these corporate and digital afforestation projects on the edges of the expanding deserts of Gansu. Bingwen, the local e-commerce employee on the frontline of bringing online marketing to the countryside, planted trees for his company, yet put forward a vision of ecology subordinated to the necessities of economics. By contrast, volunteers from the parent company, Tencent, flew into the area to engage in public works in activities reminiscent of leisure, a manual-labor camping holiday nostalgic for the Maoist past. Meanwhile, Ma Junhe, the volunteer association leader, viewed the situation as necessary for survival, reiterating what I had heard from other environmental workers such as forestry bureau employees during my time in Minqin. Meanwhile, app users in far-off locales sat behind their screens, making small alterations to their consumption habits to accrue the credits that would enable real trees to be planted in the desert by rural workers.

Rather than conforming to the idea that market reforms neatly divided time into a "before" and "after," these neosocialist transformations challenge narratives of a complete transition from a collectivist morality to individualist ethics, and from an ethos of personal sacrifice and deferred gratification of the past to a period of hedonism and immediate consumption in the present. Instead, these tendencies appear as entangled in the everyday lifeworlds of both urbanites and rural residents as they engaged with tree-planting drives. Moreover, the shared logics of labor and environment allowed empathy for hardship to flow across urban and rural fault lines, even as they merged with pity, admiration, and gratitude in complex ways. The logic of belonging suffused the motivation to work for the sake of ancestral land or future descendants, while the language of work elevated even hard rural labor through pride in greening the countryside.

Arguably, the rhetoric of ecological civilization and ecological consciousness encompasses and engulfs these diverse logics. Xi Jinping repeatedly champions this policy promise for the coming era, thereby showing that the state cares for the natural environment, the population's health, and the national future, while devolving much of the responsibility involved to citizens, local governments, and corporations. This neosocialist legacy places faith in technology, particularly by outsourcing the manual labor of environmental care through networked platforms such as apps. As part of the new green production in the countryside, tree planting offers a new avenue for employment in rural areas, which have been recast as the green lungs cleaning up urban pollution.

Conclusion

In contemporary China's neosocialist context, the good life is increasingly imagined as a green life. However, various visions coexist of what achieving a new era of ecological civilization, populated with citizen-subjects endowed with ecological consciousness, should entail. With the turn from a command to a market economy, it has been argued that the collective morality has waned with the rise of individualist ethics. However, correct conduct based on performing an internalized subjectivity and consciousness has not fully displaced displays of heroism and sacrifice. In their desire to combat environmental destruction through grassroots movements, citizens return to elements of Maoist labor logics that champion devotion and responsibility for the common good and bring them into their understandings of a greener future through ecological consciousness.

This aligns with state projects to create an ecological civilization by not only shifting material conditions from an industrial to a postindustrial service and high-tech economy but also fostering ecological consciousness as part of the socialist value system. Beyond the ideological formality of these doctrines, these concepts become aligned with previous emphasis on the Chinese Dream of happiness and well-being. This consciousness discourse allows the emergence of individual aspirations to contribute to the collective. Yet as this subjectivity merges with ideological conceptions espoused by the Chinese state, citizens position themselves in ways that diverge from the normative neoliberal trajectory of self-optimization. Instead, the internalizing discourse of the self in Chinese government policy and the historical legacy of mass activities and popular cooperation include both past legacies and future promises in a shared understanding of the neosocialist citizen-subject.

Despite these shared ecological visions, building a greener future also creates divergences, and even contradictions, along rural and urban fault lines. As urbanites pursue environmental consciousness through greening rather than by limiting their consumption, rural people become service providers, yet see themselves as doing something great for the whole of China and even the entire planet by planting trees. In the expanding cycles of growth, they continue to produce green goods and bring them to market so that they, too, can enter the brave new world of moderate prosperity. In parallel, urbanites who are constantly consuming are cast as having something missing in their lives, and they go to the countryside hoping to restore and renew their health, sociality, and environment. Environmental pressures in cities, as well as the ecological scarcity in the countryside, may be balanced out through experiences in greening the land together as a form of self-healing. While urbanites hope that their condition can be restored in the healthy, social, cooperative countryside environment, rural citizens envision becoming civilized subjects involved in green production, increasing their incomes and prospects while also caring for the environment.

Ecological civilization includes spatial, temporal, and affective notions of belonging and responsibility. It is not only the Communist Party's legitimacy in guiding the masses to the next historical stage that is at stake: in one way ecological consciousness and ecological civilization serve to connect individual responsibility with the family, the nation, and the world, through striving toward a better future. Building on a shared genealogy, everybody in China shares the responsibility for honoring previous labor and caring for the coming generations by working tirelessly for a brighter, greener future.

By both revisiting the past and representing the future, Chinese landscapes become enfolded into this narrative. The countryside is framed as the repository of past wisdom and future hope, serving as an atmospheric filter to offset pollution and degradation. Despite the inequality that carrying their double burden of environmental degradation and ecological redress creates, rural citizens retain their agency by hosting and healing their urban counterparts through their activities, while urbanites emerge as privileged green consumers of these rural greening projects, not only when they pay rural citizens to plant trees on their behalf, but also when they visit the countryside to spend a day greening the landscape. Despite these rural and urban exchanges through digital mediation and direct cooperation on tree planting, carbon projects thereby instantiate the government-backed green utopia of an ecological civilization incorporating grassroots, corporate, and state afforestation projects within its overarching goals.

Notes

All names have been changed to protect anonymity, apart from individuals who wished to be explicitly named in this research.

1   In simplified terms, the app generates "energy" from alleged "savings" in consumer habits and credits these to their users' carbon accounts. The main method for this calculation is subtracting the average carbon footprint for a particular activity (e.g., riding the subway) from a hypothetical emissions-intensive alternative (e.g., taking a taxi) and crediting the difference to the user as grams of "energy." These grams of "energy" can then be added to a virtual seedling that grows within the app. Once the digital tree has reached an adequate size, users can exchange it for an actual tree to be planted in the countryside on their behalf.

References

Anagnost, Ann. 2004. "The Corporeal Politics of Quality (*Suzhi*)." *Public Culture* 16, no. 2: 189–208.

Bakken, Børge. 2000. *The Exemplary Society: Human Improvement, Social Control, and the Dangers of Modernity in China*. Oxford: Clarendon Press.

Brandtstädter, Susanne. 2003. "With Elias in China: Civilizing Process, Local Restorations and Power in Contemporary Rural China." *Anthropological Theory* 3, no. 1: 87–105.

Bruckermann, Charlotte. 2019. *Claiming Homes: Confronting Domicide in Rural China*. Oxford: Berghahn.

Bruckermann, Charlotte. 2020. "Green Infrastructure as Financialized Utopia: Carbon Offset Forests in China." In *Uneven Financializations: Connections, Contradictions, Contestations*, edited by Chris Hann and Don Kalb, 86–110. New York: Berghahn.

Bruckermann, Charlotte. 2023. "Care for the Family and the Environment in China's Coal Country." *China Quarterly* 254: 325–39.

Ding, Iza. 2020. "Performative Governance." *World Politics* 72, no. 4: 525–56.

Hansen, Mette Halskov, Hongtao Li, and Rune Svarverud. 2018. "Ecological Civilization: Interpreting the Chinese Past, Projecting the Global Future." *Global Environmental Change* 53: 195–203.

Harms, Erik. 2014. "Civility's Footprint: Ethnographic Conversations about Urban Civility and Sustainability in Ho Chi Minh City." *Sojourn: Social Issues in Southeast Asia* 29: 223–62.

Harms, Erik. 2016. *Luxury and Rubble: Civility and Dispossession in the New Saigon.* Berkeley: University of California Press.

Herzfeld, Michael. 2005. *Cultural Intimacy: Social Poetics in the Nation-State.* New York: Routledge.

Hoffman, Lisa. 2011. "Urban Modeling and Contemporary Technologies of City-Building in China: The Production of Regimes of Green Urbanisms." In *Worlding Cities*, edited by Ananya Roy and Aihwa Ong, 55–76. Oxford: Blackwell.

Kipnis, Andrew. 2007. "Neoliberalism Reified: Suzhi Discourse and Tropes of Neoliberalism in the People's Republic of China." *Journal of the Royal Anthropological Institute* 13, no. 2: 383–400.

Liu, Xin. 2002. *The Otherness of Self: A Genealogy of Self in Contemporary China.* Ann Arbor: University of Michigan Press.

Lora-Wainwright, Anna. 2013. *Fighting for Breath: Living Morally and Dying of Cancer in a Chinese Village.* Honolulu: University of Hawai'i Press.

Lord, Elizabeth. 2020. "Theorizing Socio-environmental Reproduction in China's Countryside and Beyond." *Environment and Planning* 4, no. 4: 1687–702.

Nguyen, Minh. 2018. "Vietnam's 'Socialization' Policy and the Moral Subject in a Privatizing Economy." *Economy and Society* 47, no. 7: 627–47.

Palmer, David, and Fabian Winger. 2019. "Neosocialist Governmentality: Managing Freedom in the People's Republic of China." *Economy and Society* 48, no. 4: 554–78.

Park, Choong-Hwan. 2014. "Nongjiale Tourism and Contested Space in Rural China." *Modern China* 40, no. 5: 519–48.

Pieke, Frank. 2018. "Party Spirit: Producing a Communist Civil Religion in Contemporary China." *Journal of the Royal Anthropological Institute*, no. 24: 709–29.

Potter, Sulamith, and Jack Potter. 1990. *China's Peasants: The Anthropology of a Revolution.* Cambridge: Cambridge University Press.

Schmitt, Edwin. 2018. "Living in an Ecological Civilization: Ideological Interpretations of an Authoritarian Mode of Sustainability in China." *Critical Approaches to Discourse Analysis across Disciplines* 10, no. 2: 69–91.

Steinmüller, Hans. 2013. *Communities of Complicity: Everyday Ethics in Rural China*. Oxford: Berghahn.

Tan, Tongxue. 2016. *Shuangmianren* 双面人 (*Two-Dimensional Man*). Beijing: Shehui Kexue Wenxian Chubanshe.

Wang, Binbin. 2017. *Climate Change in the Chinese Mind: Survey Report 2017*. Beijing: China Center for Climate Change Communication.

Wang, Jing. 2019. *The Other Digital China: Nonconfrontational Activism and the Social Web*. Cambridge, MA: Harvard University Press.

Zee, Jerry. 2017. "Holding Patterns: Sand and Political Time at China's Desert Shores." *Cultural Anthropology* 32, no. 2: 215–41.

Zee, Jerry. 2021. *Continent in Dust: Experiments in a Chinese Weather System*. Oakland: University of California Press.

Zhang, Li. 2010. *In Search of Paradise: Middle-Class Living in a Chinese Metropolis*. Ithaca, NY: Cornell University Press.

Zhang, Li. 2017. "The Rise of Therapeutic Governing in Postsocialist China." *Medical Anthropology* 36, no. 1: 6–18.

Protecting the Body, Living the Good Life: Negotiating Health in Rural Lowland Laos

Elizabeth M. Elliott

Introduction: Health(care) in Late-Socialist Laos

What does it mean to live well? Beyond the suffering subject (Kleinman, Das, and Lock 1997), it has become evident that asking questions about what constitutes well-being in varied and changing contexts is crucial to understanding the priorities of contemporary life. For rural people in low-land Laos, a good life is inseparable from good health, which is vital for managing the physical tasks of village life such as farming. In the present day, this is not easy to achieve; many experience the double burden of prevalent infectious diseases combined with the increasing incidence of chronic illness associated with changes in diet, lifestyle, and the environment common to developing countries in the Global South (McMichael 2001). However, for the Lao person, well-being is more than the absence of disease: it refers to the integrity of the body, mind, and emotions, as well as social and

positions 32:1 DOI 10.1215/10679847-10890023

spiritual relationships. There are specific practices devoted to maintaining well-being that are strongly rooted in the cultural history of this region, predating but also incorporating ideas from the socialist era. Traditional methods for protecting the body have retained their popularity as new vulnerabilities and social struggles emerge.

In late-socialist Laos, the provision of state healthcare in rural areas with dispersed populations is a continuing challenge. Lao medical history reveals a fragmented story characterized by intermittent and unfinished development efforts, which change with each political era and the associated external donors. Lack of investment in the health sector under colonialism, conflict, low rates of taxation, and a focus on doctrine over technical and management skills have all inhibited the national health system's capacity to improve, and make consistent financing difficult (Sweet 2015). Salaries for government health workers are low, and gaining a position may require a number of years' experience of volunteering. It is a common practice for doctors working in the state healthcare system to also operate private pharmacies or clinics, which have rapidly increased in number since the economic reforms of the late 1980s. Recent moves to implement universal healthcare with the support of international donors (Kim and Loayza 2018) have yet to impact healthcare access substantially.

Mo ya phuen mueang ໝໍຢາພື້ນເມືອງ (village-based traditional healers) in lowland Laos are specialists in the use of plant- and animal-based medicines, which they produce from fresh local materials, and techniques such as *pao* ເປົ່າ (blowing), bonesetting, and divination. They learn through a lineage of teacher-apprentice relationships, and their practice is governed by spiritual principles that prohibit the exploitation of their patients for financial gain so they cannot directly ask for payment (Pottier 2007). Most are now elderly and their knowledge is rarely transmitted; furthermore, the loss of plant resources makes the production of herbal medicine particularly challenging (Sydara et al. 2005).

On a national level, the integration of traditional medicine into the state healthcare system is government policy (Ministry of Health 2013). However, unlike neighboring revolutionary countries, a national system of traditional medicine in Laos has not been created, perhaps partly because the weaker colonial health system did not attempt to suppress local practices (Sweet

2015). During the years following the revolution, a number of healers were drafted into the health service, mostly in rural hospitals, operating on the same premises as, but quite separately from, the biomedical departments. However, there are now extremely few traditional healers employed by government health services.[1] Traditional medicine thus has a high sociopolitical value but little practical state support or regulation, other than when produced for export (WHO 2017).

The loss of traditional healers, shortage of rural health services, and degradation of support structures means that navigating health systems has become increasingly complex and laborious for rural people. In this article I argue that rural Lao people's aspirations for a good life are fundamentally defined and impacted by their quest for health(care) and the relationships this entails.[2] The acts of seeking care and being cared for, and of creating stability in the bodily and spiritual realms are domains (Arendt 1998) in which people both strive for and articulate their vision of a good life, implementing agency within certain limitations. Their pursuit of well-being highlights vulnerabilities and interdependencies; indeed, the struggle for care can adversely affect the capacity of a person and their family to live a good life. The capacity to live, and to live well, is furthermore entwined with the life experiences and motives of the healthcare practitioners from whom they seek help.

In this article, I first define *well-being* in rural Laos, highlighting the challenges and tensions of its production in the late-socialist era. I then explore the process of negotiating care: how people experience and navigate health systems in their pursuit of well-being. I examine the motives of healthcare practitioners, emphasizing how their capacity to live a good life has an impact on the well-being of their patients. The following ethnography describes contrasting encounters of seeking care with a traditional healer and within a rural hospital to illustrate these elements.

Therapeutic Encounters

Ajan Phetsarath, a respected traditional healer, lives in a small compound with his family, who farm rice, coffee, and cassava. On the land opposite the house, there are two simple buildings, each with a low platform for sitting and sleeping. Small collections of protective objects—withered banana-leaf cones, candles, plates of flowers, and brightly colored lengths of string—have been placed in the corners of the rooms. People who are chronically ill with cancer; paralysis; or liver, digestive, or thyroid issues sleep here while receiving treatment from the healer, who visits them morning and evening, and frequently in between. Their extended families stay or visit in rotating shifts, ensuring that the sick person is never alone, bringing mattresses, mosquito nets, baskets for sticky rice, cooking utensils, and snacks. Chickens and ducks peck around the grassy area next to a small patch of forest where the healer collects medicinal plants or sends his patients to find their own.

The atmosphere is convivial; people openly discuss their health problems, sympathizing and comparing notes on treatments sought, discussing the trials of sickness and the challenges it brings to their work and family. Rarely is there any self-consciousness about speaking about problems in intimate detail. Wansai, a rubber farmer in his forties from a nearby village, describes his experiences:

> I have pain in my stomach and intestines and feel very hot inside. I don't know what the cause was—maybe something to do with food. In the past I ate everything, many things! I've been to many places for treatment already—Pakse hospital, the military hospital nearby, the Vietnamese hospital in Paksong. I had three echoes [ultrasound scans] in the Vietnamese hospital and a lot of injections, but the medicine was not correct. I stayed in the military hospital for four or five days. It helped the pain, but it didn't cure me, and it was really expensive—two million kip [$240 USD].[3] But this is still cheaper than the provincial hospital, and my nephew is a soldier so I could get better treatment. I have these medicines that I got there—I've stopped taking them now, do you know what they are? [shows three packets of tablets, including amoxycillin]. I knew Ajan Phetsarath because he treats so many people in this area. Here the treatment is very cheap, you just have to give a donation and pay your own expenses. I've been here for a few weeks already and the pain is already better, but I'm not cured yet although I hope I will be soon. It's very difficult for my family, as I cannot work now and we've spent so much money on medicines already.

Noy, a woman in her early twenties from the next district, has also been suffering from chronic intestinal pain and looks thin and pale. Her mother and sister busy themselves cleaning the area, making a fire for cooking, and ensuring there is fresh water. Her sister has a basket of plant roots and bark, which she grinds against a stone to make a thick brown liquid for Noy to drink. Phetsarath examines Noy in his medicine hut, perching on a low stool next to piles of bark, wood, roots, and leaves, with Noy and her family sitting beside him. He listens carefully to their concerns, asking questions about Noy's appetite and bowel movements, and gently palpates her abdomen.

He then invites them into an inner room with an altar containing Buddha statues, shiny offering bowls, banana-leaf cones, vases of flowers, glasses of perfumed water, a wooden elephant, and other religious objects, lit by electric candles. The predominant color in the room is soft yellow, and although a window lets in some sun, the light is muted and the atmosphere is calm, permeated by the smell of candle wax and the earthy scent of herbs. Sitting cross-legged on a pillow with his back to the altar, Phetsarath takes a plate containing white flowers picked from the garden, ten slim yellow candles, and a 20,000-kip note [\$2.30] from Noy's mother. Pursing his lips, he blows on it softly, and then onto Noy's forehead, mouthing a mantra as he does so. He prescribes a basket of plant medicines, including *ya fon* ຢາຝົນ (medicine made from roots or barks ground into cool water) and two different decoctions, for her to prepare herself.

Noy is also undergoing a series of rituals to assist her recovery. Family members prepare a boiled chicken, eggs, *lap pa* ລາບປາ (fish minced with fresh herbs), and sticky rice, make the *pha khuan* ພາຂວັນ (ritual centrepiece), and knot the lengths of slender white string. The feeling of togetherness is very strong as they work; despite the situation, the little house is full of fun and gossip. Noy is too weak to participate but she sits watching, and by the time the healer is ready to begin the soul-calling ceremony at dusk, the room is filled with people. The ceremony concludes with each of us tying a string onto her wrist and wishing her *yu di mi heng* ຢູ່ດີມີແຮງ (good health). Later I ask the healer why they held the ritual. He says its main purpose is *hai kamlang jai* ໃຫ້ກຳລັງໃຈ (to give power to the heart, boost morale).

In the other building, an older woman, Dee, diagnosed at the hospital with liver cancer, lies under a mosquito net in the corner surrounded by her family. Her teenage nieces play on their phones and giggle, and her three-year-old grandson is passed around and smiled at. Her brother tells me that it is important for all the family to stay together when one member is sick, to create *kamlang jai*. Dee's daughter sits on her bed massaging her feet, and describes their contrasting experiences in the local hospital: "It was confusing and noisy. She couldn't sleep, and nobody explained what the problem was. The medication in Lao hospitals doesn't change your condition, and sometimes when she takes it, her legs and hands swell up—the doctors are careless."

The hospital, three kilometers away along a dirt road, includes rooms for pregnancy care, delivery, examination, a laboratory, ultrasounds, pharmacy, and vaccinations, often sharing space. None of these is well-equipped or particularly clean, which seems to be largely due to age and lack of care; the delivery room has the most implements, although the beds look hard and uncomfortable and are close together, allowing for little privacy. At the front desk, a heavily pregnant woman who seems to be in the early stages of labor sits on a wooden chair filling in forms, while nurses sit watching Thai soap operas. Interactions with patients are brief, and they usually leave with two or three bags of pills from the hospital pharmacy. By 10:30 a.m. most of the staff have left.

The beginning and end of life are ever present. In the ward is another young woman, her two-day-old infant lying on a bed opposite her in the care of her relatives. She has come because she is tired after the birth and cannot drink, so she isn't practicing *yu fai* ຢູ່ໄຟ (the traditional postpartum practice of lying on a bed heated by a charcoal fire and drinking herbal decoctions). Her and the baby's wrists are wrapped in knotted white strings, and there is a small locket around the baby's neck. The mother looks exhausted and ill, as does her baby; the room lacks any extra comforts, is dirty, and smells of the nearby toilets. Inside the main consultation room, a half-naked elderly man lies on an old trolley, with no sheet over him or curtain around him. He is wearing an adult nappy and is attached to an IV drip. His wife sits holding his hand, and they both appear confused and distressed as they wait for their relatives to arrive with money to pay for the ambulance to take him to the provincial hospital in Pakse, sixty kilometers away.

Social Well-Being, Protecting the Body

In the rural southern lowlands of Laos, health, or the absence of it, is a constant preoccupation. The Lao term *sukhaphap* ສຸຂະພາບ (health) is used to describe the state of bodily health; a desirable state is *sukhaphap keng heng* ສຸຂະພາບແຂງແຮງ (strong health). This means that the person is not only free of illness but also has the strength to carry out their daily duties. Older people who lived through the revolutionary era speak with pride about their ability to withstand tough conditions, and express concern for the younger generation who ride motorbikes everywhere and value convenience over effort. While this is partly defined by notions of socialist masculinity (Creak 2015), most practices—primarily the regulation of diet, exercise, rest, and work—are rooted in traditions that predate the socialist era. Activities mentioned as beneficial to health, especially by the older generation, include rice farming, fishing, going to the forest, looking after buffalo, dancing, and gardening. The phrase *yu di mi heng* (to be well and strong) is both a description and an invocation, spoken to another who is unwell, or as a blessing.

The blood is described as the root of bodily health. If the blood isn't strong, the person will be weak and vulnerable to disease. Good blood (*luead di* ເລືອດດີ) can be created through a process of tonification (*bamlung* ບໍາລຸງ). Specific practices that may be preventive or therapeutic include the use of plant-based medicines prescribed by traditional healers or based on family knowledge. Like other Asian humoral systems (Leslie 1992), these techniques often focus on the balance of hot and cold in the body. Cooling raw medicines expel fever in the hot season, and warming decoctions during the postpartum period strengthen the uterus and ensure good blood in the future. Sauna creates a light body, expels toxins, and calms the mind (Tomecko 2009), and medicinal alcohol strengthens vitality.

But is health the same as well-being? Defined as "being well, psychologically, physically, and socioeconomically," well-being is both personally subjective and culturally mediated (Mathews and Izquierdo 2009). Health is not the only marker of well-being; as Baumeister (1991) proposes, well-being is how you feel about your health. Neil Thin (2009) proposes a further route of inquiry into "motives." To analyze motive, he suggests, "include[s] not only the desire to feel good but also the desire to have a life which is 'good' in the sense that it is meaningful and judged well by other people in accordance with social norms."

In Laos, the term *sabai* ສະບາຍ suggests a wider concept of well-being; it is "how people experience their illness and health" (Lundberg 2008). Well-being in Lao society is created and experienced in culturally specific ways that are deeply intertwined with the lives of others, an embodied "somatic mode of attention" (Csordas 1993). To ask someone if they are sabai is to ask whether they are well in a broader sense, including their happiness, familial and social relationships, spiritual state, economic status, and place in society. To be *sabai-jai* ສະບາຍໃຈ, (to have a well heart) is to be content. When I asked Noy how she was feeling, she answered, "I am *sabai-di*, but my *sukhaphap* is not good," making a distinction between being sabai and her body and physical health. While from an objective viewpoint her health was poor, her sense of wellness derived from the caring presence of her family and the treatment she was receiving. Despite her physical pain, she was encouraged to take part in social activities to boost her morale.

Being sabai is also cultivated through personal effort, particularly by avoiding damaging emotional states such as worry, and appreciating activities that are *muan* ມ່ວນ (fun, to be enjoyed). The mental-emotional state *jit-jai* ຈິດໃຈ (mind-heart) must be well balanced, especially when reflected outwardly in one's dealing with others, a process of self-regulation by "managing the heart" (Wikan 1990). This is also characterized as a balance between hot and cold: *uen jai* ອຸ່ນໃຈ (warmed heart, to have a sense of comfort) is desirable, signifying harmony with others, whereas *jai hon* ໃຈຮ້ອນ (heart which is hot, impatience) is discouraged. Cool-heartedness (*jai yen* ໃຈເຢັນ) is valued, but not a cold heart. An excess of work, emotions, or promoting one's personal qualities is to be avoided. A playful aphorism that thinking too much is likely to drive one mad is often quoted about those who demonstrate too much critical thought. One must avoid that which is *phit* ຜິດ (wrong), whether in diet or social behavior, and gravitate toward *thuek* ຖຶກ (correct, appropriate).

In the Lao context, the body and personhood are perceived as highly vulnerable to invasive forces, especially when a person is not sabai. Illness can be caused by climatic factors, toxic substances, or dangerous spiritual entities entering the person. This necessitates the use of protective techniques, which have the effect of both strengthening the person's boundaries and reestablishing their relationships with others. Blowing is a widely used therapy in which the healer, or a *mo pao* ໝໍເປົ່າ (blowing doctor), uses their accumulated therapeutic power to blow a mantra onto part of the body, or into a substance such as medicine or drinking water, which is then consumed (Pottier 2007). It is said to have a tangibly cooling effect, removing undesirable heat from the body.

Blood that is not good, extreme emotions, and lack of familial harmony all render the boundaries of the body more permeable. This allows the *khuan* ຂວັນ (souls, essence),[4] to temporarily flee the person in times of stress; they must be recalled before they become lost (Heinze 1982). When the souls leave the body the person experiences the effect as a somatic state: as one person explained, "If the *khuan* leave your body, you cannot eat or sleep." The *su khuan* ສູ່ຂວັນ or *baci* ບາສີ (soul-calling ceremony) is used to mark transitional periods. In cases of ill health, the ritual is both prophylactic and therapeutic (Tambiah 1970), as in the case of Noy. As the healer explained, its primary function is simply to "*hai kamlang jai*," to give the person the mental and emotional strength to manage a potentially difficult life event. The act of tying strings both forms and strengthens relationships, as well as protects the person's boundaries.

Weak boundaries can allow the entry of *phi* ຜີ (spirits), which may have malicious intent and can cause physical and mental illness. Blowing and string tying may suffice to remove them, or in more extreme cases, spiritual exorcism by a specialist, a *mo phi* ໝໍຜີ (spirit doctor), may be required. Sorcerous attacks by other people, such as placing objects like nails inside the body, are associated with malevolent spiritual forces said to originate from the Khmer and Isaan regions. A widespread method of protection used in the southern lowlands is provided by carrying a type of plant known as *van hom* ວ່ານຫອມ, a sweet-smelling variety of the ginger family, usually *Kaempferia galangal* L. (Vidal 1962). This may be visibly displayed in the form of an amulet around the neck for children, or hidden in the breast pocket of a shirt for men.

Although these incidents are experienced as felt bodily affliction, descriptions of magical violations of a person may also represent their social vulnerability, the perception of risks posed by other people, or a desire to restore a sense of control (Funahashi 2017; Stoller and Olkes 1987). Certainly there is much to be anxious about in the late-socialist era, and fear of external influences is a frequent topic of conversation among rural people as it becomes more difficult to maintain a closely bounded existence. Ownership of land and resources, viewed as routes to prosperity (Singh 2012), is threatened by the influx of Chinese power (Laungaramsri 2014). The consequences of environmental degradation, such as loss of dietary diversity, are having increasingly tangible effects on rural peoples' daily lives and health (Krahn 2005).

While personal well-being is dependent on guarding the body's boundaries, a good life requires living well together. In Laos, maintaining good relations with others, whether family, neighbors, officials, or the spirit world, is crucial for a person to be sabai. Social relationships have been described both as generative, producing health (Lundberg 2008), and protective, ensuring appropriate care when sick (Buchner 2011). However, while sociality may be important for well-being, extensive social obligations may have a negative effect on health, especially for women (Kim, Kang, and Choi 2018): a life that others judge to be good may come at a personal cost.

In late-socialist Laos the extended family remains the primary unit through which these benefits and strains are experienced, as well as being influenced by prevailing social norms. The term *sammakhi* ສາມັກຄີ (solidarity), popularized under socialism, is still used as a justification for encouraging "volunteer" labor (High 2006). Rituals such as the *baci* may be repurposed as a state tool for creating solidarity with rural communities (Singh 2014), showing how well-being practices may also have a performative function in representing an ideal society. The extension of perceptions of well-being to define whether a life is "good" thus imputes an additional moral and sociopolitical subtext that can provide deeper insight into certain principles of peoples' lifeworlds.

Negotiating Care

How do people in rural Laos seek and negotiate care when their health and well-being are disrupted? The descriptions above contrast encounters between patient and practitioner in two therapeutic settings: the home of the traditional healer and the rural hospital, the two most popular sources of treatment for villagers, followed by the village health worker. Other local forms of healthcare that are used less frequently include the village pharmacy, a private clinic, sellers of traditional medicine, and self-medication with herbal medicine. Farther afield are the provincial hospital and the nearby military hospital, which are consulted when local methods fail. Less than 5 percent of people reported traveling to Vientiane, more than seven hundred kilometers away, or across the border to nearby Ubon in Thailand. However, although proximity was an important factor, people were willing to travel long distances to consult practitioners reputed to be able to cure their particular problems, especially in cases of chronic illness. Villagers reported a high level of care-seeking for ill health; the various options were often used in combination, and rarely exclusively.

The modalities are defined as *ya luang* ຍາຫຼວງ (biomedicine) and *ya phuen mueang* ຍາພື້ນເມືອງ (traditional medicine) according to how "*phit* ພິດ, *san chemi* ສານເຄມີ" (toxic, containing chemicals) or "*thammasat* ທຳມະຊາດ, *sot* ສົດ," (natural, fresh) they are perceived to be. People framed their preferences in pragmatic terms such as "I don't know which is better—I just try them to see if they help me," and in statements about the effect: "*Ya luang* works quickly, but it doesn't really cure. *Ya phuen mueang* takes time, but it cures completely"; "*Ya luang* is effective, but it's toxic if you take it for more than a few days." Another distinction is between private and public healthcare provisions. Local health centers, village health workers, and state and military hospitals represent public healthcare, while the private sector includes regulated pharmacies and clinics, and the unregulated sphere of traditional medicine practitioners, traveling sellers of various "cures" including injections, pills and packaged herbal decoctions, and spiritual healing (blowing, divination, exorcism)—including Buddhist clergy.

However, behind these binary distinctions lies a heterogeneous medical landscape. The village pharmacy is run by a doctor from the hospital and his family; the village healer was a military health worker in the 1970s. Beyond the convenience of the hospital, the most-used healthcare options were offered by residents of the village with significant social roles and previous relationships with their patients. The village health worker, who visited people in the evenings to sell them small packages of drugs or IV solutions, also worked in the public health office and farmed rice. The healer had extended family networks in the village and an honorary role in the local administration. The local sharing of information and personal recommendations is paramount; people acquire, exchange, and share medicines as social commodities even when their use is contrary to the original instructions (Haenssgen et al. 2018). Medicinal plants are cultivated, found around the village, or collected in the forest to treat the ailments of family members and neighbors, and knowledge is generated through social encounters (Elliott et al. 2020).

People explained their choices based on social and familial connections even in state healthcare settings, such as relatives working in a particular hospital or the military, a common form of employment in the border areas of the south. Other studies report similar findings; in seeking care across the border in Thailand, social networks affected the choice of a healthcare provider more than socioeconomic or spatial factors (Bochaton 2015), and in rural Laos, utilizing one's social capital and network minimized the risks of being charged unofficial fees and mitigated anxiety about seeking treatment (Buchner 2011). In my research, the healers' treatments were described as strengthening the body and its boundaries, while the hospital posed risks. Hospital visits thus required additional protective measures, as shown by the knotted strings on the wrists and ankles, or *van hom*, carried in the pockets of people attending.

Negotiating the rural healthcare landscape both highlights and causes vulnerabilities. Sickness in rural Laos, as described in the cases of Wansai, Noy, and Dee, can be a difficult and resource-consuming event that profoundly affects the well-being of both the person afflicted and those close to them, who may be affected by loss of earnings, inability to provide agricultural labor, the investment of time as carers, and the cost of seeking public and private healthcare. Financial assistance is commonly provided in the form of gifts and loans from extended family, demonstrating the need for reliance on networks, and often creating substantial debts (Buchner 2011). Strategies to improve universal healthcare such as national health insurance may partially mitigate the financial strain of seeking care. However, studies show that health insurance in Laos may not significantly improve healthcare accessibility or financial protection against "catastrophic expenditure" associated with the loss of earnings (Bodhisane and Pongpanich 2017), and many patients still pay above the official fee rates for a variety of reasons (Chaleunvong et al. 2020).

In contrast, recourse to traditional healers (at least, those considered serious practitioners) was donation based, mediated by the ethical requirements of their status as initiates.

Seeking a Good Life

What can we learn about the good life from this process? For the sick person and their family, both limitations and aspirations in the search of a good life are tested. The difficulties of negotiating rural healthcare emphasize how people's choices occur within the context of structures outside their control. Thus recourse to traditional medicine is commonly understood as a response to scarcity. With limited capacity to act due to disadvantageous socioeconomic factors, rural people utilize what care is available to them.

However, this explanation does not account for agency, enacted within certain constraints. As Mol (2008) proposes, while the "logic of choice" may be erroneous and assumes personal autonomy, people are not simply passive recipients of medical authority. Patient agency may be implemented in how people engage with their own treatment and their relationships with carers. Aspirations to a good life are enacted through positive action toward well-being. Although they approached the use of medicine pragmatically, rural people consistently described experiences of interacting with the traditional healers more favorably than those with staff in state medical institutions. Following culturally familiar principles to strengthen and protect the body and establish relationships between people and with the spirit world, the healer's approach aligns more closely with the production of well-being.

This could be observed during the therapeutic encounter. The healer's consultation incorporated a series of stages, including an invitation into his therapeutic space in the presence of objects that hold symbolic meaning for the person; building trust through the creation or substantiation of relationships between the healer, the sick person, and their carers; empathetic listening to the person's illness narrative; and the use of touch in both diagnosis and therapy. Patient agency was implemented through active dialogue in which patient and healer create a shared understanding of the illness event. Few of these aspects were present at hospital consultations, which were brief and rarely included space for patients' input, or explanations of the treatment process in easily comprehensible language.

In the production of health, understanding of and involvement in one's own care is an important distinction. It has been shown that this has an impact on patient satisfaction, adherence to treatment regimes, and even the success of the treatment itself (Fischer and Ereaut 2012). Additionally, the practical participation of the sick person and their family in the preparation of medicines and rituals and even the collection of plants shows how agency is implemented through people participating in their own treatment. In contrast, rural people frequently were unsure what the medication acquired from the hospital was for, or how to use it.

Experiences of the various therapeutic settings also mark these distinctions. The therapeutic setting of the healer, such as Phetsarath's house, is a comfortable, familiar space with access to nature and room for more people to join the sick person. Family members undertake caring tasks such as preparing food, medicine, and ritual items, and provide emotional support, creating a sense of inclusiveness and safety. Soothing sensory experiences and the blurring of the boundary between the social and the therapeutic space allow the person to feel at ease, in contrast to the hospital's uncomfortable, cramped environment and lack of privacy.

But why this difference in the users' experience? Besides the varying techniques, philosophies, and settings of healthcare modalities, there is perhaps a more fundamental issue: the well-being of the healthcare providers themselves. The life experiences of staff at a state-run institution and those of individual nonregulated practitioners situated on the periphery, including their motivations, choices, systems of recompense and social status, differ. Providing care, as Mol (2008) argues, is typically characterized as a gift; but this may cast it in opposition to the mechanics of health systems, when in reality the two are entangled.

Neither the state-employed doctors nor the traditional healers in this study received substantial economic reward for their work. Satisfied patients who consider themselves cured might return to provide their healers with greater financial remuneration, but this cannot be expected. Most healers thus had other sources of income; although Phetsarath was a renowned practitioner, he still worked with his family cultivating rice, coffee, and cassava. Contrary to narratives of traditional medicine's resistance to biomedical colonization elsewhere (Wahlberg 2006), these healers expressed a desire for more government support and recognition.

Likewise, state-employed doctors often supplemented their income by opening a private clinic or pharmacy from 11 a.m to 2 p.m. and after 4 p.m., limiting their availability to hospital patients. Private health enterprises were part of the fabric of healthcare in Laos prior to 1976, and after a short hiatus, trained health staff were authorized to apply for licenses to operate private pharmacies, so state doctors diverting their energies into private healthcare is nothing new (Sweet 2015). However, after the move toward universal healthcare in 2017, which introduced a nominal fee for consultation and treatment with government providers, many doctors complained of the extra workload, confusion over paperwork, and the diversion of their private patients into public healthcare without increased returns.

Both doctors and healers were forced to diversify their incomes, and neither felt supported or valued by state structures. So what motivated them and gave them a sense of satisfaction? If "motive" is part of defining well-being (Thin 2009), this is guided by personal values as well as the desire to have a life that is judged well according to social principles. How did their lives appear as "good" according to value frameworks beyond economic reward?

The healers spoke of the satisfaction they gained from their work, and their choice to live this kind of life. Despite the disadvantages of the absence of state support, they could operate relatively freely due to the unregulated nature of their profession, and in the familiar surroundings of their homes. Their ongoing study of traditional medicine provided opportunities for intellectual stimulation and self-cultivation. They emphasized that to be able to treat patients successfully and utilize their therapeutic power safely, it is necessary to follow a virtuous lifestyle based on Buddhist principles, paying careful attention to one's actions and with the correct motivation (Coderey 2017; Pottier 2007). The healer's reputation is, therefore, closely associated with adherence to social and religious convention and the observation of these by others.

Typically, the healers occupied a significant role in the village. The almost exclusively male lineage of healers among the lowland Lao and the respect for age commonly found in Lao culture meant that they were regarded as the highest strata of the village hierarchy (Pottier 2007). Their work was thus socially and culturally valued, the subject of traditional medicine engendering enthusiasm among almost everyone to whom I spoke. Despite the pressure of the continual demand for their time and energy by people seeking care, the healers enjoyed their work and the associated social engagement. There was also an expectation of reciprocity through care provided in return, as I learned when Ajan Phetsarath became sick and became the beneficiary of many concerned visitors bearing gifts of cash, goods, or medicine.

In contrast, the rural doctors and nurses experienced more limited agency. As government employees, they often had little choice over where they were posted. Rewards for work done well were limited; arguably, the fundamental marker by which government employees were judged was obedience, including demonstrating adhesion to political ideology by attending training sessions. Although in the late-socialist era there is increasing freedom to run private medical enterprises, this is still limited by economic status and opportunity, including the loss of income as an indirect consequence of recent health insurance policies. In particular, many younger female health workers felt marginalized: they were underpaid, without opportunities for career progression, and forced to live away from their families while also encountering social pressure to marry and take on extra domestic work. Although the doctors clearly cared about their patients, they also spoke with frustration about their perception that the latter did not follow their directions or respect their diagnoses.

Constructs of the good life in terms of motives and values, whether internal (personal satisfaction, spiritual attainment, agency) or external (social recognition, reciprocity, financial gain), affected the practitioners' attitudes toward their treatment of and relationship with patients. The healers' lives were mostly oriented to the broad notion of well-being that I have outlined. But for others, restricted by the context within which they operated, tensions were created by competing notions of a good life: financial gain or a sense of control over one's life course versus adherence to sociopolitical norms. The internal conflicts encountered on entering a profession that might entail personal sacrifice have important implications for how healthcare is delivered and received.

Conclusion

Health and well-being are fundamental to the ability to live a good life in rural Laos. Indeed, aspirations to a good life and visions of well-being are defined and impacted by the process of negotiating one's health. Traditional healers are rapidly disappearing from the medical landscape, while public biomedical health services have not yet fully evolved into a trusted alternative, leaving rural people in a healthcare gap in which it is challenging to find care allied with the production of well-being. At the time of writing the COVID-19 pandemic has emphasized these vulnerabilities and the importance of protecting against dangerous external influences that threaten well-being.

In an exploration of the good life in the late-socialist era, it is important to consider motive and its wider effects. As healthcare choices are closely associated with relationships, patients' experiences of the therapeutic encounter affect their access to and satisfaction with healthcare. These experiences are strongly influenced by the practitioner's motives for providing care, guided by the desire for a life that is both meaningful and judged good according to social principles. Although lacking in financial compensation, those who feel rewarded in other ways are likely to provide care that is more acceptable to the sick person and their family. A good life in rural Laos is thus highly interdependent with the good lives of others; to live well, it is imperative to live well together.

Notes

1   This is perhaps due to the effect of the economic reforms of the 1980s, which reduced compensation for workers with a lower educational level (Sydara, pers. comm., 2016).

2   Data for this article is drawn from ethnographic research on traditional healing practices conducted in rural Champasak province during 2015–16, during which time I lived in hospital dormitories with young doctors and nurses, which provided opportunities to observe

and compare medical consultations and the lives of both patients and health care practitio-ners in rural areas.

3   Exchange rates are from the time of research.

4   There are said to be thirty-two *khuan* normally present in the body, each one resident in a different body part (referred to by the Pali word *akara*), which they are said to animate (Pottier 2007). The *khuan* belong to the person, but are also separate entities with agency.

References

Arendt, Hannah. 1998. *The Human Condition*. Chicago: University of Chicago Press.

Baumeister, Roy F. 1991. *Meanings of Life*. New York: Guilford Press.

Bochaton, Audrey. 2015. "Cross-Border Mobility and Social Networks: Laotians Seeking Medical Treatment along the Thai Border." *Social Science and Medicine* 124: 364–73. https://doi.org/10.1016/j.socscimed.2014.10.022.

Bodhisane, Somdeth, and Sathirakorn Pongpanich. 2017. "The Impact of Community Based Health Insurance in Enhancing Better Accessibility and Lowering the Chance of Having Financial Catastrophe Due to Health Service Utilization: A Case Study of Savannakhet Province, Laos." *International Journal of Health Services* 47, no. 3: 504–18. https://doi.org/10.1177/0020731415595609.

Buchner, Denise. 2011. "Stories without Endings: A Study of Illness and Disability Narratives in Rural Laos." PhD diss., University of Calgary.

Chaleunvong, Kongmany, Bounfeng Phoummalaysith, Bouaphat Phonvixay, Manithong Vonglokham, Vanphanom Sychareun, Jo Durham, and Dirk Essink. 2020. "Factors Associated with Patient Payments Exceeding National Health Insurance Fees and Out-of-Pocket Payments in Lao PDR." *Global Health Action* 13. https://doi.org/10.1080/16549716.2020.1791411.

Coderey, Céline. 2017. "The Buddhist Grammar of Healing: Building Efficacy in the Pluralistic Therapeutic Context of Rakhine, Myanmar." *Asian Medicine* 12, nos. 1–2: 233–64.

Creak, Simon. 2015. *Embodied Nation: Sport, Masculinity, and the Making of Modern Laos*. Honolulu: University of Hawai'i Press.

Csordas, Thomas J. 1993. "Somatic Modes of Attention." *Cultural Anthropology* 8, no. 2: 135–56. https://doi.org/10.1525/can.1993.8.2.02a00010.

Elliott, Elizabeth, et al. 2020. "Forest Fevers: Traditional Treatment of Malaria in the Southern Lowlands of Laos." *Journal of Ethnopharmacology* 249: 112187. https://doi.org/10.1016/j.jep.2019.112187.

Fischer, Martin, and Gill Ereaut. 2012. *When Doctors and Patients Talk*. London: The Health Foundation.

Funahashi, Daena. 2017. "In the Name of the People: Magic and the Enigma of Health Governance in Thailand." *Kyoto Review of Southeast Asia* 22, September. https://kyotoreview.org/issue-22/magic-enigma-health-governance-thailand/.

Haenssgen, Marco J., et al. 2018. "Antibiotics and Activity Spaces: Protocol of an Exploratory Study of Behaviour, Marginalisation, and Knowledge Diffusion." *BMJ Global Health* 3, no. 2. https://doi.org/10.1136/bmjgh-2017-000621.

Heinze, Ruth-Inge. 1982. *Tham Khwan: How to Contain the Essence of Life: A Socio-Psychological Comparison of a Thai Custom.* Singapore: Singapore University Press.

High, Holly. 2006. "'Join Together, Work Together, for the Common Good—Solidarity': Village Formation Processes in the Rural South of Laos." *Sojourn* 21, no. 1: 22–45.

Kim, Harris Hyun-soo, Minah Kang, and Kyungwon Choi. 2018. "Social Capital or Liability? Gender, Network Size and Self-Rated Health (SRH) among Community-Dwelling Adults in Lao People's Democratic Republic." *Social Science Journal* 56, no. 4: 617–26. https://doi.org/10.1016/j.soscij.2018.09.001.

Kim, Young Eun, and Norman Loayza. 2018. "The Drive Toward Universal Health Coverage." SSRN Scholarly Paper ID 3249565. Rochester: Social Science Research Network. https://papers.ssrn.com/abstract=3249565.

Kleinman, Arthur, Veena Das, and Margaret Lock. 1997. *Social Suffering.* Berkeley: University of California Press.

Krahn, Jutta. 2005. "The Dynamics of Dietary Change of Transitional Food Systems in Tropical Forest Areas of Southeast Asia." PhD diss., University of Bonn.

Laungaramsri, Pinkaew. 2014. "Commodifying Sovereignty: Special Economic Zone and the Neoliberalization of the Lao Frontier." *Journal of Lao Studies* 5, no. 1: 29–56.

Leslie, Charles. 1992. "Interpretations of Illness: Syncretism in Modern Ayurveda." In *Paths to Asian Medical Knowledge,* edited by Charles Leslie and Allan Young, 177–206. Berkeley: University of California Press.

Lundberg, Kristin Vivian. 2008. *Women Weaving Well-Being: The Social Reproduction of Health in Laos.* Lawrence: University of Kansas.

Mathews, Gordon, and Carolina Izquierdo. 2009. *Pursuits of Happiness: Well-Being in Anthropological Perspective.* New York: Berghahn.

McMichael, Tony. 2001. *Human Frontiers, Environments, and Disease: Past Patterns, Uncertain Futures.* Cambridge: Cambridge University Press.

Ministry of Health. 1996. "Policy on the Promotion of TM in Lao PDR." Lao PDR: Ministry of Health.

Mol, Annemarie. 2008. *The Logic of Care: Health and the Problem of Patient Choice.* London: Routledge.

Pottier, Richard. 2007. *Yu Di Mi Heng; être bien, avoir de la force; essai sur les pratiques théra-peutiques Lao* (*Yu Di Mi Heng: To Be Well and Strong: Essay on Lao Therapeutic Practices*). Paris: EFEO.

Singh, Sarinda. 2012. *Natural Potency and Political Power: Forests and State Authority in Contemporary Laos.* Honolulu: University of Hawai'i Press.

Singh, Sarinda. 2014. "Religious Resurgence, Authoritarianism, and 'Ritual Governance': 'Baci' Rituals, Village Meetings, and the Developmental State in Rural Laos." *The Journal of Asian Studies* 73, no. 4: 1059–79.

Stoller, Paul, and Cheryl Oakes. 1987. *In Sorcery's Shadow: A Memoir of Apprenticeship among the Songhay of Niger.* Chicago: University of Chicago Press.

Sweet, Kathryn Dawn. 2015. *Limited Doses: Health and Development in Laos, 1893–2000.* Singapore: NUS.

Sydara, K., S. Gneunphonsavath, R. Wahlström, S. Freudenthal, K. Houamboun, G. Tomson, and T. Falkenberg. 2005. "Use of Traditional Medicine in Lao PDR." *Complementary Therapies in Medicine* 13, no. 3: 199–205. https://doi.org/10.1016/j.ctim.2005.05.004.

Tambiah, S. J. 1970. *Buddhism and the Spirit Cults in North-East Thailand.* Cambridge: Cambridge University Press.

Thin, Neil. 2009. "Why Anthropology Can Ill Afford to Ignore Well-Being." In *Pursuits of Happiness: Well-Being in Anthropological Perspective*, edited by Gordon Mathews and Carolina Izquierdo, 23–44. New York: Berghahn.

Tomecko, Denise. 2009. *Buddhist Healing in Laos: Plants of the Fragrant Forest.* Bangkok: Orchid Press.

Vidal, Jules. 1962. "Les plantes utiles du Laos (VII)" ("Plants Used in Laos [VII]"). *Journal d'agriculture tropicale et de botanique appliquée* 9, no. 11: 502–24. https://doi.org/10.3406/jatba.1962.2680.

Wahlberg, Ayo. 2006. "Bio-Politics and the Promotion of Traditional Herbal Medicine in Vietnam." *Health: An Interdisciplinary Journal for the Social Study of Health, Illness and Medicine* 10, no. 2: 123–47. https://doi.org/10.1177/1363459306061784.

Wikan, Unni. 1990. *Managing Turbulent Hearts: A Balinese Formula for Living.* Chicago: University of Chicago Press.

WHO (World Health Organization). 2017. "Meeting on Strengthening Quality Assurance of Traditional Medicines, Seoul, Republic of Korea, 1–3 March 2017: Meeting Report." Manila: WHO Regional Office for the Western Pacific. https://iris.wpro.who.int/handle/10665.1/13632.

Summer Happiness: Performing the Good Life in a Tibetan Town

Fan Zhang

> Look! The male voice is sonorous as a long golden horn,
> Look! The female voice is melodious as a golden Tibetan trumpet.
> Hearing the lyrics, please look!
> The Maitreya Dharma Wheel Monastery [Lithang Monastery] sits on the elephant's
>   trunk with auspicious streams running by.
> May the lama with health,
> May the homeland with happiness,
> May the earth without disasters.

This song, accompanied with the white-mask dance, opens *Alce Lhamo* (*Sister Goddess*),[1] a theatrical performance at Lithang's annual summer festival.[2] The festival includes mountain sacrifice, *Sister Goddess*, horse racing, camping, and feasting. It starts in the town seat of Lithang and spreads to all of

positions 32:1   DOI 10.1215/10679847-10890036

its villages over several months. Like Carnival, it interrupts the tedious daily routine and forms a space of ritual, theater, and amusement.

This article studies the monthslong performance of happiness and the local vision of the good life in Lithang. As ethnic Tibetans, the people of Lithang are easily labeled "peripheral," "minority," or "subaltern," in contrast to the Han, the majority and default participants in Chinese modernity. Ethnic studies of China tend to highlight the violence of the Chinese state and the sufferings of ethnic subjects in the modernizing process (Liu 2011; Mueggler 2001; Yeh and Coggins 2014). Thus, they often take the performance of happiness by the ethnic groups such as the Miao and the Tibetans as epiphenomena of the suffering reality, concealing a structure of inequality and differences that is produced and reproduced translocally and transnationally by a whole set of multicultural and transnational mechanisms (Adams 1996; Schein 2000).

Nonetheless, as Michael Herzfeld (2016) argues, performances shape social relations rather than just being epiphenomena of the real world. By studying the poetics of the Greeks' performances, Herzfeld illustrates the cultural intimacy between state ideologies and the rhetoric of everyday life, and a social poetics of essentializing differences through performance. The concept of cultural intimacy reveals the common ground between the individual and the state, as well as the cultural engagement of the common people and the elites in the formation of state ideology. Taking my cues from Herzfeld, I see performance as real as any other action rather than as symbolizing an idealized vision or concealing a power structure. I focus on the poetics and politics of performance as ritual, heritage, and tactics to illustrate the ways in which the government, the monastery, and the global media are included in the local vision of the good life and the local system of heroism, underscoring a dynamic of intimacy between the individual and the state as well as between the local and the global.

Lithang has been labeled "the highest town in the world" and "the county of poverty" by the Chinese government, due to its high altitude, hostile climate, poor road conditions, and underdeveloped industry. It seems the least likely place to talk about happiness and the good life. However, locals are often heard rejoicing at their *norbu sacha* (treasure land). This reveals a different vision of a good life, as expressed in their performance: life's treasure rests not only in wealth but also in good karma and merit (May the lama be with health), fertile land (May the homeland be with happiness), and cosmological balance (May the earth be without disasters). It clearly extends beyond the position of individuals in the state (beyond power and politics), to that of human beings in the world (to virtue and poetics). Such a vision not only demonstrates the autonomous spaces of action within the confines of social positions but also enriches the value frameworks of the good life in postsocialist political economies, as explored in this issue. In Lithang, *Sister Goddess* performances are on the one hand a way of negotiating for autonomy and profit with the local government and the global market, and on the other hand, a way of communicating with the deities, bringing fertility to the land, pacifying demons, and accumulating merit.

As the Chinese philosopher Zhao Tingyang (2004) proposes, visions of the good life arise more from possible lives than from life possibilities. Possible lives rest on the very ontologies of being-in-the-world, while life possibilities are realized through social and political processes. Similarly, Michael Jackson (2011: xi) defines the idea of well-being as grounded "in the mystery of existential discontent," which leads to the sense that "one may become other or more than one presently is or was fated to be." In line with their emphasis on the ontological frame, I raise the concept of *cosmological poetics* to articulate the local understanding of well-being that encompasses both the political-economic and the ontological dimension. Cosmological poetics refers to the connectedness of being and well-being with natural and supernatural beings (see also Elliott's article in this issue for a similar conception of well-being in Laos). This approach sees ritual performance as not only engaging with social processes but also regenerating the social at the ontological and existential levels.

In the following, I first outline in section 1 the origin and development of the two *Sister Goddess* troupes in Lithang, one of laymen and the other of monks, and the tension between them. I don't simply attribute their tension to political violence or the modernizing process; instead, I argue that the tension also arises from their pursuit of heroism. In Lithang, heroism means the capacity of navigating through various power centers such as the state and the market, and becoming a hero is a goal of life. It is the basis of cultural intimacy and the key to understanding the local vision of the good life. It also illuminates a different perspective from a top-down one that easily treats the state as a violent hand transforming ritual into heritage. As I further demonstrate in section 1, both the laymen and the monks engage actively with this process and strive to become an officially recognized heritage so as to "eat the government." Further, different from the perspective of globalization, as I discuss in section 2, though Lithang is definitely at the margins of the world system, by connecting with the cosmopolitan centers on the screen, the local people incorporate the globe into their system of heroism. Despite being officialized and commercialized as cultural heritage, the ritual aspects of the performances are maintained, and local people see them as the foundation of their well-being. Therefore, in section 3, rather than highlighting the rupture between modernity and tradition, I describe how the performance dissolves it. In section 4, I discuss how cosmological poetics is mediated through the performance to demonstrate the local vision of well-being: the interconnectedness of humans, land, mountains, cosmic power, and supernatural beings that is crucial to local people's sense of happiness and heroism.

My contribution goes beyond articulating the local vision of a good life. I further argue that the local view of well-being provides a broader value framework for our conceptualization of the good life that breaks the illusive scales of top-down and local-global and the dichotomies of modernity against tradition, politics against poetics. We tend to scale up from the individual to the state to the global, or from the individual to society to nature, as if these concepts are concrete and discrete entities external to one another. However, the cultural intimacy and cosmological poetics I illustrate in the article challenge these scales and highlight how individuals incorporate and coordinate all the agents and networks to craft a better space of being in the world.

1. Eating the Government: Hero, History, and Heritage

The local people in Lithang believe that the Living Buddha of Lithang Monastery, the Second Kyagon (1909–49), first introduced *Sister Goddess* to Lithang. They consider the Living Buddha an exemplary hero: he was versatile at negotiating with various economic and political powers in Nanjing,

Lhasa, and India, and his collaboration with the government of Republic China greatly influenced the regional politics of Kham and the formation of the modern Chinese state in the early twentieth century (He 1989: 13; Litang xianzhi bianzhuan weiyuanhui 1996: 510–13). He is a hero to whom the locals attribute the introduction of *Sister Goddess*. It is said that he led a team to Lhasa in 1941 to learn the performance. After five years the team returned and started to perform regularly at his birthday celebrations, which soon merged with the summer festival. This undocumented narrative has been reiterated by the monks and introduced to me by local officials.

Similar to the life history of the Living Buddha, the local monastic and governmental histories also feature Lithang's connections with political centers and its role in regional history. As the local government's documented history goes, Lithang was established as a garrison by the Yuan court in the thirteenth century and continued to function as an important garrison between Chengdu and Lhasa during the Qing Dynasty (Litang xianzhi bianzhuan weiyuanhui 1996). As the local monastic history goes, Lithang Monastery was founded by the Third Dalai Lama at the end of the sixteenth century, which officially made Lithang a parish of the Gelug School of Tibetan Buddhism (N. L. Gyatso 2005: 241–42). The Gelug School was patronized by the Qing court, and Lithang Monastery was the biggest monastery in Kham until the early twentieth century. Lithang was thus governed both by local rulers who were recognized by the Qing court and by high monks who were entitled by Lhasa, the two ruling agents often being from the same family (Litang xianzhi bianzhuan weiyuanhui 1996: 511). During the Republic era Lithang interacted with Lhasa and Nanjing through its monastic and bureaucratic system. Since the 1960s, however, the monastic influence in Lithang has declined when the central government tightened its policies in the Tibetan region. Although the current reincarnation of the Living Buddha still holds a position in the central government, he is not as influential as the previous incarnation was. At the same time the influence of the local government has been rising and it dominates the local life. A large proportion of the local population earn their living from local governmental infrastructure and cultural projects. The locals describe such a way of earning bread from working in or for the government as "*Jago sama*" (eating the government). It has become an ideal way of life locally.

Regardless of the changing relationship between religion and politics, the state in various forms remains the foundation of local life. Far from the assumption of "naive natives," Lithang's people understand the role of politics well and actively manipulate state policies; rather than visualizing the state as hostile and invasive, distant and unreachable as the top-down perspective assumes, they draw it into a relationship of cultural intimacy.

Contrary to Lithang's own highlight on its centrality, being part of Kham, a region characterized by its "tribal" situation, linguistic variation, segmentary loyalties and feuds, and lack of institutionalized religion and systematized philosophy, Lithang actually is a geographical and cultural margin to both Central Tibet and the hinterland of China. It is popularly seen as the birthplace of merchants, warriors, and bandits, part of the autonomous social and political spaces referred to by James Scott (2009) as Zomia. However, the local people did not escape from the state as Scott has assumed, but passionately embrace the state. To understand the reason, it is necessary to introduce the concept of heroism in Lithang. Similar to the Greek and Yi understandings of manhood (Herzfeld 1985; Liu 2011), Lithang's people cherish heroism and easily turn daily life into social gestures of exaggeration and bombast, battle and feud. However, the Kham heroism does not simply refer to a Robin Hood–like spirit or any outlaw action, but implies flexibility, mobility, and an ability to manipulate and mobilize multiple forces and agents such as the state or the market. As Tenzin Jinba (2017) points out, far from being a space of Zomia, Kham has been intensively involved with the dominant political and cultural powers of the Indian-Hindu, Han-Confucian, and Theravada-Tibetan Buddhist states and civilizations.

The people of Lithang respect heroes because heroes embody connections and mediate power. Lithang's heroic figures are continuously commemorated and their birthplaces, residences, life stories, and personal items are carefully preserved as sources of empowerment. Today the house in which the Living Buddha was born is still carefully maintained by Happiness Village. Through this connection, Happiness Village claims to be the exclusive donor of *Sister Goddess* performances. Although inviting performers, purchasing material for costumes and masks, setting up tents, and providing food for the performers involve great expense and intensive labor, the villagers see such donations as a good way of accumulating merit and prestige.

Moreover, the monk performers are mostly originated from Happiness Village, thus their performances are seen as being imbued with the power of the Living Buddha.

Lithang people's desire to become heroes leads them to engage actively with the state. In collaboration with the local government, the layman performers have become new heroes and challenged the prestige of Happiness Village as donor and its monk performers. In the 1980s, Rainbow Village invited some former monk performers to help them organize a troupe of laymen to perform occasionally on holidays and at festivals, because the monk troupe had been dismissed during the Cultural Revolution. In the 1990s, with the central government's more liberal religious policies, Happiness Village's monk performers revived their performance at the summer festival. Meanwhile Rainbow Village's layman troupe was thriving under the patronage of the local government. At first the laymen performed only in their own village, while the monks performed across the entire region. Gradually, with the development of tourism, the local government invited the laymen to perform in the town's central square during the tourist season, and as a result they established a good reputation among the tourists and the locals. In 2008, the *Sister Goddess* troupes in the neighboring towns of Bathang, Serda, and Derge were officially recognized as national Intangible Cultural Heritage. This triggered Lithang's sense of heroism and a desire to be nominated as cultural heritage themselves. Endorsed by the local government, the layman troupe was officially recognized as Intangible Cultural Heritage at the prefecture level in 2018.

Although only recognized by the prefecture government, having their performance officially recognized as cultural heritage brings the troupe repute, income, and opportunities. Their employment by the local government secures them a stable salary, and they are able to take on a mobile and cosmopolitan life. They perform representing Lithang in megacities such as Shanghai, Beijing, Chengdu, and Kunming. With local government recommendation, they appear in movies, shows, and newspapers. The local government also sponsors Tibetan- and Chinese-language classes for them as most of them are illiterate, and their new language skills enable them to communicate with broad audiences. As pious Tibetan Buddhists, the layman performers show great respect to the monk performers, and never felt equal to them, but official recognition has greatly increased their reputation and confidence.

The troupe leader, Lobsang Tamba, became a completely different person once their performance was recognized as cultural heritage. A former artisan monk with moderate art and literary training, he had renounced his monastic life in his thirties to marry. He and his wife ran a not very profitable craft studio and were thrown into poverty after bearing three children. The couple sent two sons to the monastery to improve their life. Compared to his previous quiet and sullen demeanor, Lobsang Tamba is now a successful "eater of the government" and a confident and eloquent local hero, frequently shaking the hands of high officials, appearing in the popular media, and touring big cities with the troupe.

This section has shown how the state, in the form of officials, policies, subsidies, and certificates, represents not only authority from afar but also a resource that can be mobilized. An outsider might expect the intimacy between the local government and the layman performers to lead to injustice and inequality, but the locals respect it, as it embodies a capacity for contracting relations with powerful agents and benefiting from mobilizing them.

2. Screening Differences: The Local and the Global

Janet Gyatso (2005: 3) has cautioned the field of Tibetan studies to be aware of "Tibet's Hollywoodization," the tendency to romanticize or demonize Tibet through scholarly production to feed the popular imagination, because such a tendency imprisons Tibet in Shangri-La, rendering the real life-worlds of the Tibetans irrelevant (see also Lopez 1998; Sakya 1994). This perspective somewhat underestimates the subjectivity of the local people in appropriating the "Orientalist images." This section demonstrates how the people of Lithang practice self-Orientalizing strategies to plug themselves into the global world.

As mentioned, more and more people in Lithang are becoming "eaters of the government." This accompanies the central government's overall switch from building a modern society to building *xiaokang* 小康 (a moderately prosperous society) (Zhonggong zhongyang wenxian yanjiushi 2016).[3]

Such an ideological turn is followed by policies of redistributing wealth and power nationwide. Instead of investing in already-developed economic zones, the central government introduced poverty-alleviating policies and relief for underdeveloped regions including Lithang. In this way Lithang's local government began to invest in infrastructure and tourism that absorb local labor. The nomination of *Sister Goddess* as cultural heritage in 2018 and the construction of the *Sister Goddess* Museum in 2019 are part of this process.

Realizing that the exotic *Sister Goddess* masks and costumes attract domestic and international tourists, the local people have taken advantage of this Orientalist image to brand Lithang as a town of mystery and romance. The museum's walls are decorated with masks and costumes, and the museum employs the layman troupe to perform during the tourist season. Adjusting to the museum's schedule and available space, the troupe has cut the three-day performance to two hours and reduced the cast of more than twenty performers to four or five. The local government has installed lighting facilities in the old town and arranged performances in the town square at night. The museum, the decorations, the lights, the dance, and the music strongly shape the local visual and acoustic landscape. Increasing numbers of Lithang inhabitants have opened restaurants, hotels, and bars, and run other tourist businesses. The embellished old town has become the new center of the local world.

The mysterious and romantic image of Lithang attracts a wide range of visitors, including investors. In 2018, parts of the movie *Looking for Rohmer* were shot in Lithang. The layman troupe joined the international cast side of Chinese movie stars and foreign actors. The movie is a life and death romance, and ultimately, a story of salvation in Tibet. The layman troupe's *Sister Goddess* performance in the movie represents a path to salvation. Through encountering, watching, and joining the performance, the main character recovers from the trauma of his lover's death.

Chris Berry (2019) points out that this movie follows the trend of othering Tibet, in which salvation is featured through exotic symbols rather than actual human interaction. Indeed, the layman troupe appears on the screen as a circus and their performance is reduced to a thin story and an exhibition of exotic masks and dances. However, behind the scenes the layman performers also participated in the fabrication of the story and the exhibition of their mysterious symbols. Lobsang Tamba, the troupe leader, wrote the script for the *Sister Goddess* performance in the movie, demonstrating his adaptation to the popular exoticization and romanticization of Tibet. He drew the plots from one of the most popular *Sister Goddess* scripts, transformed the religious story into a love story, and added more mask dances in the choreography. The troupe even made new costumes in brighter colors, and more exaggerated masks for the movie performances.

The layman performers enjoy showing off their photos with the stars and foreigners, regardless of the open promotion of the film as a "gay movie." For them the othering process means connection, mobility, and cosmopolitanism. At its basic level, the economic profit derived from such media engagement alleviates these nomads' dependence on their scant production of potatoes and yak meat and the unpredictable market for highland herbs and mushrooms that they used to rely on for their livelihoods. More than just a way of gaining profit, the experience of working as part of an international team has given them a way into a bigger world and made them heroes in the eyes of other locals, who consider them brave in their venture out into the world, connecting with the cosmopolitan actors, and benefiting from their courage and connections. Lobsang Tamba showed me a photograph of himself with the entire cast of the movie with the same pride as when he showed me his certificate of cultural heritage. The framed photograph hangs on the wall in the main entrance to his house as a badge of honor and a symbol of his cosmopolitanism.

By repositioning the local in the global, this section has illustrated how the local people are capable of essentializing differences as a way of creating intimacy with the global world, not simply out of economic rationality but also from their desire to embrace difference and their ability to imagine life against a bigger picture than their own.

3. Modernity on the Surface: Ritual and Theater

The story above seems to be one of a rupture in which the secular regime overruns the religious regime and secular actors overshadow monastic actors. As Arjun Appadurai (2005) suggests, modernity is often featured as rupture, and through electronic and virtual media the expressive space of art, myth, and ritual in the transcendent realm has descended to the quotidian life. However, this section illustrates how in Lithang ruptures appear only on the surface, while in their deeper lives people experience the continuous entanglement of the secular and the transcendent, with the *Sister Goddess* performance seen as a simultaneously ritualistic and theatrical mechanism that amalgamates this-worldly fortune and other-worldly merit.

During performance, on the one hand, the performers welcome and even invite their audiences to take photographs and videos, because the resulting exposure in the local and global media is a way of establishing connections and harvesting respect. On the other hand, the performers are concerned when their masks are exposed to cameras. They usually keep their own masks, unlike those specially made for museum exhibition and media display, under a white cloth. For the local people, these items possess sacred and dangerous transformative power. Wearing them entails a transformation from ordinary human performers into demons, animals, heroes, and gods, in which normally the heroes and gods, assisted by the good animals, prevail and kill the demons. Lithang people see this transformation as actual rather than symbolic. They believe that the masks and costumes possess supernatural power, and thus the mask dances influence their karma and their bodies. To avoid waking the demons, they cover the demon masks with cloth, avoid touching them, and only uncover them for performances. A monk performer who plays the role of a demon attributes his rheumatism to the health-damaging action of touching the contagious demon mask. In the same vein, the layman troupe has to invite a monk to play the role of monk due to the profane karma-damaging action of laymen wearing monk costumes.

In this sense, being recognized as cultural heritage never really causes rupture for the troupe. The ritualistic aspect remains the core value of the performance. Although performing for different audiences in different spaces, both troupes start with ritualistic mask dances to enact the power of the masks. They take this step as a guarantee of the authenticity and authority of their performances. Meanwhile, the enactment of the transformative power is also and always associated with secular profits. Especially, it is critical in the two troupes' competing claims to heritage and museum.

For the monks, the authenticity of their performance is guaranteed by their connection with the Buddhist teachings, the Living Buddha, and the institutional transmission of the standardized scripts and techniques of the performance. The head lama of the monk troupe, Lama Phurba, who received the highest Buddhist degree after twelve years of study in India and is thus well respected by the locals as a cosmopolitan figure, told me that the monk performers summon the power of Buddha through mask dance. He highlighted that *Sister Goddess* is not entertainment but an entertaining way of spreading the Buddhist teachings, and thus accuracy is important, because wrong words bring bad karma to both performers and audience. He expressed his concern that due to their illiteracy, the layman troupe frequently improvises new lyrics and deviates from the Buddhist classics. Lama Phintso, the leading monk performer, highlighted descendance and techniques. He pointed out the differences between their three-dimensional blue masks and the flat masks of the laymen, and emphasized that the monks' much more complicated technique was introduced by the Living Buddha from Lhasa. He also reiterated his experience as the disciple of a prestigious monk who trained in Lhasa with the Living Buddha, the strict training in vocal and body techniques that he received, and his teacher's close relationship with the Living Buddha. He believes that the layman group's performance techniques do not meet the standards required to qualify as cultural heritage.

In contrast, the laymen's shamanistic capacity to navigate freely among the cosmic forces, government power, and local and global media illustrates their performative authenticity. They believe their mask dance provokes the power of the three realms of the universe, which clearly corresponds to the pre-Buddhist shamanic tradition (Xie 1988). This releases them from the Buddhist duty of maintaining accuracy in performance, so they frequently improvise lyrics and steps and incorporate new trends, bringing them popularity among the tourists, employment at the museum, and exposure to global audiences. When touring local festivals and rituals from village to village, they disseminate new government policies as well as local and global news. Such flexibility and cosmopolitanism lead them to wider popularity.

The competing claims of the two troupes have shaped the cultural heritage narrative and the materialization of the museum. In China, individual and collective heritage is often appropriated by the local government to represent its administrative achievements and local prestige in order to secure economic and political resources from the central government (Chen 2015). Lithang also witnessed fierce debates on which troupe was qualified as inheritor of *Sister Goddess* representing Lithang. With their sense of heroism, officials from Happiness Village and Rainbow Village value safeguarding the prestige and resources of their own people more highly than their official task of preserving cultural heritage. As a compromise to the differing interests of the officials involved, the layman troupe received a certificate as inheritor while the monk troupe was recognized as orthodoxy in the museum. The laymen are paid to perform in the museum, pose for photographs, and produce masks for display, while the monks ensure that the museum displays their standard narrative, scripts, and techniques and officially supports their orthodoxy. Such an appropriation of the laymen's performance as representing Lithang and the redistribution of profits to both troupes illustrate the cultural intimacy rather than tension between the government and the local people.

This raises criticism of studies contending that the surge in heritage is a consequence of modernity (Foster and Gilman 2015; Hafstein 2018), and studies concluding that authenticity and agency are part of the modernist project (Bauman and Briggs 2003; Bendix 1997), out of which actors transform their folkloric past into a possession (Herzfeld 2016). In Lithang, the different groups' competing claims are not simply made with reference to the modernizing process: the sense of heroism, pursuit of prestige, concern about bad karma, and desire to accumulate merit are all present.

4. Cosmological Poetics: The Landscape of Well-being

The above analysis has explored how the local people incorporate the state and the market into their vision of a good life, and how a sense of heroism shapes their ways of achieving it. This section applies the concept of cosmological poetics to highlight the local vision of the connectedness between social well-being and cosmological balance, which broadens the value framework of political economy in the conceptualization of well-being.

As mentioned, Lithang people see their hometown as "treasure land,"

and understand the treasure in life as resting not only in wealth, but also in good karma and merit, fertile land, and cosmological balance. They often attribute their treasure in life to Lithang's blessed geography that was mapped out by the Third Dalai Lama who founded Lithang Monastery as the center the local world. As expressed in the performance, "the Maitreya Dharma Wheel Monastery [Lithang Monastery] sits on the elephant's trunk." The locals believe that Lithang manifests as a crouching elephant with the monastery on its trunk, leading the way. Surrounding the monastery, the eight villages of the old town are visualized as being carried on the elephant's back arranged in the shape of a lotus flower. Further, the monastery, villages, and mountains are imagined as integral parts of a mandala, with four sacred mountains embracing the flower from the four directions. Elephants, lotus flowers, and mandalas symbolize empowerment, luck, and safety in Buddhism.

The locals thus perform sacrifices at the sacred mountains every year to assure continuing blessings and protection, order and good fortune, and land fertility. *Sister Goddess* performance constitutes a significant part of the sacrifice. As the monks explained, burning pine branches and chanting sutras at a mountain sacrifice before the performance can drive away unhappy land spirits, and the *Sister Goddess* performance can satisfy the water dragon residing under the mountains that is in charge of water, rivers, floods, and rain. In this sense, the land and the mountains are not seen as an inert world of material supporting the production of yaks, potatoes, and caterpillar fungus, but as agents with emotions, desires, and reason, which demand respect, amusement, and awe. Once their emotions and desires are tended to, they regulate the water by bringing the necessary rainfall and preventing floods. Such a vision of well-being embeds nature in the human world through the landscape, the mountain sacrifice, rainfall, and the cultivation of yaks and caterpillar fungus.

In recent years the government's infrastructure projects have reshaped the old town with new roads and buildings, and the shape of the lotus flower is no longer recognizable. The local people make even more luxurious and majestic mountain sacrifices to counterbalance the destruction. They attribute the increased mobility, connection, job opportunities, and wealth brought by the new infrastructure to their auspicious land and pious sacrifices.

Local livelihoods depend heavily on the land: the grasslands feed the yaks, and the mountains produce various flora and fauna, including caterpillar fungus, matsutake, and other expensive herbs and mushrooms that cannot be mass-produced. With rapidly increasing demand in recent years, the caterpillar-fungus season brings in a handsome income. The local people thus perform more enthusiastic mountain sacrifices in hope of securing stable production and weather conditions.

To increase local well-being, the local government also participates in the mountain sacrifice. Each year before the *Sister Goddess* performance, when the monks travel clockwise on horseback to each of the four sacred mountains to make their sacrifices, government cars lead the way. During the performance, local officials and commoners mingle in the crowd, burning juniper branches, offering wind-horse flyers, replacing old prayer flags with new ones, and reciting the scriptures of each individual mountain deity. In this spectacle the assumed boundaries between the state and the social, the secular and the sacred, the human world and the natural world dissolve, giving way to an imagination of the good life in which cosmological balance takes center stage.

It is believed that the sacrifice increases overall well-being, while each person's individual portion is ultimately decided by their karma and merit. According to Buddhist teaching, karma is written at one's birth according to one's previous life cycle, while merit is accumulated by conducting good deeds throughout the current life. Thus local people respect those who are capable of finding valuable highland herbs and make good sales, whose yaks are strong and fertile, who have fast horses and win the race, who profit from government projects and the development of tourism, who can afford a modern home, and who get opportunities to be sponsored by the government or exposed in the outside world. They see fortune as the product of karma and merit rather than part of the structure of inequality.

As such, the natural and social realms are connected with individual lives through karmic operation and the cosmic movement. We have long assumed a clear division between nature and culture, and between the secular and the sacred. However, in the vision of the Lithang people, political power, economic gain, individual achievement, ritual performance, and the ecological order are seen as closely related through the system of karma and merits.

Conclusion

We tend to reach for concepts such as power and politics, inequality and injustice when discussing the necessary conditions for a good life. They are significant because they open up possibilities in the lives of local people. However, by focusing on these alone we miss the local visions of possible lives from which we can learn to expand our own vision of well-being. People in Lithang have a much broader scale of well-being, which, as expressed in the *Sister Goddess* performance, encompasses supernatural (May the Lama with health), human (May the homeland with happiness), and natural (May the earth without disasters) dimensions, illuminating how we can expand and reframe the limited scope of our discussion.

I therefore propose the concept of cosmological poetics to include natural and supernatural beings in the discussion. When framing a discussion, politics is usually seen as more real than poetics. Yet the case of Lithang shows that poetics acts to coordinate the cosmic order, supernatural power, and natural beings, which are perceived by the local people as the basis of well-being (see also Elliott, this issue; Kleinod-Freudenberg and Chanthavong, this issue).

Far from being just a zone of Zomia, the state has long been embedded in the local imagination and realization of the good life as potential resources and relationships that can be mobilized for a better life. Contrary to the Appaduraian idea that the global mediascape pushes the local into the global, I have repositioned the global in the local, showing how local people incorporate cosmopolitanism into their system of heroism and prestige. Such intimacy between the individual and the state, and between the margins and the cosmopolis, breaks the illusive scales of top and bottom, local and global.

In short, the local landscape of connectedness, in which history and myth, ritual and theater, merit and karma, money and market, as well as the local, the state, the cosmopolitan, and the cosmological, are folded into the local life-world and its people's vision of the good life. This landscape of connectedness defies the reified dichotomies between ritual and theater, poetics and politics, and tradition and modernity.

Notes

1 I recorded it during Lithang's 2019 summer festival. While translating it into English, I try to keep the original Tibetan way of expression. *Sister Goddess*, sometimes translated as Tibetan Opera, is a traditional performance that may derive from sources such as the ceremonial spectacles of the Tibetan imperial period (seventh–ninth century), local songs and dances, and Indian Buddhist dramas (Henrion-Dourcy 2015; Fitzgerald 2018). In Lithang, the performance follows a prescribed three-stage procedure: prelude, main story, and coda. The prelude includes a white-mask dance and a blue-mask dance; the main stories are based on the popular *Eight Classics of Sister Goddess*, and the coda incorporates local songs and dances.

2 Literally, the festival is called Dbyar Skyid (Summer Happiness). It celebrates the end of *dbyar gnas* (summer retreat; in Sanscript *varśa*), a three-month retreat in the monastery during the monsoon season to avoid stepping on insects (Buswell and Lopez 2014: 960).

3 Xiaokang was previously raised as a goal to be achieved through the modernizing process. It was reset by the current regime as a new political ideology, adopting the Confucian view of well-being that encompasses both economic growth and the broad distribution of wealth, cultural diversity, and ethical pursuits among the various ethnic populations.

References

Adams, Vincanne. 1996. "Karaoke as Modern Lhasa, Tibet: Western Encounters with Cultural Politics." *Cultural Anthropology* 10, no. 4: 510–46.

Appadurai, Arjun. 2005. *Modernity at Large: Cultural Dimensions of Globalization*. Minneapolis: University of Minnesota Press.

Bauman, Richard, and Charles L. Briggs. 2003. *Voices of Modernity: Language Ideologies and the Politics of Inequality*. Cambridge: Cambridge University Press.

Bendix, Regina. 1997. *In Search of Authenticity: The Formation of Folklore Studies*. Madison: University of Wisconsin Press.

Berry, Chris. 2019. "Pristine Tibet? The Anthropocene and Brand Tibet in Chinese Cinema." In *Chinese Shock of the Anthropocene: Image, Music, and Text in the Age of Climate Change*, edited by Kwai-Cheung Lo and Jessica Yeung, 249–73. Singapore: Springer Singapore.

Buswell, Robert E., and Donald S. Lopez. 2014. *The Princeton Dictionary of Buddhism*. Princeton, NJ: Princeton University Press.

Chen, Zhiqin. 2015. "For Whom to Conserve Intangible Cultural Heritage? The Dislocated Agency of Folk Belief Practitioners and the Reproduction of Local Culture." *Asian Ethnology* 74, no. 2: 307–34.

Fitzgerald, K. 2018. "'My Beautiful Face, the Enemy of Dharma Practice': Variations in the Textual History of Nangsa Ohbum." *Asian Ethnology* 77, nos. 1–2: 145–68.

Foster, Michael Dylan, and Lisa Gilman, eds. 2015. *UNESCO on the Ground: Local Perspectives on Intangible Cultural Heritage.* Bloomington: Indiana University Press.

Gyatso, Janet. 2005. "Presidential Address, Tenth Seminar of the International Association of Tibetan Studies." *Journal of the International Association of Tibetan Studies Seminar*, no. 1: 1–5.

Gyatso, Ngawang Lobsang, the fifth Dalai Lama 五世达赖喇嘛阿旺洛桑嘉措. 2005. *Yishi—Sishi Dalai Lama zhuan* 一世—四世达赖喇嘛传 (*Hagiographies of the First to the Fourth Dalai Lama*). Translated and compiled by Chen Qingying 陈庆英 and Ma Lianlong 马连龙. Beijing: Zhongguo Zangxue.

Hafstein, V. T. 2018. "Intangible Heritage as a Festival; or, Folklorization Revisited." *Journal of American Folklore* 131, no. 520: 127–49.

He, Yong 何勇. 1989. "Lithang jiefangchuqi de minzushangye" 理塘解放初期的民族商业 ("Commerce of Lithang in the Early Phase of Liberation"). *Minzu yanjiu* 民族研究 (*Ethnic Studies*), no. 2: 12–17.

Henrion-Dourcy, Isabelle. 2015. "*rNgon-pa'i 'don*: A Few Thoughts on the Preliminary Section of a-Lce Lha-Mo Performances in Central Tibet." *Études mongoles et sibériennes, centrasiatiques et tibétaines*, no. 46: 1–18.

Herzfeld, Michael. 1985. *The Poetics of Manhood: Contest and Identity in a Cretan Mountain Village.* Princeton, NJ: Princeton University Press.

Herzfeld, Michael. 2016. *Cultural Intimacy: Social Poetics and the Real Life of State, Societies, and Institutions.* New York: Routledge.

Jackson, Michael. 2011. *Life within Limits: Well-Being in A World of Want.* Durham, NC: Duke University Press.

Litang xianzhi bianzhuan weiyuanhui 理塘县志编纂委员会 (Compiling Committee of the Gazetteer of Lithang). 1996. *Litang xianzhi* 理塘县志 (*Gazetteer of Lithang*). Chengdu: Sichuan renmin.

Liu, Shao-hua. 2011. *Passage to Manhood: Youth Migration, Heroin, and AIDS in Southwest China.* Stanford, CA: Stanford University Press.

Lopez, Donald S. 1998. *Prisoners of Shangri-La: Tibetan Buddhism and the West.* Chicago: University of Chicago Press.

Mueggler, Erik. 2001. *The Age of Wild Ghosts: Memory, Violence, and Place in Southwest China.* Berkeley: University of California Press.

Sakya, Tsering. 1994. Introduction to *Resistance and Reform in Tibet*, edited by Robert Barnet. London: Hurst.

Schein, Louisa. 2000. *Minority Rules: The Miao and the Feminine in China's Cultural Politics*. Durham, NC: Duke University Press.

Scott, James. 2009. *The Art of Not Being Governed: An Anarchist History of Upland Southeast Asia*. New Haven, CT: Yale University Press.

Tenzin, Jinba. 2017. "Seeing Like Borders: Convergence Zone as a Post-Zomian Model." *Current Anthropology* 58, no. 5: 551–75.

Xie, Jisheng 谢继胜. 1988. "Zangzu Samanjiao de sanjie yuzhoug jiegou yu linghun guannian de fazhan" 藏族萨满教的三界宇宙结构与灵魂观念的发展 ("The Structure of the Tripartite Universe and the Concept of Souls in Tibetan Shamanism"). *Zhongguo zangxue* 中国藏学 (*China's Tibetology*), no. 4: 100–112.

Yeh, Emily T., and Chris Coggins. 2014. *Mapping Shangrila: Contested Landscapes in the Sino-Tibetan Borderlands*. Seattle: University of Washington Press.

Zhao, Tingyang 赵汀阳. 2004. *Lun Keneng Shenghuo: Yizhong guanyu xingfu he gongzheng de lilun* 论可能生活: 一种关于幸福和公正的理论 (*On Possible Lives: A Theory on Happiness and Justice*). Beijing: Renmin daxue.

Zhonggong zhongyang wenxian yanjiushi 中共中央文献研究室 (Study Office of CPC Central Committee Archive). 2016. *Xi Jinping guanyu quanmian jiancheng xiaokang shehui lunshu zhaibian* 习近平关于全面建成小康社会论述摘编 (*Compilation of Xi Jinping's Thoughts on Comprehensively Building a Xiaokang Society*). Beijing: Zhongyang wenxian.

Spirits with Morality: Social Criticism and Notions of a Good Life in Laos through the *Bangbot* Imaginary

Michael Kleinod-Freudenberg and Sypha Chanthavong

In Asia's late-socialist countries, animist worldviews have survived colonialism, warfare, state socialism, and capitalist modernization in everyday lived experience. In Laos, the existence of many kinds of spirits is unquestioned across the social board. This article seeks to contribute to recent discussions on animism in Southeast Asia (Arhem and Sprenger 2016; Endres and Lauser 2012; Mueggler 2001; Sprenger and Grossmann 2018; Taylor 2007) and, more specifically, Laos (Kleinod 2020; Sprenger 2018) by tapping the rich repertoire of folklore to uncover notions of the good life in late-socialist Laos. Empirical data provided by folklore, when contextualized, is useful for understanding social relations and experiences of rapid societal change (Abrahams 1983; Bauman 1983; Dundes 1980; Oriole 2000). Such notions tend to include political criticism, as folklore allows people "to talk indirectly of reality and to freely express ideas and feelings which they often

positions 32:1   DOI 10.1215/10679847-10890049

would not dare to state in other ways" (Oriole 2000: 292). Such an indirect approach seems appropriate where, as in Laos, a vocal civil society is largely absent, and discontent is indirectly expressed.

Relying on fieldwork (2011–14 by the first author, 2019 by both authors), we focus here on the imaginary[1] of a peculiar sort of forest spirit that is currently almost unknown in the literature: the *bangbot*. We argue that this imaginary, which directly links notions of morality with undisturbed forest, provides an excellent entry point into socioecological criticism and alternative visions in Laos at a time when development is largely coterminous with deforestation.[2] The bangbot can thus be seen as representatives of a good life, a measure against which to critically (and indirectly) comment on the morality of late socialism in the Lao People's Democratic Republic (PDR). However, as we will demonstrate, the amount and quality of such criticism varies according to historical context and social structure. More precisely, we argue that in the early 1900s the bangbot legitimized rural leaders in the context of colonialism, whereas today they represent an increasing urban environmentalism reflecting the emergence of new urban milieus. While under colonialism the bangbot legitimized a most powerful, violent social criticism among rural milieus, today the potential for social criticism—as uttered through this imaginary—is highest in urban accounts and lowest in rural accounts. We furthermore observe that the critical potential of today's bangbot seems rather tame compared to their role in past violent anti-colonial revolt under rural leaders: they have become role models combining modern sustainability thinking with an idealized Laoness, and are expressive of recent sociostructural shifts such as the emergence of new socioecological and adventurous sections among the educated, urban middle class.

We lay out this argument first by situating the bangbot in the recent political-economic context of Laos as a resource frontier, and outlining the specifics of this imaginary. We then present in detail the ways in which bangbot appeared during the anti-colonial struggle as well as today in various local settings. This Buddho-animist-ecological imaginary links directly with Elliott's article (this issue) on traditional Laotian notions of well-being and addresses ecological awareness as part of modern aspirations to a good life (Bruckermann, this issue; Zhang, this issue). Thus, in the vision of the bangbot as spirits with morality, questions of subjectivity, inequality, ecology, and cosmology converge, challenging the dichotomy of nature and culture and speaking to anxieties and aspirations in late-socialist Asia (see Nguyen, Wilcox, and Lin, this issue; Zhang, this issue).

Frontier Capitalism and the Bangbot Imaginary

Many parts of the Lao PDR can be characterized as frontiers of global capitalism where the "cheap" appropriation of resources and labor overrides capitalization, implying ecological plunder and inequality (Moore 2015; Barney 2009). The frontier character of the Lao economy is reflected in the official policy of *han thi din pen theun* ຫັນທີ່ດິນເປັນທຶນ ("turning land into capital"), for instance in the form of large-scale concessions for hydropower plants, plantations, and mining (Baird 2011; Dwyer 2007; Kenney-Lazar, Dwyer, and Hett 2018). In Laos modernization is often coterminous with deforestation, while the equal distribution of the economic participation and benefits meets various challenges characteristic of rentier states and conditions of "primitive accumulation" (Baird 2011; Barma 2014). One reason that resources and labor on capitalist frontiers are cheap is that human reproduction relies at least partly on uncommodified subsistence networks (Moore 2011) to which, in turn, animist imaginaries are integral (Kleinod 2020; Kleinod, Duile, and Antweiler 2022). Therefore, the focus on bangbot in this political-economic context is directly related to a main thrust of this special issue: the question of how some groups' pursuit of the good life excludes and even harms other groups. In other words, animist imaginaries persist not so much despite transformations but because of the latter's specific quality. Throughout the history of Laos as a People's Democratic Republic, animism had an ambivalent position: although officially regarded as superstitious, and thus discouraged, "many of the officials in charge of policing the instructions [concerning "superstition"] were implicated in the self-same deeply rooted cultural practices" (Evans 2002: 202). Today animism ties into Lao modernization and has even become iconic of the national culture, as in the ubiquitous *baci* ບາສີ, or *soukhwan* ສູ່ຂວັນ (wrist-tying ritual).

In this diverse cosmos of spiritual beings, the bangbot occupy a rather exceptional position which in turn can speak directly to the perceived morality of Laos's recent development and related notions of a good life.

Because imaginaries, as defined here, are integral and subject to the vicissitudes of everyday survival on the frontier, a core meaning for bangbot is difficult to establish, as will become clear. There are, however, two aspects that all our informants agreed on: bangbot are invisible (the literal translation of bangbot, "hidden in the shade," is taken as meaning "invisible"), and bangbot are spirits with morality. Along with the *phi tahaek* ຜີຕາແຮກ (guardian spirit of the rice fields), bangbot are the only benevolent nature spirits.[3] They are generally imagined as "people like us," although they are invisible and live a devout Buddhist village life in remote, inaccessible forest places. They are thus similar but morally and meritoriously superior to humans. This definition as moral superhumans sets them apart from humans and other forest spirits. According to a modern account (see the Nam Kat case below), bangbot exist in a dimension different from and parallel to the human one due to their higher karmic status, which explains why they are invisible and can move incredibly fast or be in different places at the same time. They make themselves visible only to humans with a pure heart, whom they may help in various ways. Villagers are set on the right track home when lost in the forest or are invited for a visit to a bangbot village, or their clothes and tools are repaired, all on the condition of absolute honesty.[4]

Central to our argument is the connection established in this imaginary between moral purity and the deep, remote, and inaccessible forest, as this potentially allows for framing criticisms of Lao modernity as materialized in deforestation (see Singh 2012). This peculiar context of meaning—the direct link between morality and undisturbed forest—allows for evaluation of the morality of development in a late-socialist resource economy (see Nguyen, Wilcox, and Lin, this issue). Relatedly, the element of moral superiority confers political legitimacy or social credibility (symbolic capital) on those using such narratives, as those allegedly in touch with bangbot must be morally worthy, and it indicates a vision of the good life in terms of harmonious and honest socioecological relations. In the following we provide various accounts of bangbot ordered according to our overall argument of a historical shift of their critical potential from rural to urban milieus.

The Bangbot in the Past: Anti-colonial Revolt

The critical and even emancipatory potential of the bangbot is demonstrated by their role in one turbulent period of early colonial history in Laos, the Phu Mi Bun ຜູ້ມີບຸນ ("Man with Merit") revolt in 1901–36 (see Baird 2013; Ishii 1975; Gunn 2003; Ladwig 2014; Murdoch 1967). Ong Keo was the first leader of this long uprising against colonial administrative impositions, primarily the head tax. Not only his devout, meritorious life but also, and certainly as a consequence of this, a bangbot entitled him to be a leader. This is documented in Pholsena (2006: 130), who quotes a seventy-five-year-old informant whose father was a fighting companion of Ong Keo's:

> One evening, Pha Ong heard the Phi Bang Bot, who came down on his horse. But he couldn't see him. He could only hear him. Ong Keo was in the spirit house. He learnt the chants and the prayers from the Phi Bang Bot during three days and three nights. After the third night, Ong Keo saw the candles in the spirit house. He still couldn't see the Phi Bang Bot but his horse only. From then on, Ong Keo had the power. If he ordered the buffaloes to crush, they would; if he told people to fight against each other, they would. So everybody, without exception, in Meuang Thateng believed that he was a Pha Ong, the most powerful; that he could defeat the French. And Ong Keo said that he wanted to defeat the French because they were oppressing the people.

This quotation marks the earliest historical appearance of the bangbot, at least to our knowledge, right in the center of the anti-colonial struggle, framed and legitimized by a "tradition of sorcery and invulnerability" (131). It thus appears that in the historical context of anti-colonial resistance the bangbot lend rural leaders legitimacy by conferring magical powers of invincibility rather than Buddhist moral purity, even if these cannot be neatly separated (see Holt 2009). As Geoffrey Gunn (2003: 142) argues, the Phu Mi Bun revolt was revolutionary only in the sense that it sought to "restore a pre-capitalist past by way of the magical invocation of traditional deities." The power derived from Phi Bang Bot was rebellious, and it was mainly directed against a foreign power, the French. Today Ong Keo is celebrated as a quasi-revolutionary hero.

The Bangbot Today: An Emerging Glocal Environmentalism

Today the bangbot appear in a context that differs from the early colonial situation both politically and ecologically. The recent tension between environmental plunder and forest protection was not an issue in colonial Laos (Cleary 2005). The following empirical accounts of bangbot narratives are ordered on a continuum of explicitness regarding social criticism that also tends to reflect the socioecological distinction between rural and urban. We suggest that today the most explicit criticism is found in urban bangbot narratives as part of a new form of glocal environmentalism expressive of a transforming social structure.[5]

The Bangbot as Everyday Tricksters

The densely forested Phou Khao Khuay National Protected Area is located to the north and east of Vientiane Capital. A militarized buffer between the capital city and Hmong insurgent strongholds in the Xaysomboun region around Phou Bia, Phou Khao Khuay was one of the first ecotourism destinations in Laos, and it is a bangbot hotspot. Judging from informal conversations, young urban people from Vientiane enjoy camping in the forest overnight, and we return to this in our last case. A monk at Vat Phabat Vang Noi, a ten-year-old forest monastery at the fringes of Phou Khao Khuay, confirmed that bangbot are all around, and that Thai monks cross the Mekong to meditate there and get in contact with them.

For the ethnic Khmu and Lao villagers of Ban Hatkhai, bangbot have an everyday quality: boys or girls are seen bathing in the river, only to disappear in an instant. Recently, bangbot kept our host's brother in a cave for seven days. He had been fishing with a friend and suddenly disappeared from view, waking up in a cave guarded by a huge snake that would not let him out. He was provided with Lao-style food. On the seventh day, the snake had gone and he could leave, gradually waking from a dreamlike state as he made his way back to the village. Another informant recalled a day in his childhood when his sister had disappeared: together they had been following their parents to the rice field, and suddenly she was gone. From 8:00 a.m. to 2:00 p.m. she was hidden by the side of the pathway. No one could see or hear her, whereas she could see and hear villagers looking for her without success. Only the sacrifice of a pig made her reappear. In such accounts, bangbot appear, like other spirits (with which they partly merge), as everyday tricksters to be reckoned with, as they may coop you up for unclear reasons, extort a sacrifice (as in the case with the disappeared sister), or even take your rice. According to our argument that the critical potential of bangbot narratives hinges on the nexus of morality and undisturbed forest, such low amount of morality as found in recent rural accounts indicates that here the critical potential is minimal or nonexistent. This comes out in a rare bangbot story told by a village elder, which exemplifies the contrast with the role the bangbot played in the anti-colonial revolt described in the previous section. In the early 1960s in the Pathet Lao camps not far from Ban Hatkhai, a soldier conversant with magical ways grills the skin of a white buffalo, thereby rendering a bangbot village visible and catching one of its inhabitants as a recruit. The bangbot makes a great soldier, often the first to attack and killing many of the enemy. About ten years later he argues with his superior and deserts to settle in Pha Muang, where he marries and enjoys his time between home and field. Following Laos's independence his former superior sets out to find him; as he approaches Pha Muang the bangbot's wife points him to the field, but as he goes there to catch him he can only see the buffalo. So he leaves empty-handed. The bangbot dies three years later. This account frames bangbot in the same magical perspective encountered in the case of Ong Keo, above. However, instead of the aloof, superior spiritual power lending political potency and legitimacy, in this case they are rather normal actors in human relationships. This is also indicated by the idea that bangbot can be forced into visibility by certain ritual procedures in order to employ them for human purposes, such as in the anti-imperialist struggle.

The Bangbot as Bad Conscience

There is more socioecological criticism in terms of the morality of modernization in this case of a Katang sacred forest in the National Protected Area of Dong Phou Vieng in eastern Savannakhet Province.[6] The dense vegetation on this small 180-ha patch of old-growth forest contrasts sharply with the surrounding area. The local Katang consider it inhabited and protected by a *phi mueang* ຜີເມືອງ (powerful territorial spirit) who, on choosing this place to live, gathered villagers to move into the forest with him, whereby they turned into bangbot living in a village inside this forest. The territorial spirit established taboos on the cutting of trees and the hunting and killing of two species of monkey. As conservationists have classified the latter as endangered, the spirit forest is additionally protected by a conservation project. This seems necessary given the extractive context of illicit trade in wildlife and precious timber in which villagers are also involved (Coudrat, Duckworth, and Timmins 2012). In this context, the critical potential of bangbot becomes tangible when considering the relationship between them and humans; according to villagers, the bangbot used to help them by lending or repairing tools and clothes in return for their honest behavior, such as appearing on time for an appointment or returning borrowed items according to the agreement. This theme is also expressive of the related dimensions of cosmology and care (see Nguyen, Wilcox, and Lin, this issue; Elliott, this issue), but it turns this nexus upside down: according to informants among the village elite, this relationship deteriorated as the villagers became increasingly dishonest. They did not return what was borrowed anymore, or started spying on the little helpers as they were repairing their tools. These bangbot may now be gone, or perhaps they simply no longer show themselves; in either case, the help-for-honesty relationship has ceased to exist, and according to other informants this is also common elsewhere. There are interesting parallels here to the monkeys mentioned previously: not only are they, like the bangbot, principally invisible and seen only when willing to be seen, they are also increasingly leaving the forest, where they can be, and are being, hunted. As both the bangbot and the monkeys are protected by the territorial spirit residing in that forest, these changes must accord with the spirit's will and are thus legitimate.

We suggest that it is possible to read this narrative of the deterioration of the relationship between bangbot and villagers not only as a comment, in the animistic idiom, on deteriorating ecological relations in terms of increasing dishonesty, but also as (self-)criticism in disguise, conveying a bad conscience about one's own role in this, even if it is due more to economic necessity than to choice. With the following case, we switch from rural accounts to urban ones, where bangbot embody a more explicit form of ecological criticism.

The Bangbot as Endangered Species

This case brings us to Xay District of Oudomxay Province, in the north of Laos. The forest of Nam Kat, and particularly its waterfall, was developed as a tourism destination around 2010. Since 2016 the Nam Kat Yorlapa Lodge has offered first-class accommodation as well as various tours and activities in the forest.[7] Reportedly owned by a successful and well-connected Lao businessman, the venture represents a new stage in the professionalization of ecotourism in Laos. This can be understood from the style and content of its promotional films, one of which relates a bangbot story that is sociologically revealing. "Bangbot (Love that Breaks through Dimensions)"[8] is professionally produced by Una Studios and tells the story of a young teacher, Na, who stays at Nam Kat Yorlapa Lodge. On an eco trek he is followed by a young bangbot lady and, drawn to a strange sound beside the trail, disappears right next to his guide. While the lodge staff mount a search operation, the young man finds himself in the bangbot dimension. Through a gate indicating the place as "Khmu Capital" (see below), he enters a village inhabited only by young and attractive females and their governess. He learns that in a former life he and one of the girls, Khuan, had been a couple and that she has been waiting for him for a long time. He also learns how to leave this world, and finally does so.

The young teacher also learns about bangbot lore, and one detail is central to our argument: in one scene, Khuan tells Na that humans, as well as bangbot, are lucky to have someone "thinking like the owner of Nam Kat" because "humans and bangbot, despite different worlds, use the same resources.... The water we use comes from Nam Kat. The forest where we find our food is the forest around Nam Kat. Only, humans cannot see bangbot." The ambivalence of bangbot, their being and not being of this world, is used here to lend legitimacy to those who protect the forest, elevating the "owner of Nam Kat"—who can be equated in this context with the owner of the Nam Kat Yorla Pa lodge and its attendant ecotourism activities— to the protector of these moral superhumans who thereby virtually become an endangered species. Importantly, what would vanish with them if they go is not just their honesty and purity but also a supposedly traditional Lao style of living in harmony with nature, as conveyed by pictures of clear water, a clean and simple village, and the absence of modern markers;

attractive women dressed in decent and decorous amalgams of ethnic symbolism express harmony between the various ethnic groups, as promoted by state policy.[9] Na entering the bangbot village through a gate saying "Khmu capital" identifies Khmu ethnicity and the status of the Khmu as original inhabitants of Lao territory with bangbotness. Saving the bangbot by protecting the forest, the Nam Kat Yorla Pa venture simultaneously saves proponents of both moral purity and national culture. In this context, a rather explicit criticism of "endless human longing," as uttered by the bangbot lady Khuan, lends credibility to particular political-economic interests by drawing partly on traditional animistic lore and partly on globalized modern environmentalism. In this sense the bangbot as an endangered species discourse is an example of the politics of aspiration in late-socialist Asia (see Nguyen, Wilcox, and Lin, this issue).

This case reflects the emergence of new urban groups and milieus in the country's social structure. The movie-form hints at increasingly professionalized media production in the context of emerging subcultural milieus indicating the differentiation of the urban middle classes (see Rehbein 2017). Environmentalism is becoming increasingly popular among urban youth. As the owner of the film studio that produced the film *Bangbot* stated in an interview, apart from promoting the lodge, one main objective of the film was to raise awareness of the need to protect the forest among the young. For him, bangbot lore is not superstition; but even if it was, it makes people protect the forest, which is better than not believing in anything while resources dwindle year by year.

Ideas of a simple and happy life related to sustainability are equally present in Western conservationism and ecotourism, as well as in traditionalist sufficiency-economy ideals. Our last case expands on the glocal nature of urban bangbot narratives, and the nostalgia implied in a revolutionary's account.

The Bangbot as Role Models

While criticism was still rather reluctantly expressed in the previous case, it is explicit in this account of the bangbot as role models for a good life. In an upper-middle-class neighborhood of Vientiane Capital lives a well-known and respected writer who, now in his late seventies, has authored

well over a hundred books about Lao history, national heroes, and Buddhism. He joined the Pathet Lao at the age of sixteen and was thus an
early and respected member of the Lao revolutionary movement. After the
American War he returned to his birthplace, Vientiane, to write. Today he
continues to produce books, aiming at two hundred titles, distributing them
for free in order to promote morality and religion. He regards this as necessary in the face of the increasing immorality in the younger generations and
the current political regime.

He contrasts this current situation with the bangbot, as civilized and
enlightened beings practicing the *sinsip* ສິນສິບ (ten monastic precepts),[10] lik-
ening them to *thep* ເທບ (gods) or *thewada* ເທວະດາ (angels). He agrees that
they are role models for a traditional Lao way of life, which is clearly more
desirable than the current dishonesty, corruption, and violence. He first
heard about the bangbot at the age of fourteen from his mother, who was
from the Phou Khao Khuay area (see above); she had borrowed clothes and
necklaces from bangbot in a cave for a village festival. He was not very interested at the time, but now he would like to go to the bangbot of Phou Khao
Khuay and live with them. He had already tried to get into contact with
them, but it has not worked out so far. Instead, he lives the life of a hermit
in the capital city among piles of his books.

What does this account have to offer beyond mere nostalgia? It is exactly
this nostalgia, coming from a former revolutionary, that is telling for Laos's
postwar trajectory and late-socialist condition. It speaks to the way and the
degree to which the late-socialist society has taken up the project of a socialist revolution (see Nguyen, Wilcox, and Lin, this issue), including, according to Kaysone Phomvihane in 1977, the creation of "a new type of socialist
man . . . with a spirit of collective mastery, who profoundly loves the country and socialism and who has a clear spirit of internationalism" (Kaysone
Phomvihane, quoted in Stuart-Fox 2002: 159). The challenges of the socialist
project in a war-devastated Southeast Asian country of subsistence peasants
became obvious with the failure of its key building block: collectivization.
Today, however, the "spirit of collective mastery" has become ruthless competitive individualism and corrupt politics, resulting in inequality and environmental degradation and leaving only nostalgia for a precolonial past as a
last resort for criticism. Nostalgia, moreover, also "point[s] towards certain

visions of the future, expressing diverse hopes and fears about the kind of world that future generations will inhabit" (Berliner 2012: 770). As mentioned, such nostalgia is also strikingly present in powerful global discourses on sustainability and ecological modernization, and in the ways these play out as conservation projects. This version of the bangbot as "angelic" role models thus expresses the double-sidedness of late-socialist transformations (see Nguyen, Wilcox, and Lin, this issue). It can be seen as a taming of Ong Keo's violent criticism, but it also makes possible a new global environmentalist ethic expressing sustainability issues in traditional animistic idioms.

One of the author's grandsons was present at our interview. In his early twenties, he had lived in the US for about eight years and had returned to help his grandfather. Well mannered and handsome, proud of his Laoness and fluent in Lao and English, he described one of his own overnight stays in the jungle of Phou Khao Khuay: upon waking up to noises as if in the middle of a village, but unable to see anyone or understand the language, he interpreted this as clearly a bangbot experience. This exemplifies not only the considerable cultural capital accumulated abroad by descendants of former revolutionaries, but also how the nostalgia expressed in the grandfather's bangbot account is transferred to a young generation of urban intellectuals. We met several young, well-educated cosmopolitan Laotians (e.g., a female forestry scientist in her twenties who had studied for her MA and PhD in England) who enjoy staying overnight at Phou Khao Khuay, witnessing inexplicable events that they attributed to the bangbot.

This return to Phou Khao Khuay sums up our case studies, which have examined the changing interpretation of bangbot from everyday tricksters to role models for a good life. This trajectory is one of increasing socioecological criticism, with a move from rural to urban accounts culminating in the emergence of new glocal environmentalisms expressive of recent shifts in the country's social structure.

Conclusion

As seen in the figure of the bangbot, precapitalist worldviews have survived the violent ruptures of modern Lao history, refashioned according to experienced realities. Those worldviews are thus not remnants but active ingredients of Lao modernization reinterpreted according to historical situation, social position, and subjective aspiration. We have argued that the potential of the bangbot for social criticism depends on context as well as historical and social positionality: these beings are not automatically carriers of critical visions of a good life. This chapter accords with Li Zhang's (afterword, this issue) call to attend to the distinct socioeconomic conditions that give rise to a particular set of aspirations. Among these conditions, differences between rural and urban notions (Bruckermann, this issue) were bound up with the historical dimension: while in the early 1900s the bangbot legitimized rural leaders in the context of colonialism, today they reflect the social and environmental consciences of newly emerging urban milieus. It is in such urban, rather than rural, bangbot narratives that criticism and visions of a good life are currently expressed.

The rise of the bangbot as role models combining modern environmentalism with an idealized Laoness is expressive of the mindset of new socioecological and adventurous milieus among the educated urban middle class.[11] Since the great majority of the educated urban class fled the country after 1975 (Evans 2002: 178), newly emerging educated milieus are drawing from the resources of socialist intellectuals, but are also cocreated by international organizations such as conservation NGOs. They are able to provide their Lao employees with a salary that supports a modern middle-class lifestyle and build on and further nurture a critical awareness of social and environmental challenges.[12] Closely related is the creation of adventurous middle-class groups via the growing tourism business, in which ecotourism plays not a small part. For example, the founder of Laos's most established ecotourism company is the son of another revolutionary writer, born in wartime in the Pathet Lao stronghold of Vieng Xay. A widely traveled and ambitious man, he now embodies the successful adventurous Lao entrepreneur. Many employees of ecotourism companies aspire to the habitus and lifestyle of their Western customers, displaying environmental awareness and an urban, modern savoir-vivre, including political criticism. While the idea of revolution does not appear prevalent in these middle-class sections, it is present among young intellectuals destined for a career in the state apparatus, some of whom are increasingly vocal about the absence of the socialist-revolutionary ideals of the past.

In this context, the violence that the bangbot legitimated in the past appears to have vanished, to be replaced by largely silent criticism and escapism. While the bangbot legitimized a most powerful, violent social criticism among rural milieus under colonialism, today very little social criticism, as uttered through this imaginary, is found in rural accounts. The most pronounced criticism is present in urban interpretations of the bangbot as role models and an endangered species. The vision of a good life according to such bangbot imaginaries is one of rural sufficiency, an economy in harmony with the natural environment, piously Buddhist, and based on fine Lao customs. In the past, bangbot were instrumental in conferring political power to leaders of rural ethnic milieus. Today, in contrast, it appears that 1) critique through the bangbot imaginary is most clearly uttered from specific urban positions, and 2) compared with its past involvement in anti-colonial revolt, this criticism is now tamed, civilized, and "Buddhicized." Just as Ong Keo is part of the official discourse, the spirit that conferred his powers on him has become an icon of ecologically modern Laoness epitomizing recent sociostructural transformations and the deeper integration of this late-socialist Asian country into late-global capitalism.

Notes

1   Notions of the concept *imaginary* vary considerably (see Strauss 2006). Our use of the term refers to a specific complex of meanings—here, bangbot lore—as part of an encompassing social ontology that is largely in line with Taylor's (2004) notion of social imaginary (see also Baumann and Rehbein 2020) and which, in Laos, involves an animistic worldview (see, e.g., Arhem and Sprenger 2016; Holt 2009). The bangbot imaginary is a culture-specific lens constituted by the peculiar confluence of animist and Buddhist sociocultures (Rehbein 2011) with the recent socio-environmental problematic of late-socialist development in Laos. An imaginary is thus a defined complex of meaning and internal coherence that is dynamic around a more or less fixed core, in this case involving variations on the idea of moral superhumans residing in the deep jungle to address recent socioecological conditions.

2   In this respect, this article is about the ways in which spirit imaginaries provide moral commentaries on modern developments in the tradition of Aihwa Ong's (1987) classical study, as well as "hauntological" works inspired by Derrida's (1994) *Specters of Marx* (e.g., Comaroff and Comaroff 1999, 2018; see also Blanes and Santo 2013).

3   As related by Bualei Phengsaengkham, who wrote his MA thesis on forest spirits in Laos (see Phengsaengkham 2015).

4 This imaginary also plays into and fuses with the myth of *muang laplae* เมือง ลับแล ("hidden kingdom or city") in Thailand, a hidden kingdom inhabited only by women. In this narrative thread, bangbot women need to reach out to male humans to find a spouse (see Luangphasi 2000, and the Nam Kat case under the header "The Bangbot as Endangered Species"). Another thread that imagines bangbot as monks seems to draw on the auspicious figure of the forest monk (Tambiah 1984; Taylor 1993). In fact, many informants claim that laplae and bangbot are one and the same; and both can be seen or visited first of all by Buddhist monks.

5 For accounts of Lao social structure see Rehbein 2007, 2011, 2017.

6 For details on this area and its socioecological context, see Kleinod 2017 and Kleinod et al. 2022.

7 See Yorla Pa (website), https://namkatyorlapa.com (accessed October 26, 2023).

8 See Una Film Studios's video, https://www.youtube.com/watch?v=Rg31I7PI34w (September 30, 2017).

9 Such as dresses that mix certain features of Laos's ethnic trinity, i.e., the Lao of the lowlands, mountain slopes, and mountaintops, iconized in many expressions of national discourse such as bank notes (see Tappe 2007).

10 That is, obeying the ten prohibitions: do not kill, steal, have sex, lie, drink alcohol, eat between the afternoon and the early morning, dance or sing, decorate the body, put one's foot on a pillow, or receive gold and money.

11 For example, for Germany, see BMU and BfN 2018.

12 We draw here from observation from fieldwork on ecotourism in National Protected Areas in Laos. For an analysis of socioecological and expeditive milieus' creation of habitats of authenticity, and also regarding Laos, see Kleinod and Schneickert 2020.

References

Abrahams, Roger D. 1983. "Interpreting Folklore Ethnographically and Sociologically." In *Handbook of American Folklore*, edited by Richard M. Dorson, 345–50. Bloomington: Indiana University Press.

Arhem, Kaj, and Guido Sprenger, eds. 2016. *Animism in Southeast Asia*. London: Routledge

Baird, Ian G. 2011. "Turning Land into Capital, Turning People into Labour: Primitive Accumulation and the Arrival of Large-Scale Economic Land Concessions in the Lao People's Democratic Republic." *New Proposals* 5, no.1: 10–26.

Baird, Ian G. 2013. "Millenarian Movements in Southern Laos and North Eastern Siam (Thailand) at the Turn of the Twentieth Century: Reconsidering the Involvement of the Champassak Royal House." *South East Asia Research* 21, no. 2: 257–79.

Barma, Nazneen H. 2014. "The Rentier State at Work: Comparative Experiences of the Resource Curse in East Asia and the Pacific." *Asia & the Pacific Policy Studies* 1, no. 2: 257–272.

Barney, Keith. 2009. "Laos and the Making of a 'Relational' Resource Frontier." *Geographical Journal* 175, no. 2: 146–159.

Baumann, Benjamin, and Boike Rehbein. 2020. "Rethinking the Social: Social Ontology, Sociocultures, and Social Inequality." In *Social Ontology, Sociocultures and Inequality in the Global South*, edited by Benjamin Baumann and Daniel Bultmann, 6–22. London: Routledge.

Bauman, Richard. 1983. "The Field Study of Folklore in Context." In *Handbook of American Folklore*, edited by Richard M. Dorson, 362–68. Bloomington: Indiana University Press.

Berliner, David. 2012. "Multiple Nostalgias: The Fabric of Heritage in Luang Prabang (Lao PDR)." *Journal of the Royal Anthropological Institute* 18, no. 4: 769–86.

Blanes, Ruy, and Diana Espírito Santo, eds. 2013. *The Social Life of Spirits*. Chicago: University of Chicago Press.

BMU and BfN. 2018. *Naturbewusstsein 2017: Bevölkerungsumfrage zu Natur und Biologischer Vielfalt. (Nature Awareness: Social Survey on Nature and Biological Diversity.)* Berlin: Federal Ministry for the Environment, Nature Conservation, Building, and Nuclear Safety (BMU)/ Federal Agency for Nature Conservation (BfN).

Cleary, Mark. 2005. "Managing the Forest in Colonial Indochina c.1900–1940." *Modern Asian Studies* 39: 257–83.

Comaroff, Jean, and John L. Comaroff. 1999. "Occult Economies and the Violence of Abstraction: Notes from the South African Postcolony." *American Ethnologist* 26, no. 2: 279–303.

Comaroff, Jean, and John L. Comaroff. 2018. "Occult Economies, Revisited." In *Magical Capitalism: Enchantment, Spells, and Occult Practices in Contemporary Economies*, edited by Brian Moeran and Timothy de Waal Malefyt, 289–320. Cham, Switzerland: Palgrave Macmillan.

Coudrat, Camille, John Duckworth, and Robert J. Timmins. 2012. "Distribution and Conservation Status of the Red-Shanked Douc (Pygathrix Nemaeus) in Lao PDR: An Update." *American Journal of Primatology* 74: 874–89.

Derrida, Jacques. 1994. *Specters of Marx: The State of the Debt, the Work of Mourning and the New International*. New York: Routledge.

Dundes, Alan. 1980. *Interpreting Folklore*. Bloomington: Indiana University Press.

Dwyer, Mike. 2007. "Turning Land into Capital. A Review of Recent Research on Land Concessions for Investment in the Lao PDR." A Report Commissioned by the Working Group on Land Issues, Part 1. Vientiane: CIDSE-Laos.

Endres, Kirsten W., and Andrea Lauser, eds. 2012. *Engaging the Spirit World: Popular Beliefs and Practices in Modern Southeast Asia*. New York: Berghahn.

Evans, Grant. 2002. *A Short History of Laos: The Land in Between*. Crows Nest, Australia: Allen & Unwin.

Gunn, Geoffrey C. 2003. *Rebellion in Laos: Peasant and Politics in a Colonial Backwater*. Bangkok: White Lotus.

Holt, John C. 2009. *Spirits of the Place: Buddhism and Lao Religious Culture*. Chiang Mai, Thailand: Silkworm.

Ishii, Yoneo. 1975. "A Note on Buddhistic Millenarian Revolts in Northeastern Siam." *Journal of Southeast Asian Studies* 6, no 2: 121–26.

Kenney-Lazar, Miles, Michael Dwyer, and Cornelia Hett. 2018. "Turning Land into Capital: Assessing a Decade of Policy in Practice." A Report Commissioned by the Land Information Working Group (LIWG). Vientiane, Laos: LIWG.

Kleinod, Michael. 2017. *The Recreational Frontier: Ecotourism in Laos as Ecocapitalist Instrumentality*. Göttingen, Germany: University of Göttingen.

Kleinod, Michael. 2020. "Social Ontologies as World-Making Projects: The *Mueang-Pa* Duality in Laos." In *Social Ontology, Geocultures, and Inequality in the Global South*, edited by Benjamin Baumann and Daniel Bultmann, 119–35. London: Routledge.

Kleinod, Michael, Timo Duile, and Christoph Antweiler. 2022. "Outwitting the Spirits? Toward a Political Ecology of Southeast Asian Animism." *Berlin Journal of Critical Theory* 6, no. 1: 127–76.

Kleinod, Michael, and Christian Schneickert. 2020. "Habitats of Authenticity: The Ecological Crisis, World-Ecological Praxeology and the Capital Structure of 'Uncapitalized' Spaces." *Environmental Sociology* 6, no. 3: 279–90. https://doi.org/10.1080/23251042.2020.1759491.

Ladwig, Patrice. 2014. "Millennialism, Charisma and Utopia: Revolutionary Potentialities in Premodern Lao and Thai Theravada Buddhism." *Politics, Religion, and Ideology* 15, no. 2: 308–29.

Luangphasi, Duangxay. 2000. *Chao Sao Bang Bot (Bang Bot Bride)*. Vientiane, Laos: Lao Youth.

Moore, Jason W. 2011. "Transcending the Metabolic Rift: A Theory of Crises in the Capitalist World-Ecology." *Journal of Peasant Studies* 38, no. 1: 1–46.

Moore, Jason W. 2015. *Capitalism in the Web of Life: Ecology and the Accumulation of Capital*. London: Verso.

Mueggler, Erik. 2001. *The Age of Wild Ghosts: Memory, Violence, and Place in Southwest China*. Berkeley: University of California Press.

Murdoch, John B. 1967. "The 1901–1902 'Holy Man's' Rebellion." *Sciences* 5: 78–86.

Ong, Aihwa. 1987. *Spirits of Resistance and Capitalist Discipline: Factory Women in Malaysia*. Albany: State University of New York Press.

Oriole, Carme. 2000. "Jokes about National Groups in Andorra." *Fabula* 41; nos. 3–4: 285–93.

Phengsaengkham, Bualei. 2015. *A Study of the "Ghost" Characters in Lao Folktales* (in Lao). MA thesis, National University of Laos.

Pholsena, Vatthana. 2006. *Post-war Laos: The Politics of Culture, History, and Identity*. Singapore: Institute of Southeast Asian Studies.

Rehbein, Boike. 2007. *Globalization, Culture, and Society in Laos*. London: Routledge.

Rehbein, Boike. 2011. "Differentiation of Sociocultures, Classification, and the Good Life in Laos." *SOJOURN: Journal of Social Issues in Southeast Asia* 26, no. 2: 277–303.

Rehbein, Boike. 2017. *Society in Contemporary Laos: Capitalism, Habitus and Belief*. London: Routledge.

Singh, Sarinda. 2012. *Natural Potency and Political Power: Forests and State Authority in Contemporary Laos*. Honolulu: University of Hawai'i Press.

Sprenger, Guido. 2018. "Buddhism and Coffee: The Transformation of Locality and Personhood in Southern Laos." *SOJOURN: Journal of Social Issues in Southeast Asia* 33, no. 2: 265–90.

Sprenger, G., and K. Grossmann. 2018. "Plural Ecologies in Southeast Asia." *SOJOURN: Journal of Social Issues in Southeast Asia* 33, no. 2: ix–xxi.

Strauss, Claudia. 2006. "The Imaginary." *Anthropological Theory* 6, no. 3: 322–44.

Stuart-Fox, Martin. 2002. *Buddhist Kingdom, Marxist State: The Making of Modern Laos*. Bangkok: White Lotus.

Tambiah, Stanley J. 1984. *The Buddhist Saints of the Forest and the Cult of Amulets*. Cambridge: Cambridge University Press.

Tappe, Oliver. 2007. "A New Banknote in the People's Republic: The Iconography of the Kip and Ideological Transformations in Laos, 1957–2006." *International Quarterly for Asian Studies* 38, nos. 1–2: 87–108.

Taylor, Charles. 2004. *Modern Social Imaginaries*. Durham, NC: Duke University Press.

Taylor, James L. 1993. *Forest Monks and the Nation-State: An Anthropological and Historical Study in Northeastern Thailand*. Singapore: Institute of Southeast Asian Studies.

Taylor, Philip, ed. 2007. *Modernity and Re-enchantment: Religion in Post-revolutionary Vietnam*. Singapore: Institute of Southeast Asian Studies.

Afterword: What Good Life, and Why Now?

Li Zhang

Since attending and speaking at the conference titled "The Good Life in Late-Socialist Asia: Aspirations, Politics, and Possibilities" at Bielefeld University in Germany in September 2019, I continue to ponder several unanswered questions. Why do we seem to be obsessed with the notion of the good life? And why at this particular historical moment in late-socialist societies? What is particular about the pursuit of the good life in these places where socialism, capitalism, and globalization intersect? Are there any better alternatives to desire while living in a time of heightened precarity, anxiety, contingency, and impasse? Today, as we face a serious global pandemic brought about by a novel coronavirus, these questions become even more pressing. Indeed, as COVID-19 rages across the world bringing the global economy to a near halt and causing massive loss of life, widespread human suffering, and profound uncertainty about the future, we cannot help but

positions 32:1   DOI 10.1215/10679847-10890062

ask whether the good life, or even the normal life, is possible at all in the immediate future. What will a decent life look like in this surreal age of frequent public health crises? In this afterword, rather than commenting on each individual article in this rich and timely collection, I would like to offer my recent thoughts on some of the broader questions with which many contemporary scholars are still grappling.

Let us begin by returning to Lauren Berlant's acclaimed book, *Cruel Optimism* (2011), which has questioned the widespread enthusiasm generated by the good life discourses across the globe. With a profound and blunt unpacking of the harsh reality beneath such optimism and fantasies, Berlant reveals how often that which one desires and dreams of can become the very obstacle to one's flourishing. She raises a number of poignant questions about the existential crisis facing us: What happens when the good-life fantasies start to fray? Is it better to hold on to cruel optimism, or to have none at all? What is the price of embracing or rejecting our conventional ways of handling the variety of challenges facing us today? In my view, the power of Berlant's book is not that she offers easy answers or a way out of the impasse that many of us are facing. It is that, by poking numerous holes in the upward-mobility, good-life fantasies, she moves us to confront the complexity and (im)possibility of living and thriving in this contemporary world marked by precarity, insecurity, and crisis.

Yet the publication of Berlant's book did not completely dampen talk of hope, resilience, and well-being in academia, let alone the general population's pursuit of a better life regardless of circumstances and obstacles. On the contrary, it seems to have stimulated more and more interest in exploring the power and complexity of optimism, even in the face of the ruins of shattered dreams: "the anthropology of hope" (see the curated collection of *Cultural Anthropology*, "Reclaiming Hope" [Kirksey and LeFevre 2015]), "the anthropology of the good" (Robbins 2013), and "the anthropology of wellbeing" (Fischer 2014), to name but a few. This special issue joins the growing body of literature critically examining why, despite potential pitfalls, disappointments, and cruel betrayals, people around the world continue to be drawn toward the good-life saga, finding constant inspiration and strength in the process. More importantly, these scholars seek to show that such dreams and the desire to attain a better life are always historically situated, and thus assume different meanings and significance in specific social and political contexts.

The renowned cultural theorist Stuart Hall once suggested that the concept of "race" can be regarded as a "floating signifier." As such, its "meaning is relational, and not essential, and can never be finally fixed, but is subject to the constant process of redefinition and appropriation (Hall 1997: 8). Further, all floating signifiers consist of an "endless process of being constantly re-signified, made to mean something different in different cultures, in different historical formations, at different moments of time" (8). Yet floating signifiers are powerful and long-lasting, because they can adjust, mutate, and reemerge. I find Hall's insight extremely helpful and pertinent to thinking about what the increasingly pervasive idea of the good life suggests in different contexts in our present time. I argue that the good life has also become a powerful floating signifier, whose meaning is constantly being redefined and appropriated in specific historical and cultural contexts, or what Ilana Gershon (2019: 404) calls "multiple social orders that are interconnected and contingent." While this specific floating signifier circulates across different social orders, it also gains new meanings and is contested in diverse ways, as Gershon demonstrates. To speak of the good life is not to refer to any universal, fixed, idealistic scheme of living well. Rather, we need to attend to the distinct socioeconomic condition that gives rise to a particular set of aspirations and determinations, as well as to the obstacles, struggles, and prices that emerge in this process (Chua 2014). It is this historically conditioned pursuit—guided by resilient human spirits and yet, at the same time, accompanied by pain and suffering—that the authors of this special issue seek to unpack. As a floating signifier, the meaning of the good life is inevitably unstable, diverse, and relational because "the meaning of a signifier can never be finally or trans-historically fixed" (Hall 1997: 8). Further, as people, ideas, and information move across the porous boundaries between social orders, we are likely to see certain commensurable and incommensurable elements emerging in their understanding of what the good life means in the process.

What does it mean, then, to pursue the good life in late-socialist Asian countries such as Vietnam, Laos, and China today? Despite their different social and cultural traditions, these three societies share a great deal in common. They all embraced socialist political and economic systems at one point in history, and then sought economic reforms through varying degrees of marketization and commercialization beginning in the late 1970s and early 1980s. They all pursued a market-based mixed economy rather than full privatization, yet socialist political ideology and authoritarian control are still very much alive. The shared socialist experience and a bifurcated political-economic system remain important to our understanding of the meanings and implications of the quest for the good life. There are at least four elements worth exploring here.

First, striving for a brighter future and hoping to move forward and upward is not a novel idea for people living in late-socialist societies. But there has been a remarkable shift in terms of the focus of this endeavor: a move from the promotion of primarily state-defined collective welfare and national well-being to private individuals' cultivation of personal and family happiness, prosperity, and harmony. If in the past, the national longing generated by official efforts largely eclipsed individual desires, in the last two or three decades personal aspirations to success, well-being, prosperity, and family harmony are increasingly sanctioned and even exalted in official and popular discourses. An early sign of this fundamental change was expressed vividly in a famous slogan coined by Chinese leader Deng Xiaoping in the 1980s: "To get rich is glorious!" For the first time in Chinese socialist history, individuals were encouraged to pursue personal prosperity and getting ahead of others was not seen as a punishable wrongdoing. This emerging aspiration to a comfortable life quickly inspired millions of Chinese to seek new ways of generating private wealth.

Further, if the vision of a better life was largely singular and top-down in the past, this time it has become rather diverse and bottom-up. There has been a shift from glorifying lofty national goals of strengthening the country to indulging in everyday consumer desires, fighting for cleaner air, creating better residential spaces, and individual well-being to reflect their concept of a meaningful good life. For instance, some younger generations of middle-class Chinese are keenly interested in living a healthier life, raising a perfect child, maintaining good mental health, and enjoying clean air and safer food with the aid of new science and technologies, including psychological science, environmental science, and cutting-edge biomedicine such as stem-cell treatment (Bruckermann, this issue; Greenhalgh and Zhang 2020; Kuan 2015; Song 2017; Wahlberg 2018; Yang 2015; Zhang 2020). Meanwhile, older urban residents tend to seek various forms of traditional *yangshen* 养生 (life-nurturing) practices such as martial arts, qigong, dance, and meditation to improve and transform everyday life (Chen 2003; Farquhar and Zhang 2012). In more recent years, we have seen a resurgence of the national quest for what the Xi regime advocates as the "New China Dream." However, this new effort by the party-state to define the good life is not likely to over-shadow the myriad existing and emerging dreams and yearnings of ordinary people at the grassroots.

Second, in the context of recent socialist history marked by brutal class struggles, ideological campaigns, and political turmoil, the ability and opportunity to talk openly about one's good-life fantasy and take action to fulfill personal dreams are themselves a daring political acts because, just thirty years ago, such undertakings were unimaginable or not endorsed by the socialist state. It is in this troubled socialist context that anthropologist Arthur Kleinman (2011: 267) suggests that "the quest for happiness is one of the most important stories in China today." Indeed, against the backdrop of devastating economic crisis and violent political struggles between party factions in Laos, Vietnam, and China, it was bold for ordinary people to embrace and act on their own dreams and hopes despite the political risks, particularly in the early years of the reform and opening. The yearning for personal joy and family prosperity is a hallmark of the late-socialist era, across the three countries and beyond.

Third, although the quest for material comfort, wellness, and upward mobility in the three transforming societies is deeply personal and intimate, it is not primarily driven by individualism; rather, it is profoundly social. This form of sociality is foremost embedded in concrete families, friends, and local communities rather than expressed through abstract notions of the nation-state. Teresa Kuan's (2015) work on the politics of parenting in China demonstrates that child-rearing is often an interactive process driven by the desire to secure a brighter future for not only one's child, but also the family as a whole. My own research on the rise of psychotherapy in Chinese cities further suggests that young middle-class professionals seeking new psychotherapy and training do not wish to retreat into the private self but hope to become more resilient people, better at managing their families and social worlds (Zhang 2020). This task involves a dialectic process of what I call *disentangling* (engaging with a private and safe space to undertake the psychological work of self-exploration) and *reembedding* (returning to one's social nexus to perform duties and obligations as a more effective person) through psychological counseling. This special issue adroitly reveals the socially embedded nature of the pursuit of the good life in a number of areas including access to electricity, transportation, health care, and migration among Laotians, Vietnamese, and Chinese. Attending to one's family, community, and social nexus is a key element of attaining a desirable life.

Finally, some groups' quests for the good life and modernity can be accompanied by the massive dispossession and devastation of others. This is the case for each of the three societies concerned here, and beyond (see Harvey 2005). Among the many examples, let me highlight just three: the anthropologist Erik Harms (2016) lucidly demonstrates this dual process by juxtaposing two striking images of luxury and rubble in his study of Vietnam's urban redevelopment. Saigon's march to global modernity is undeniably built on the shattered dreams of the poor and disenfranchised. Based on her research among waste traders in Hanoi, Minh Nguyen (2019) shows that Vietnamese middle-class aspirations for wealth and success are inseparable from dirty, harsh labor performed by those in the recycling economy. Nguyen argues that, here, waste and wealth, anguish and enjoyment are inseparable in the search for the good life. It has become clear that in such scenarios one person's dream can easily be another's nightmare. My own research in urban China shows that Kunming's middle-class residents' search for private paradises in the form of gated commercial housing compounds comes at the great expense of the interests of long-term, relatively poor residents. The latter, who had lived in the city core for generations, were pushed out ruthlessly without adequate compensation to make room for the city's modernization (Zhang 2010). This polarity of simultaneous urban development and massive displacement, security and exclusion, enhancement and marginalization, frequently plays out in the march toward spatial modernity far beyond Asia (Herzfeld 2009; Low 2004).

The good life as a floating signifier will attract numerous people in different situations for many years to come, especially at times of intensified insecurity and crisis, as well as new opportunities for radical change. No matter what form it takes—passionate aspiration, resilient hope, cruel optimism, or mirage—people will continue to endow it with different meanings, values, and significance based on their specific life circumstances in order to endure hardship, push through a life of deadlock, and eventually flourish. In my view, the yearning and willpower to live well and live better under late-socialist conditions and beyond, despite such challenging circumstances as the current global pandemic, are not expressions of delusion. They are rather a story of embracing an everyday politics that validates the human propensity for happiness, well-being, and recognition, against the odds.

Notes

I thank Minh Nguyen and Phill Wilcox for inviting me to deliver the keynote speech at the conference at Bielefeld University, and am grateful for the opportunity to engage with the conference participants' wide range of fascinating research and lively discussions.

References

Berlant, Lauren. 2011. *Cruel Optimism*. Durham, NC: Duke University Press.

Chen, Nancy. 2003. *Breathing Space: Qigong, Psychiatry, and Healing in China*. New York: Columbia University Press.

Chua, Jocelyn Lim. 2014. *In Pursuit of the Good Life: Aspiration and Suicide in Globalizing South India*. Oakland: University of California Press.

Farquhar, Judith, and Zhang Qicheng. 2012. *Ten Thousand Things: Nurturing Life in Contemporary Beijing*. New York: Zone.

Fischer, Edward F. 2014. *The Good Life: Aspiration, Dignity, and the Anthropology of Wellbeing*. Stanford, CA: Stanford University Press.

Gershon, Ilana. 2019. "Porous Social Orders." *American Ethnologist* 46, no. 4: 404–16.

Greenhalgh, Susan, and Li Zhang, 2020. *Can Science and Technology Save China?* Ithaca, NY: Cornell University Press.

Hall, Stuart. 1997. "Race, The Floating Signifier." *Media Education Foundation*, https://www.mediaed.org/transcripts/Stuart-Hall-Race-the-Floating-Signifier-Transcript.pdf.

Harms, Erik. 2016. *Luxury and Rubble: Civility and Dispossession in the New Saigon.* Oakland: University of California Press.

Harvey, David. 2005. *A Brief History of Neoliberalism.* Oxford: Oxford University Press.

Herzfeld, Michael. 2009. *Evicted from Eternity: The Restructuring of Modern Rome.* Chicago: University of Chicago Press.

Kirksey, Eben, and Tate LeFevre, curators. 2015. "Reclaiming Hope." Curated collection, *Cultural Anthropology.* https://journal.culanth.org/index.php/ca/catalog/category/reclaiming-hope.

Kleinman, Arthur. 2011. "Quests for Meaning." In *Deep China: The Moral Life of the Person,* contributed to by Yunxiang Yan, Jing Jun, Sing Lee, Everett Zhang, Pan Tianshu, Wu Fei, and Guo Jinhua, 263–90. Oakland: University of California Press.

Kuan, Teresa. 2015. *Love's Uncertainty: The Politics and Ethics of Child Rearing in Contemporary China.* Oakland: University of California Press.

Low, Setha M. 2004. *Behind the Gates: Life, Security, and the Pursuit of Happiness in Fortress America.* New York: Routledge.

Nguyen, Minh. 2019. *Waste and Wealth: An Ethnography of Labor, Value, and Morality in a Vietnamese Recycling Economy.* Oxford: Oxford University Press.

Robbins, Joel. 2013. "Beyond the Suffering Subject: Toward an Anthropology of the Good." *Journal of the Royal Anthropological Institute* 19, no. 3: 447–62.

Song, Priscilla. 2017. *Biomedical Odysseys: Fetal Cell Experiments from Cyberspace to China.* Princeton, NJ: Princeton University Press.

Wahlberg, Ayo. 2018. *Good Quality: The Routinization of Sperm Banking in China.* Oakland: University of California Press.

Yang, Jie. 2015. *Unknotting the Heart: Unemployment and Therapeutic Governance in China.* Ithaca, NY: Cornell University Press.

Zhang, Li. 2010. *In Search of Paradise: Middle-Class Living in a Chinese Metropolis.* Ithaca, NY: Cornell University Press.

Zhang, Li. 2020. *Anxious China: Inner Revolution and Politics of Psychotherapy.* Oakland: University of California Press.

Contributors

Charlotte Bruckermann is an anthropologist specializing in imaginaries of carbon and the role of green labor in the creation of Chinese ecological civilization. Since her doctoral research (DPhil 2013, University of Oxford) she has conducted several years of ethnographic fieldwork across China, including among families in a decarbonizing coal region, emissions experts and carbon footprint app developers in urban centers, and afforestation workers in various rural carbon offset sites. She is a lecturer and researcher at the Department of Social and Cultural Anthropology and the Global South Studies Center of the University of Cologne.

Sypha Chanthavong is an environmental law lecturer and director of Graduate Programs of the Faculty of Law and Political Science at National University of Laos, based in Vientiane, Lao PDR. His research interests focus on environmental and natural resource laws, particularly water, land, forest, climate justice, and local people's rights related to natural resource management.

positions 32:1   DOI 10.1215/10679847-10890075
Copyright 2024 by Duke University Press

Elizabeth M. Elliott is a medical anthropologist working in Laos and Southeast Asia. She has a background in Asian medicines and her PhD dissertation is one of the only detailed studies of traditional medicine in Laos, based on long-term ethnographic research with rural healers, communities, and medical staff in the southern lowlands, including ethnopharmacological documentation of medicinal plants and remedies. She recently completed a postdoctoral fellowship with the Science, Technology, and Society cluster in the Asia Research Institute, National University of Singapore, and currently works as an applied anthropologist within public health focusing on people-centered and community-led approaches.

Kirsten W. Endres is head of a research group at the Department Anthropology of Economic Experimentation, Max Planck Institute for Social Anthropology, Halle/Saale (Germany). Her research interests include state-society relations, markets and trade, urban planning, infrastructure, electricity, and colonialism. Her current work examines the history of electrification in Vietnam during the French colonial period.

Jiazhi Fengjiang is lecturer in social anthropology at the University of Edinburgh. She is completing a book on the political, moral, and economic lives of ordinary people who strategized volunteering and charitable work in coping with political-economic restructurings in contemporary China. Before joining the University of Edinburgh, she worked at the Max Planck Institute for the Study of Religious and Ethnic Diversity as a postdoctoral researcher and at Princeton University as a Fung Global fellow.

Arve Hansen is researcher at the Centre for Development and the Environment at the University of Oslo and leader of the Norwegian Network for Asian Studies. He has worked in and on Vietnam more than a decade and has published widely on consumption, the middle classes, and development in the country. He is the author of *Consumption and Vietnam's New Middle Classes: Societal Transformations and Everyday Life* (2022) and the coeditor of several books, including *Consumption, Sustainability and Everyday Life* (2023) and *The Socialist Market Economy in Asia: Development in China, Vietnam, and Laos* (2020).

Michael Kleinod-Freudenberg is currently postdoctoral researcher and scientific coordinator at University of Cologne's Global South Studies Center. His dissertation, "The Recreational Frontier: Ecotourism in Laos as Eco-rational Instrumentality" (2017), sheds light on the "world-praxeological" implications of ecotourism in Laos, combining insights from critical theory, Bourdieusian practice theory, and eco-Marxian approaches. This combination of perspectives also informs Michael's other works, such as those on animism, utopianism, and socio-ecological theorization. With praxeological transformation studies as a central point of orientation, one of his key interests is in how the manifold non-identities with the capitalist metabolism might add up to its meaningful overcoming.

Sandra Kurfürst is professor of cross-cultural and urban communication at the Department of Social and Cultural Anthropology, University of Cologne. She is cospeaker of the Global

South Studies Center. Her research interests include urban studies, youth, gender, and social movements in Southeast Asia. Sandra has worked on public spaces and public spheres in the city of Hanoi. In her recent book *Dancing Youth: Hip Hop and Gender in the Late Socialist City* she examines youth's aspirations and desires embodied in hip-hop dance in the larger context of post-socialist transformation, urban restructuring, and changing gender relations.

Jake Lin is assistant professor of political science at the University of Texas, Rio Grande Valley. He is also an associate fellow at the Faculty of Sociology, Bielefeld University in Germany. He was Japan Society for the Promotion of Science postdoctoral fellow in 2017, based at Tokyo University of Foreign Studies after receiving his PhD from Victoria University of Wellington, New Zealand. His current research explores labor migration and social policy reconfigurations in Global China and Vietnam as part of the European Research Council Starting-Grant Project WelfareStruggles (no. 803614). His works are published in *Global Public Policy and Governance*, *Journal of Contemporary Asia*, and *Socialism and Democracy*.

Minh T. N. Nguyen is professor of social anthropology at Bielefeld University and visiting professor at University of Social Sciences and Humanities, Vietnam National University, Hanoi. Her research focuses on labor and work, care and welfare, migration and mobility in Vietnam, China and Southeast Asia. She is the Principal Investigator of the European Research Council Starting-Grant Project WelfareStruggles (no. 803614) and the author of *Vietnam's Socialist Servants: Domesticity, Gender, Class, and Identity* (2014) and *Waste and Wealth: An Ethnography of Labour, Value, and Morality in a Vietnamese Recycling Economy* (2018, winner of the Society for the Anthropology of Work Book Prize 2019).

Phill Wilcox is research associate at Bielefeld University, Germany. Her research interests include the anthropology of development, aspiration, and future making. She is the author of *Heritage and the Making of Political Legitimacy in Laos: The Past and Present of the Lao Nation* (2021). Her current work considers China as a (new) driver of development in the Global South.

Roberta Zavoretti is a social anthropologist, sinologist, and the author of *Rural Origins, City Lives: Class and Place in Contemporary China* (2017, 2021). She has published extensively on kinship, gender, and family politics in China, and has taught at several universities in the United Kingdom and Germany. Roberta presently works in the prevention of gender discrimination and abuse, applying the methodological insights of ethnographic research in policy-making contexts.

Fan Zhang is assistant professor of anthropology at Peking University (China). Her research concerns ethnic studies, historical anthropology, and anthropological theory. She has carried out historical and ethnographical studies in Tibet and Sichuan. Her major publications include "Edicts and the Edible: Digesting Imperial Sovereignty in Lhasa" (2021), "Reorienting the Sacred and Accommodating the Secular: the History of Buddhism in China (*rgya* *nag chos 'byung*)" (2016), and "Transcendent Space, Mandala, and Our Holy Empire: Multiple Spatial Imaginations of Mount Wutai and Multiple Identifications in the Eighteenth Century" (2019, in Chinese).

Li Zhang is professor of anthropology at the University of California, Davis. She is the author of *Anxious China: Inner Revolution and Politics of Psychotherapy* (Honorable Mention, Victor Turner Book Prize in Ethnographic Writing), as well as two previous award-winning books, *Strangers in the City* and *In Search of Paradise*. She also coedited two books: *Privatizing China, Socialism from Afar* and *Can Science and Technology Save China?* She was a 2008 John Simon Guggenheim fellow and the president of the Society of East Asian Anthropology (2013–15).

Erratum for Editorial Collective, *positions* 31, no. 4 (2023).

Errors were made to the Editorial Collective listing on the journal's masthead in the print version of *positions* 31, no. 4. The double crosses should have been placed next to the names of Donald Lowe, Miriam Silverberg, and Marilyn Young. These errors have been corrected in the online version.

https://doi.org/10.1215/10679847-11071129

Keep up to date on new scholarship

Issue alerts are a great way to stay current on all the cutting-edge scholarship from your favorite Duke University Press journals. This free service delivers tables of contents directly to your inbox, informing you of the latest groundbreaking work as soon as it is published.

To sign up for issue alerts:

1. Visit **dukeu.press/register** and register for an account. You do not need to provide a customer number.

2. After registering, visit **dukeu.press/alerts**.

3. Go to "Latest Issue Alerts" and click on "Add Alerts."

4. Select as many publications as you would like from the pop-up window and click "Add Alerts."

read.dukeupress.edu/journals

Printed and bound by CPI Group (UK) Ltd, Croydon, CR0 4YY

13/04/2025

14656480-0001